# MUSEUMS, EXHIBITIONS, AND MEMORIES OF VIOLENCE IN COLOMBIA

This book explores how recent Colombian historical memories are informed by cultural diversity and how some of the country's citizens remember the brutalities committed by the Army, guerrillas, and paramilitaries during the internal war (1980–2016).

Its chapters delve into four case studies. The first highlights the selections of what not to remember and what not to represent at the National Museum of the country. The second focuses on the well-received memories at the same institution by examining a display made to commemorate the assassination of a demobilized guerrilla fighter. The third discusses how a rural marginal community decided to vividly remember the attacks they experienced by creating a display hall to aid in their collective and individual healing. Lastly, the fourth case study, also about a rural peripheric community, discusses their way of remembering, which emphasizes peasant oral traditions through a traveling venue. By bringing violence, memory, and museum studies together, this text contributes to our understanding of how social groups severely impacted by atrocities recreate and remember their violent experiences. By drawing on displays, newspapers, interviews, catalogs, and oral histories, Jimena Perry shows how museums and exhibitions in Colombia become politically active subjects in the acts of reflection and mourning, and how they foster new relationships between the state and society.

This volume is of great use to students and scholars interested in Latin American and public history.

**Jimena Perry** is a Latin American Scholar. She earned a BS in Anthropology from the Universidad de Los Andes in Colombia, an MPhil in Social Anthropology from the University of Cambridge, UK, and a Ph.D. in History from the University of Texas at Austin. She is also a public historian and the Project Manager of Explorers of the International Federation for Public History since 2018.

# Global Perspectives on Public History
*Edited by Dr. Kristin O'Brassill-Kulfan, Rutgers University*

This series explores the work of public historians and the contested histories they engage with around the world. Authored by both scholars and practitioners, volumes focus on cases where complex histories and diverse audiences meet and examine public representations of history. The series aims to link professional discussions of different historical methodologies with broader dialogues around commemoration, preservation, heritage, and interpretation in diverse geographical, cultural, social, and economic contexts. The co-existence of both global and regionally specific volumes in the series highlight the wide range of innovative new projects and approaches on offer. These books will provide students, researchers, and practitioners with new case studies and helpful analytical tools to confront the (mis)representations of history they encounter in their work and as members of twenty first century communities.

**Public in Public History**
*Edited by Joanna Wojdon and Dorota Wiśniewska*

**Public History in Poland**
*Edited by Joanna Wojdon*

**Public History for a Post-Truth Era**
*Fighting Denial through Memory Movements*
Liz Sevcenko

**Museums, Exhibitions, and Memories of Violence in Colombia**
*Trying to Remember*
Jimena Perry

# MUSEUMS, EXHIBITIONS, AND MEMORIES OF VIOLENCE IN COLOMBIA

Trying to Remember

*Jimena Perry*

NEW YORK AND LONDON

Designed cover image: View of the main display of the Hall: The 200 photographs of Granada's victims seen upon entrance to the hall of never again in Granada, Antioquia, Colombia. Photograph by Jimena Perry, 2017

First published 2023
by Routledge
605 Third Avenue, New York, NY 10158

and by Routledge
4 Park Square, Milton Park, Abingdon, Oxon, OX14 4RN

*Routledge is an imprint of the Taylor & Francis Group, an informa business*

© 2023 Jimena Perry

The right of Jimena Perry to be identified as author of this work has been asserted in accordance with sections 77 and 78 of the Copyright, Designs and Patents Act 1988.

All rights reserved. No part of this book may be reprinted or reproduced or utilised in any form or by any electronic, mechanical, or other means, now known or hereafter invented, including photocopying and recording, or in any information storage or retrieval system, without permission in writing from the publishers.

*Trademark notice*: Product or corporate names may be trademarks or registered trademarks, and are used only for identification and explanation without intent to infringe.

*Library of Congress Cataloging-in-Publication Data*
Names: Perry Posada, Jimena, author.
Title: Museums, exhibitions, and memories of violence in Colombia : trying to remember / Jimena Perry.
Other titles: Trying to remember
Description: New York, NY : Routledge, 2023. |
Series: Global perspectives on public history | Includes bibliographical references and index. |
Identifiers: LCCN 2022060798 (print) | LCCN 2022060799 (ebook) | ISBN 9781032255699 (hbk) | ISBN 9781032234885 (pbk) | ISBN 9781003283997 (ebk)
Subjects: LCSH: Political violence—Museums—Colombia. | Public history—Colombia. | Collective memory—Colombia. | Colombia—Politics and government—1974- | Victims of political violence—Colombia—History. | Museums—Political aspects—Colombia. | Museums and community—Colombia. | Museo Nacional de Colombia. | Civil war—Colombia—History—21st century. | Civil war—Colombia—History—20th century.
Classification: LCC F2253.5 .P47 2023 (print) | LCC F2253.5 (ebook) | DDC 986.1—dc23/eng/20230306
LC record available at https://lccn.loc.gov/2022060798
LC ebook record available at https://lccn.loc.gov/2022060799

ISBN: 978-1-032-25569-9 (hbk)
ISBN: 978-1-032-23488-5 (pbk)
ISBN: 978-1-003-28399-7 (ebk)

DOI: 10.4324/9781003283997

Typeset in Bembo
by codeMantra

For Muno and Tata, my parents

For Gloria Elcy Ramírez, Gloria Elcy Quintero, Soraya Bayuelo, and all the victims and survivors of the Colombian armed conflict.

# CONTENTS

*List of figures* ix
*List of tables* xi
*Acknowledgments* xiii

Introduction 1
   *A Never-Ending Story? Violence in Colombia 15*
   *Colombia's Violent Background 17*
   *Memory Museums and Exhibitions in Colombia and Latin America 21*
   *Colombia's Cultural Diversity 27*

1   Throwing in the Towel: Representations of Political Violence in Colombia's National Museum and Their Polemics   32
   *Remembering and Omitting Violence at the National Museum of Colombia, 2001 34*
   *The Storied History of the National Museum of Colombia 36*
      Headquarters of the National Museum of Colombia 42
   *Reactions to Elvira Cuervo de Jaramillo Towel Initiative 44*
   *Historic Artifacts 49*
      The Director's Public Life 52
   *The Founding Father of the FARC-EP, Tirofijo, and His Victims 56*
   *Conclusions 63*

2 Lives Ended in Their Prime: Political Violence at the
   National Museum of Colombia                                                69
   *The National Museum of Colombia Innovative Pathways 71*
   *Carlos Pizarro Leongómez: From Elite to Commander of the M-19 74*
      *The Palace of Justice Siege in Ya vuelvo: A Multi-Sided History 77*
   *"Ya Vuelvo Should Stay": Positive Reactions to the Exhibition 81*
      *Two Other Candidates Killed in 1989: Luis Carlos Galán Lives, Bernardo Jaramillo Does Not 83*
      *The Military Outrage: Ya vuelvo Does Not Belong in the National Museum of Colombia 88*
   *Representations and Remembrances of Carlos Pizarro Leongómez and His Struggles to Achieve Colombian Peace in Ya vuelvo 89*
   *Auspicious Historical Memories: Ya vuelvo's Sensible Reception 95*
   *Conclusions 99*

3 Memory, Healing, and Justice: The Hall of Never Again,
   Granada, Antioquia                                                        105
   *"Museums are for the dead": The Hall of Never Again's Challenge 109*
   *Memory and the Hall of Never Again 116*
   *Paths to Transitional Justice in Colombia 117*
   *The Hall of Never Again: Location, Violence, and Its Representations 121*
   *The Bitácoras and Ways to Remember 134*
   *Conclusions 138*

4 Memory and Intangible Heritage: The Traveling Museum
   of Memory and Identity of Montes de María, El Mochuelo    143
   *Immaterial or Intangible Heritage in Colombia 145*
   *The Violence in Montes de María 150*
   *Representations of Violence at El Mochuelo 157*
   *Nature of El Mochuelo 165*
   *Conclusions 170*

Final Thoughts                                                                173

*Bibliography*                                                                *185*
*Index*                                                                       *199*

# FIGURES

2.1 Picture by Catalina Ruíz, Curator of *Ya vuelvo*. Bogotá, 2011     79
2.2 View of the opening of Ya vuelvo. Picture by Catalina Ruíz. Bogotá, 2011     92
3.1 This image is a view of the wall that displays the approximate 200 victims of the recent armed conflict in Granada, Antioquia. Picture by Jimena Perry, 2017     114
3.2 View of Granada's church from the bus station. Photograph by Jimena Perry, August 2017     122
3.3 Entrance to the Hall of Never Again. Photograph by Jimena Perry, 2017     124
3.4 View of the main display of the Hall: The 200 photographs of Granada's victims. Photograph by Jimena Perry, 2017     126
4.1 A man in San Jacinto municipality observing the timeline of the known massacres of Montes de María. Pictures taken by the members of the Corporation Collective of Communications Line 21     159
4.2 The members of the Collective took these pictures a few days before launching of the site. The original 2008 idea changed significantly when the museum opened in 2019. Pictures taken by the members of the Corporation Collective Line 21     162
4.3 The "Tree of Life," where 700 cards with victims' names hang. Giovanni Castro, curator of the venue, is sitting below. Pictures taken by the members of the Corporation Collective of Communications Line 21     164
4.4 Soraya Bayuelo at the entrance of El Mochuelo. Picture taken by the members of the Corporation Collective Line 21     164

# TABLES

| | | |
|---|---|---|
| 0.1 | Memory Sites in Colombia, 2022 | 22 |
| 1.1 | Genre | 57 |
| 1.2 | Ethnic Group | 57 |
| 1.3 | Age | 57 |
| 1.4 | Disability | 57 |
| 3.1 | Massacres Committed in Granada, Antioquia, 1998–2004 | 127 |
| 4.1 | Some Massacres Perpetrated in the Montes de María Region between 1991 and 2007 | 151 |

# ACKNOWLEDGMENTS

There are many people and institutions I want to thank because without them this book would not have been possible. I am extremely grateful for their support and encouragement during this process.

I will always be proud for my training as a scholar at the University of Texas at Austin. The Department of History not only has the most professional and amazing professors but also has one of the best programs for Latin American History. I want to particularly thank Professor Seth W. Garfield, for whom I only have words of gratitude and admiration. His incomparable historiographical knowledge and analytical skills inspired me to do the best work I could. Dr. Garfield's generosity and devotion to his colleagues also are qualities of a great professional. He taught me how to become a scholar, a researcher, and a true historian. I will always be grateful for his academic mentorship and feel very fortunate for being one of his former students. Other professors who supported my work and deserve special recognition are Benjamin Claude Brower, whose class Trauma and History sparked my interest in memory and violence studies; Virginia Garrard, who always had words of encouragement for me and my research; and Donna DeCesare, whose invaluable feedback helped me shape my project.

In Colombia, there are many people who deserve special recognition, especially those whom I had the honor to interview. In the town of Granada, Antioquia, I thank Gloria Elcy Ramírez, Gloria Elcy Quintero, Claudia Milena Giraldo, Jaime Montoya, Sonia Bermúdez, Wilder Ceballos, and Edwin Giraldo. In Medellín, the staff of the Museo Casa de la Memoria. In Montes de María, Caribbean Colombian region, I thank Soraya Bayuelo and Giovanni Castro. In Bogotá, I am grateful to Elvira Cuervo de Jaramillo, María Victoria de Angulo de Robayo, Daniel Castro, Antonio Ochoa, Catalina Ruíz, Samuel

Monsalve, and María Paola Rodríguez, all related to the Museo Nacional. I also thank journalist and activist Patricia Lara and artist Lorena Luengas for their valuable input to my work. To the staff of the Centro Nacional de Memoria Histórica, before the appointment of Darío Acevedo as its director, all my gratitude for their help and guidance. To my dear and beloved friend Clara Isabel Botero, who introduced me to the museum world, I am forever indebted. Her memory is present in this work.

The following institutions were pivotal for my research, and I want to acknowledge them: Centro de Memoria, Paz y Reconciliación (Bogotá), Museo de la Policía (Bogotá), Museo del Caribe (Barranquilla), and Museo Comunitario de San Jacinto (Montes de María). I also want to acknowledge the support and friendship I have found in the public history community. They have become critics and examples to follow, the conversations we have sustain my professional path. They are María Elena Bedoya, Thomas Cauvin, and my colleagues of the International Federation for Public History, too many to count, but they know who they are and how appreciative I am for having them as peers.

Finally, I am grateful to my family. My father, who passed away some years ago, was a historian too, and I hope to make him proud from wherever he is. To my mother and my brother my most sincere gratitude due to their unconditional affection and support for my work. Finally, I would not have been able to get this far without Luisa Perry, my daughter. She inspires me every day to be a better version of myself. Her love and example are the beacons that illuminate my life.

# INTRODUCTION

On June 19, 2022, Colombians elected a demobilized guerrilla fighter as their president and a Black woman as vice president (2022–2026). In addition, on June 28th, the Truth Commissioners, after four years of fieldwork and research, presented the Final Report of the Truth Commission. This Colombian agency was launched in 2017 within the framework of the Peace Agreement of 2016, with the aim to elucidate the truth about the armed conflict, promote coexistence, and avoid the repetition of atrocities offering all citizens a comprehensive explanation of what happened during the internal war. The Truth Commission is part of the transitional justice mechanisms, thus is temporary and extrajudicial. The other instruments are the Jurisdicción Especial para la Paz, JEP (Peace Special Jurisdiction), and the Unidad para la Búsqueda de Personas dadas por Desaparecidas, UBDP (Missing Person Search Unit).[1]

These two major events are milestones in the country's recent history. It is the first time that Colombians voted for a left leaning government and want to face the magnitude about the horrors of the internal war. For a nation traditionally ruled by two political parties: liberals and conservatives, these affairs have positive significance, particularly for marginalized populations. However, large segments of Colombian inhabitants do not embrace inclusion and are critical of the new country leaders and the report, even though they claim to be open-minded and not racist.

The mentioned affairs are also changing the Colombian memory scene, tampered by radical right-wing actors. Since 2016, when President Juan Manuel Santos (2010–2018) signed the Peace Agreement with the Fuerzas Armadas Revolucionarias de Colombia-Ejército del Pueblo, FARC-EP (Revolutionary Armed Forces of Colombia-People's Army) guerrilla, the efforts of achieving national reconciliation have been shattered by political players who do not

DOI: 10.4324/9781003283997-1

believe this is the way to end the country's internal war. Their positions go as far as denying the existence of an armed conflict. Instead, right-wingers talk about terrorism, common criminal activities, informal employment, and internal migration, ignoring completely the voices of local minorities, their victim and survivor status, memory, and their right to reparation and justice. Thus, the historical memories struggle in Colombia is contentious, dangerous, and revolutionary. In this context, the two occurrences become extremely significant, sparking the ambition of most Colombians to live in peace. The election of the candidates of the political party Pacto Histórico (Historical Pact), Gustavo Petro as president and Francia Márquez as vice president, evidences the Colombians' desire to find alternatives to the conventional country's rule. The coalition they belong to, created in 2021, is composed of representatives of the left and center left, which follow progressive, social democrat, and socialist democrat ideologies and strongly believe in the country's need to achieve peace.

This novel memory scenario brings challenges to academics, researchers, activists, victims, and survivors who have listened to horror stories during the last two decades but now have the chance to overcome them and envision a better present and future. I started this investigation in 2014 when President Santos was still in office and fighting for the Peace Agreement with the FARC-EP. Then came the worldwide news of the plebiscite, in which the country's citizens voted no for peace. After that, Colombians polarized between those who wanted an end to the armed conflict and those who do not believe national reconciliation can be obtained under the given terms of the accord, which included no incarceration for the demobilized FARC-EP members but specific areas for their reincorporation into civilian life. Since then, some politicians, such as former minister of justice and interior and right-winger Fernando Londoño, have voiced their efforts to "shred the agreement with the FARC-EP,"[2] totally disregarding victims and survivors of brutalities.

Armed conflict deniers were emboldened by Iván Duque's presidency (2018–2022), whose mandate ended on August 7, 2022, and caused upheaval in almost all sectors of Colombian affairs. His stands about historical memory, for instance, were highly explosive, causing discomfort, distrust, and concern in victims associations, human rights activists, NGOs, and citizens who do not follow the logic of war. During his mandate, he appointed an armed conflict negationist as head of the National Center for Historical Memory, who resigned when the new nation leaders got elected and was summoned by the JEP to give explanations about his actions during his appointment. However, the damage inflicted was significant. Duque also privileged narratives of paramilitaries, rich landowners, military men, and the conventional political class in the project of nation building, taking advantage of the considerable percentage of Colombian citizens who believe in right-wing positions and his historical memory policies. Since the new government took office on August 7, 2022, there have been many developing issues and discussions left out in this book. As I write this introduction, multiple debates are taking place responding to the new airs blowing throughout the country; their outcomes are subject of ongoing research and a future publication.

Using this dynamic context as a backdrop, *Museums, Exhibitions, and Memories of Violence in Colombia, 2000–2014: Trying to Remember* presents four case studies of historical memory representations of brutalities endured by urban and rural communities during the nation's armed conflict since the decade of 1980s until 2014. This work is part of a broader effort in the social sciences and humanities to understand the interactions between memory, documentation, transitional justice, and cultural heritage. Although this book focuses on Colombia and on the different historical memories created by the state and grassroots communities, my hope is that these case studies contribute to the needed discussion for providing a regional narrative about the production of historical memories in Colombia as part of the public history field, its practices, and its implications. My wish, in addition, is that they inspire nonconventional ways of approaching the mentioned issues and place them in a Latin American regional context.

This work engages with the study of memory sites, exploring how different human groups use museums and exhibitions as aids to grieve and restore social fabrics destroyed by war. Through ethnographic fieldwork and archival research, this investigation highlights the significance of cultural diversity among communities in Colombia that come to decide which memories are worth passing on to new generations. Hence, *Museums, Exhibitions, and Memories of Violence in Colombia, 2000–2014* addresses four questions: How does a public history framework informs the study of historical memories of violence and its representation in memory sites in Colombia? Which narratives do Colombians privilege as historical memories?

How is violence represented differently in the country's varied memory sites, museums, and exhibitions? And what is the role of these places in Colombian society? I am interested in how elite and marginal communities create narratives of national belonging, with the attendant rights and privileges of citizenship and social inclusion.

To answer the previous questions, I resort to the relationship between public history and social justice. This approach which addresses community initiatives to be heard and acknowledged in the nation, their voices, and projects informs the cases presented in this book. In the Colombian and Latin American context, it is not possible to understand public history without taking a stand in favor of justice, victims, survivors, and their right for representation. As historians Sebastián Vargas and Amada Carolina Pérez note, although in recent years Colombian public historians and the field have gained prominence in the country, there are several academics, researchers, and activists who have practiced it, sometimes unknowingly, since 1960.[3] Aware that history is a public matter not limited to classrooms, they work in museums, libraries, universities, media and communication, and the government. In addition, noteworthy events have taken place in Colombia. For instance, in 2016, the Third International Conference of the International Federation for Public History (IFPH) took place in Bogotá, Colombian public historians and their concerns to the forefront, which comprise museums and other exhibitions sites, films, documentaries, historical novels, anniversaries and commemorations, re-enactments and living history, public policies, transitional justice commissions, television, radio, websites, social media, and justice.

Another example of the interrelation of public history and social justice occurred during the country's 2021 social unrest which caused at least 46 dead in a little more than a month.[4] The disturbances were sparked by a long history of poverty, inequality, lack of representation of minorities, and corruption. After years of silence and keeping their heads down, Colombians realized that the signing of the Peace Accord in 2016 opened the door for fair and non-discriminatory ways of living. The 2021 protests were also fueled by Duque's government management of the Covid-19 pandemic, which was successful at the beginning. However, by April 2021, deaths broke records aggravated by the government's brutal response to the wave of grassroots protests sweeping the nation. One of the most significant waves of demonstrations happened when president Iván Duque made an ill-considered move, announcing that he planned to implement a wide-ranging new tax structure on goods and income streams such as pensions, basic foodstuffs like eggs and coffee, and public utilities, including electricity and water. He also sought to procure more revenue from diverse economic sectors, including the publishing industry and software development. The nation mobilized *en masse*, led by youth—who face extremely high unemployment rates—and representatives from indigenous, Afro-Colombian, and other severely marginalized groups. Under the pandemic, the number of people living in extreme poverty grew by 2.8 million. The proposed tax reform pushed people over the edge because it made evident the economic and social inequalities faced by the lower and middle class in Colombia, which the pandemic exacerbated.[5]

In this hectic social context, students and young people lost their lives and body parts such as eyes, and the killing of social leaders increased, rising to more than 140 in 2021 only. Marginal groups such as the Indigenous and Black populations took advantage of these circumstances to strengthen an initiative started by the Namuy Misak community in 2020 by knocking down the statue of the Spanish conquistador Sebastián de Belalcázar (1480–1551) in the city of Popayán in the south-west of Colombia. This significant act brought up the desire of the Colombian Indigenous population to rewrite their history of exclusion and oppression. More statues fell after the ones mentioned. The same community removed a second statue of Belalcázar in the south-western city of Cali, and a few days later they destroyed an effigy in Bogotá representing Gonzalo Jiménez de Quesada, the conquistador who founded the city in 1638.

Encouraged by the Misak people, in June 2021, in the northern city of Barranquilla, anti-government protesters toppled the statue of Christopher Columbus, and during the same month, strikers attempted to tear down the statues of Columbus and Isabella I of Castile also in Bogotá and painted them red, which led the culture ministry to remove the figures "for safety reasons."[6]

The removal of statues in Colombia reminded scholars and activists of the link between public history and social justice which can be traced in Latin America to the decade of 1980s when Argentinian sociologist Elizabet Jelin got involved with human rights movements in her country.[7] Her reflections, at the time, alluded to the need for social justice in the South Cone and the region. Since then, researchers from other states of the region, such as Colombian historian Gonzalo Sánchez, also started to think about how victims and survivors of violent and traumatic events remembered and represented in the present their justice demands.[8] Jelin´s concerns during the 1980s were related "to the ways in which a society and its legitimate authorities, as represented in a democratic state, confront a violent past in which all the principles for peaceful coexistence were crushed and violated." This tension noted by the sociologist is still present in Latin America, where there is an evident tension between the state and grassroots communities' narratives of the atrocities committed during war. What can the state do to bring country and society back into the fold of the "normal" world? How can a state establish a global presence free from the shameful drags of the past when neither amnesty nor amnesia is acceptable in a cultural climate that has given a prominent place to memory worldwide? The meanings of the past were elaborated in the years immediately following the transition to democracy after the South Cone dictatorships condemned violence, especially the state terrorism responsible for human rights violations. The focus was on civil and political rights rather than on social or economic ones. In the case of Argentina, the emphasis on human rights violations became particularly clear in 1985 when the former heads of the military governments were brought to trial in Buenos Aires. Both the report of the Comisión Nacional sobre la Desaparición de Personas, CONADEP (National Commission on the Disappearance of Persons), and the trial shared an interpretive framework that depoliticized the sociopolitical conflict. An interpretation of repression as a "violation of human rights," as stated in 1996 by Kathryn Sikkink in her article "The Emergence, Evolution, and Effectiveness of the Latin American Human Rights Network," soon gained acceptance. Before that time, domination and social and political struggles were interpreted in terms of class struggle or national revolutions. The incorporation of the framework of "human rights violations" was, in this context, a true paradigmatic revolution. According to it, human beings possess certain inalienable rights regardless of their actions and even of their will. The concept also implies that state institutions are the main entities responsible for enforcing and protecting these rights. Since then, memory policies followed this framework.

As part of the growing memory field in Latin America and the relation between public history and social justice, from May 11 to 13, 2021, the project Explorers of the IFPH held the online conference *Public History, Museums, and Digital Communities in Latin America*. During this event, Latin American researchers presented their projects related to public history which ranged from local museums to social justice, digital humanities, archives, cemeteries, and historical memories. These three days displayed the state of the art of the field in the region leaving interesting questions and unfinished discussions. One of them relates to public history's state of the art in Latin America, and others noted that despite a considerable number of public history research, academics, activists, politicians, and artists have emphasized on regionalism rather than globalization, and now there is a need for transnational perspectives as well. Professionals from Guyana, Chile, Ecuador, Brazil, Colombia, Guatemala, Mexico, and Brazil presented their current work, which shed light on the need to encourage reflections not only as individual countries but also as a region.

This event followed one that took place in 2017 organized by the Getty Research Institute Symposium in Los Angeles called the *Birth of the Museum in Latin America*. On this occasion, Latin American researchers addressed the new scholarship on the origins of museums in their countries. The presentations included interdisciplinary perspectives on the creation, identity, and current issues of the institutions in the region. Scholars from Argentina, Panama, Costa Rica, Mexico, Brazil, Germany, and the USA discussed the long-lasting questions: What is a museum? How are collections of Latin American origin distributed across museums and private collectors globally? What challenges has colonialism created for Latin America? What makes for a successful museum and its intended public? Which are alternative models for the display of Latin American objects? Which are the problems that Latin American museums currently face?[9]

These two conferences illustrate how intellectuals, activists, and artists have conducted public history and social justice research for a long time in the region. Even though we can trace the origins of public history to the 1970s and even before,[10] the interest in the field has raised significantly in the last 30 years. Currently, there are several researchers and disciplines interested in public history, which can be seen in the new scholarship produced, such as the works of Professor Andrew Rajca, who wrote in 2018 *Dissensual Subjects: Memory, Human Rights, and Postdictatorship in Argentina, Brazil, and Uruguay*; the ethnographer Joseph Feldman's 2021 *Memories before the State. Postwar Peru and the Place of Memory, Tolerance, and Social Inclusion*; the Professor of Spanish Aurelia Unamuno's 2020 *Entre fuegos, memoria y violencia de Estado: Los textos literarios y testimoniales del movimiento armado en México*; and the academics Karina Oliva Alvarado, Alicia Ivonne Estrada, and Ester E. Hernández 2017 *U.S. Central Americans: Reconstructing Memories, Struggles, and Communities of Resistance*, just to name a few. These authors are reconfiguring innovative ways to approach museums, archives, and memory by using transverse axes to answer some of the ever-present questions in public history. Queries such as who has the right to the past, the tensions between official and non-official historical memories, the function and role of museums in society are part of the topics dealt with by the mentioned authors, but they are providing a wider scope. For instance, Rajca's work focuses on Argentina, Brazil, and Uruguay. He delves into the studied relationship between art and politics using the slogan "never again" to find differences and similarities in historical memories production in post-dictatorship contexts.

Although we can talk about remembrance, commemorations, memorialization, and forgetting in the region since the early twentieth century and even before, *Museums, Exhibitions, and Memories of Violence in Colombia, 2000–2014* focuses on what has been called the memory turn of the second half of the twentieth century. In this context, scholars such as Michael Lazzara state that there are three definitive periods in the region related to memory and its analysis. First, he mentions a time between the 1980s and 1990s characterized by the concern for traumatic memories, the forms remembrances took, the reflections on transitions to democracy, and the challenges this implied. A second wave, following Lazzara, took place in the mid-to-late 1990s and was determined by the works of Argentinian sociologist Elizabeth Jelin and the Social Science Research Council and Ford's Foundation cosponsored project, "Collective Memories of Repression in the Southern Cone." Thanks to this initiative, analysis and discussions about archives, memorials, sites, pedagogies, and institutions gained visibility, and the result was a wide array of scholars and publications addressing the topic in Latin America. Although these two junctures focused mostly on the aftermath of the South Cone dictatorships recollections and representations, the field started to expand its scope and included other Latin American countries that also had problematic pasts, such as Peru, Colombia, El Salvador, Guatemala, Nicaragua, Brazil, and Mexico. A third moment related to approaches to the field came with the turn of the century, when memory studies continued to broaden their geographical scope in the region, its topics, and places of study and research. This regional reach included marginal and rural areas and questions related to local memories. Within this framework, scholars came to the realization that even though the starting point for memory studies in Latin America was the violence of some Southern Cone countries, the experiences and concepts produced in these contexts were not relatable to other territories, such as Colombia and Mexico, where violence has never left.[11]

The three waves mentioned by Lazzara also implied shifts in the questions and attention devoted by scholars and activists about which topics to explore within the memory field. From concerns about what and who remembers or forgets examined during the first moment, in the following one the inquiries were more related to the conflictive character of memory itself: Who has the right to remember, who is worth remembering, and how do "truths" play a definitive stance in memorialization. Another significant topic of research during the last two periods is which memories should be passed on to future generations and for what reasons. Currently, the field is constantly growing and bringing to our attention forgotten marginal characters who produce memories in several diverse ways. In 2022, Michael Lazzara and Fernando Blanco published the edited volume *Los futuros de la memoria en América Latina: Sujetos, políticas y epistemologías en disputa* (*Memory's Futures in Latin America: Subjects, Politics, and Epistemologies*) in which they provide a state-of-the-art perspective of memory. This book delves into the three mentioned above moments hinting to the need to take the representations and remembrances beyond the past and realize that the region is undergoing dramatic changes that deserve inclusion in the memory field. Corruption, an acute crisis of neoliberal economic models, strong claims for all kinds of rights, massive protests, and the still strong presence of the right, demand reflections immersed in "memory's futures." Lazzara and Blanco, following historian Andreas Huyssen, insist that the memory field needs a transformative renovation, reframing its effect on conventional historiography and other disciplines without denying the undeniable. They also concur with Huyssen on his statement about the need to have more than remembrances of past injustices; instead, the scholars insist, what is crucial for the advancement of the discipline are debates about memory's incidence in democracy, about its influence in contemporary contexts, and about how they open and close actions, oppose the established orders, and promote social change. These considerations trigger new questions such as, How to get involved currently with the memory field research going on since 1960? Which voices do we still need to unveil? Do "post-transitions" require novel analytical frameworks? If so, which ones? Or shall these coexist with the ones of the 1970s, 1980s, 1990s, and 2000s? Which kinds of memories are necessary to build the democracies we dream of?[12]

Commonly, historical memory research in Latin America and its concerns focus on the representation and remembrance of violent and traumatic events and what is called difficult heritage. Popularized by anthropologist Sharon McDonald, she talks about the value of displaying a problematic past and the ways in which people react to these exhibitions. According to McDonald, depending on their background, age, social status, and political views, observers will have different impressions of what they are seeing. Perhaps, instead of horrifying the viewers, showing difficult heritage can spark criticism and innovative thoughts about identity.[13]

Associated to McDonald's approaches to heritage, the memory field started to gain significant notoriety in Latin America during the decade of 2000s, when Argentinian sociologist Elizabeth Jelin pioneered the project "Collective Memories of Repression in the Southern Cone," already mentioned.[14] This initiative promoted the analysis and comprehension of traumatic memories in the region and included archives, memorials, sites, pedagogies, and fieldwork. Her influence was not confined to Argentina, Chile, and Paraguay; its impact reached Mexico, Peru, El Salvador, Guatemala, Nicaragua, Brazil, and Colombia. Meanwhile, since the 1980s, historian Gonzalo Sánchez was also paving the way for memory studies in the region. He states that in Colombia's case, for instance, memory is associated with fractures, divisions, and cultural distress. He also refers to vast historical memories of violence that prevail in the country due to the large number of victims and survivors of brutalities. He emphasizes, as well, the relevance of testimonies for preventing state officials from forgetting. Therefore, recalling and representing violent past events acquire different meanings, due to the selectivity and positionality of Colombians' memory. To omit certain violent accounts or the reluctance to talk about the brutalities endured by members of several communities does not mean people ignore what happened. On the contrary, it denotes how Colombians want future generations to remember the brutalities endured from 1980 to the early 2000. Sánchez echoed Jelin when affirming that the activation of memories is a fraught process due to the diverse and politically divides that memories trigger. Starting with the analysis about Colombia's internal conflict and his active participation in academic efforts to explain and understand the ongoing violence, Sánchez became as crucial as sociologist Elizabeth Jelin to understand the growing Latin American memory field.[15]

Within this framework, I address the ever-present inquiry of whose memories are the ones represented. I borrow this interrogation from French philosopher Paul Ricouer's *Memory, History, Forgetting*.[16] Although this book is not about memory proprietorship, it is fundamental for my discussion to acknowledge who decided what, how, why, and when to remember atrocities. To analyze memories' creation allows us to understand which cultural decisions came into play when omitting certain accounts of brutalities. In this sense, silences are unlike forgetting because, according to Ricoeur, the difference between amnesia, in its clinical meaning, and to forget, is that the first one does not leave traces. Thus, a community's decision not to represent a violent event past is the product of an intentional cultural deliberation and its historical legacies. Building on Ricoeur's work, sociologist Elizabeth Jelin states that "dealing with memories entails paying attention to remembrance and forgetting, to narratives and acts, to silences and gestures. Knowledge and information are at play, but so too are emotions, lapses, voids, and fractures." This applies to the Colombian cases explored in *Museums, Exhibitions, and Memories of Violence in Colombia, 2000–2014*. The museums and exhibitions of the social groups explored demonstrate that in recalling a violent act, for instance, there is simultaneously an exercise of forgetting. In this sense, and concurring with Jelin, "memory is selective, full memory is impossible."[5]

In each one of the chapters of this book, I highlight the significance of memories of political violence in a specific museological context. In Chapters

1 and 2, I examine the relationship between memory, documentation, and forgetting, contrasting a failed initiative of the Director of the National Museum of Colombia and a successful exhibition in the same institution about artifacts and life stories of renowned guerrilla leaders. In these chapters, I adhere to Jelin's definition of memory, as stated in *State Repression and the Labors of Memory*: "memory is not an object that is simply there to be extracted, but rather it is produced by active subjects that share a culture and an ethos." Therefore, Ricoeur's question "whose memory?" arises again in direct relationship with Jelin's query "where is memory?" Her interrogation builds on Ricoeur's insistence on the fact that conflict emerges when there are a variety of recollections. The diversity of memories clash, she insists, when each one tries to become the most accurate, visible, truthful, and vivid—in other words, hegemonic—making remembrances and their representations subjects of "political struggle." However, states Jelin, collective remembrances bring people together and strengthen their sense of belonging to a group or community. "Furthermore, especially for oppressed, silenced, or discriminated groups," she notes, "the reference to a shared past often facilitates building feelings of self-respect and greater reliance in oneself and in the group." In *Museums, Exhibitions, and Memories of Violence in Colombia, 2000–2014*, I concur with Jelin when she claims that the victims of atrocities are those who should be the main protagonists when producing historical memories. The diversity of remembrances should be part of projects of nation building.

Historian Michael Rothberg agrees with Jelin's arguments by underscoring the need for comparisons rather than exclusions. For him, memory production is more than "a one-way street."[17] Inspired by Rothberg's multidirectional memory concept, which calls our attention to "the dynamic transfers that take place between diverse places and times during the act of remembrance and helps explain the spiraling interactions that characterize the politics of memory," I analyze how Colombian survivors of violence have made claims for inclusion, participation, and visibility from the state. In Chapters 1 and 2, I show how varied cultural backgrounds also set the scene for the aesthetics of remembrance. Thus, artifacts that reflect "alternative" kinds of experiences may not find space in patrician institutions such as the National Museum. To demonstrate this point, I resort to sociologist Pierre Bourdieu's concept of cultural capital, which includes matters of class and taste. For the sociologist, this is the academic and non-academic, inherited, social knowledge, behaviors, and skills that demonstrate our cultural competence; therefore, our status in society depends on:

> [...] activities such as the visual arts [museum narratives], or playing a musical instrument, [...] presuppose a cultural capital generally acquired outside the educational system and are (relatively) independent of the level of academic certification [...], the correlation with social class, which is again strong, is established through social trajectory [...][18]

Bourdieu's insights help clarify why taste and class become status markers that permeate exhibition contents in shrines of high culture, such as the National Museum of Colombia. Moreover, the representations of violence in official institutions aimed at producing historical memories are reflective of the politics and cultural capital of their curators and their perceptions of the war. Chapter 1 presents the debates surrounding an intimate object of a perpetrator, a guerrilla leader, at the National Museum of Colombia in 2001. Although in hindsight, we can think that the display of such an object is necessary for an encompassing understanding of the armed conflict, the readers will find that within the socio-political context of the time, such initiative was impossible. In fact, it never came true. On occasion, time and distance from the violent episodes are necessary to remember and represent them. During 2001, the country was amid guerrilla's attacks to the country's infrastructure and civilians, causing a deep disdain for the attackers. However, the project of acquiring the personal objects of the guerrilla leader sparked questions about who Colombians should remember, how, and why. Chapter 2 is a sequel to the former one. There, I discuss an exhibit that took place at the National Museum of Colombia in 2010. It was about the life of a demobilized guerrilla leader who ran for president in 1991 but encountered death when a hired hitman shot him 45 days after launching his campaign. As opposed to the main character of Chapter 1, the one in Chapter 2 was accepted and loved by Colombians, especially after laying down his arms. I argue that he had the country's citizens' approval because he belonged to a traditional, well-known family and had a wealthy background, while the guerrilla leader of the first section was poor, uneducated, and came from a peasant family. In Chapter 2, I remember the year 1991 as a traumatic time for Colombians, not only because of the demobilized guerrilla member's murder but also because of the assassination of other two presidential candidates. Of the three, two won a place in Colombians' memory by having a commemorative exhibition 20 years after their magnicide; the third one, militant of the Colombian Communist Party, did not. Thus, in Chapter 2, I ask the question of which are some of the elements that come into play when deciding who Colombians should remember.

Chapters 3 and 4 of *Museums, Exhibitions, and Memories of Violence in Colombia, 2000–2014* contrast with the first two because they are devoted to grassroots initiatives, which usually have a complicated relationship with the government. These examples of community memory sites highlight some examples of how marginalized and local social groups recall the atrocities they endured during the recent armed conflict. In Chapter 3, I address the case of the Salón del Nunca Más (Hall of Never Again) in Granada, Antioquia, a township in the Department of Antioquia, whose capital is Medellín, to explore, through pictures, written testimonies, and material culture, the relationship between memory and transitional justice in poor peasant communities. Here, I also engage in conversation with museum scholars such as Hilde Klein, Tony Bennett, Silke

Arnold di Simine, Ivan Karp, Steven Levina, Irina Podogrny, Margaret Lopes, Gyan Prakash, Steve Stern, and Paul Vergo to ponder on the nature and role of museums. For instance, for the inhabitants of Granada, the Hall of Never Again is not a museum, although in some circumstances it poses like one. The idea in Chapter 3 is not to give definitions about the institution but to understand how diverse sites serve their own communities.

The main sources examined in Chapter 3 are called *bitácoras*, journal-like notebooks displayed at the Hall of Never Again. They pair with the approximately 200-picture exhibition of Granada's victims of atrocities since 1980. At the Hall, survivors, relatives, and friends of the absent ones grieve and communicate with them through the *bitácoras*, where they write to the departed. In their pages, there are accounts of violence, descriptions of the township, and narratives about the sorrow of losing loved ones to violence. These devices are fundamental for understanding the nature of the Hall due to the interactions they register and trigger. In addition, they are healing tools and records of Granada's recent history. Currently, the Hall of Never Again houses almost 200 *bitácoras*, which are public records. They are meant for the public to read them and are part of the site's creator's goal of causing a long-lasting impact on those who visit the Hall. Frequently, during Hall's tours, the guides will read excerpts of the *bitácoras* to the audience. Lastly, this chapter is aimed to examine the relationship between memory sites and transitional justice in Colombia, considering the Special Peace Jurisdiction (Jurisdicción Especial para la Paz, JEP) created in 2016, as a part of the Integral System for Truth, Justice, Reparation, and No Repetition within the Peace Agreement frame. Although we can talk about transitional justice in Colombia since 2005, the JEP is a significant step to know the reality and magnitude of the atrocities committed before 2016. The JEP will not last more than 20 years. In this context, I insist that the content found at the Hall of Never Again, for instance, as in the other memory Colombian sites, should become fundamental contributions for the policies aimed at achieving the long-awaited peace.

Finally, Chapter 4 of *Museums, Exhibitions, and Memories of Violence in Colombia, 2000–2014,* examines the Museo Itinerante de la Memoria e Identidad de Los Montes de María, aka El Mochuelo (Traveling Museum of the Memory and Identity of Montes de Maria), and its emphasis on oral histories and local culture in the Colombian Caribbean. It was named after a traditional songbird of the region, and each time the venue travels, it is referred to by its creators as flights. Through this case study, I explore the connection between memory and cultural heritage and how it informs the remembrances of the recent country's violence. Grassroots venues and exhibits encapsulate the insistence of human rights scholars and advocates on memory as a key component for communities in their struggle against cycles of violence, impunity, inequality, and marginalization. This venue has unique features which deserve a closer look. It is a peripatetic institution and not only an itinerant exhibition, which makes it noticeable, especially due to the conditions of the area. Usually, Montes de María has hot weather and basic public utilities, such as water and electricity, that can be spotty, circumstances that make moving El Mochuelo around difficult. Therefore, the venue's architecture is made of materials found in the area and has an easy to carry, assemble, and disassemble structure.

Another of El Mochuelo's qualities is the way the members of the 15 communities of the area and its creators decided to remember and represent the brutalities inflicted upon them since 1980. They chose not to allude directly to the violence but to rely on their own traditional oral expressions, which has become a cultural inventory exercise. The venue displays songs, poems, and stories of Montes de María and even has devoted a space for live storytellers. El Mochuelo producers understand the country's internal war as a part of their history that does not define them; instead, they want the public to remember them as "people of words." When the museum moves or "flies" like the people of the area say, it also activates knowledge exchanges because the stories it accounts for are different among the municipalities and townships it serves. Thus, El Mochuelo is constantly updating its displays and generating new contents, which in turn encourages the region's inhabitants to preserve their culture. This is also an example of how local and marginalized communities decide what kind of memory device and institution serves them better.

To delve into the issues in Chapters 3 and 4, I consider philosopher and sociologist Maurice Halbwachs' concepts of autobiographical and collective memory, developed in his book *On Collective Memory*. For Halbwachs, social groups share memories, knowledge, and information that are definitive for their identity. Members of a community interpret what they see and live as members of a collective, which in turn determines how they approach events.[19] The interaction between what he has called autobiographical, instead of individual, and collective memory is what constitutes historical memory. When people come together to remember not only the brutalization but also the accomplishments of those departed, they resort to their collective memory, to the social institutions of the group. The shared memories also come from autobiographical memory of the individuals, those who personally experienced the motive of commemoration.

In relation to the analysis of memory sites and its dynamics, also addressed in Chapters 3 and 4 of this book, I draw on the scholarship of academics such as Charumbira, Hakk, Alon Confino, Richard Terdiman, LaCapra, Coehn, Carol Lansing, Marilyn Lake, Kevin Walsh, and T. Benton. Other fundamental text that has influenced the conception of intangible heritage is Jay Winter's *Sites of Memory, Sites of Mourning: The Great War in European Cultural History*, which focuses on the nine million French, British, and German citizens who died during the First World War (1914–1918) and the ways in which the mourning processes took place. Winter presents literary, cinematic, and architectural topics that aided in commemoration projects.

In addition, I rely on historian Pierre Nora's definition of what he calls *lieux de mémoire* (sites of memory). In his book, *Realms of Memory. The Construction of the French Past. Vol I* Nora argues that these places emerge because memory is not spontaneous. The author claims that social groups frequently suppress rituals related to the past due to their decision to privilege the present. Hence, museums, archives, cemeteries, and other memory sites become ritualized spaces used by communities to preserve their remembrances and commemorate what is relevant for their culture. Thus, for Nora, memory is quite distinct from history in the sense that the first is alive, in permanent evolution, subject to the dialectic of remembering and forgetting, and "capable of lying dormant for long periods only to be suddenly reawakened." For Nora, as well, modern memory is archival, "it rests entirely on the materiality of the trace, on the immediacy of the record, on the visibility of the image." History on the other hand, "is the reconstruction, always problematic and incomplete, of what is no longer."[20] *Museums, Exhibitions, and Memories of Violence in Colombia, 2000–2014* concurs with Nora in the sense that the state agents or grassroots communities that actively created the memory sites and exhibitions analyzed here had specific agendas and templates in mind when ritualizing and commemorating traumatic past events. For the main actors involved in the creation of the venues presented in this investigation, memory becomes a tool to create new political dialogues and historical landmarks.

In *Museums, Exhibitions, and Memories of Violence in Colombia, 2000–2014*, I emphasize how through museums and exhibitions, communities and individuals activate their memories in plural because there is never only remembrance in society, a process even more fraught in a culturally diverse and politically divided nation like Colombia. Historian Gonzalo Sánchez, in his book Guerras, Memoria e Historia (*Wars, Memory, and History*), states that in Colombia's case, memory is associated with fractures, divisions, and cultural distress.[21] Sánchez refers to vast historical memories of violence which prevail in the country due to the substantial number of victims and survivors of brutalities. He emphasizes, as well, the relevance of testimonies for preventing state officials from forgetting. Therefore, recalling and representing violent past events of Colombians' memory, as discussed throughout this investigation. To omit certain violent accounts or the reluctance to talk about the brutalities endured by members of communities does not mean people ignore what happened. On the contrary, it denotes how Colombians want future generations to remember the brutalities endured from 1980 to the early 2000. In addition, historian Steve Stern calls our attention to the restrictive binary dichotomy between remembrance and forgetting that narrows the analysis of the topic, which is much more nuanced. Stern insists on considering that memory making implies silence making. I believe this applies to Colombia.

Introduction 15

## A Never-Ending Story? Violence in Colombia

In 2005, during the second mandate of right-wing president Álvaro Uribe Vélez (2002–2006; 2006–2010),[24] Congress issued the controversial Ley de Justicia y Paz or Ley 975 de 2005 (Law of Justice and Peace or Law 975 of 2005). This regulation aimed to demobilize the members of the Autodefensas Unidas de Colombia, AUC (United Self-Defense Forces of Colombia), a far-right paramilitary and drug trafficking organization, responsible for many of the atrocities committed during the country's armed conflict from 1997 to 2006. If we read between the lines, notes historian Marco Palacios, Law 975 absolved these armed groups from any accountability for brutalities. According to Palacios in his book *Violencia pública en Colombia, 1958–2010 (Public Violence in Colombia, 1958–2010)*, "This law was a great victory for the paramilitaries because it provided impunity for almost all their crimes against humanity... and only 7% of the demobilized were judged according to the Law." That same year, a group of researchers created the Grupo de Memoria Histórica (Group for Historical Memory), which criticized the law. Anthropologist Pilar Riaño and anthropologist and historian María Victoria Uribe stated that this regulation "was a way to exonerate the paramilitaries of the crimes committed."[22] For instance, the vague phrasing of the law made it difficult to distinguish who was a victim, implying that the paramilitaries could also fit in the category:

> For the purposes of this law, victim is the person who individually or collectively suffered direct damage due to temporary or permanent injuries which cause physical, psychic, or sensory disability, emotional suffering, financial loss, or lessening of their fundamental rights. The damage should be a consequence of transgressing the country's criminal law by armed groups outside the law.
> 
> Victim is also the spouse, partner, and first-degree relatives, first civil degree of the direct victim, when dead or disappeared.
> 
> Colombians also acquire the victim condition regardless of whether the authorities identify the author of the punishable conduct, apprehend, prosecute, or convict him or her without regard to the family relationship between the author and the victim.[27]

Another critique to the law was the leniency for members of the paramilitaries who confessed to crimes. As a result, some of them had reduced sentences or were set free.[23]

This legislation, however, set in motion a national movement devoted to remembering, representing, and creating historical accounts of the violence since the 1980s in Colombia. Thus, in 2011, the Congress issued the Ley de Víctimas y Restitución de Tierras de 2011 (Law for Victims and Land Restitution of 2011), an outgrowth of Law 975, which in turn encouraged the official foundation of the Centro Nacional de Memoria Histórica, CNMH (National Center for Historical Memory). This law advanced a definition of victims, as expressed in its Article 3:

> For the purposes of this law, victims are those persons who individually or collectively had suffered damage due to events occurred from January 1, 1985, on. These acts should be consequences of infractions of the International Humanitarian Law or severe violations to the Human Rights international norms, happened within the internal armed conflict.
> 
> [...] There are also victims the spouses, permanent partners, same sex couples and relatives with first degree of consanguinity, first relative of the direct victim, in case they died or disappeared. In the absence of these, there are also victims the relatives in second degree of ascendant consanguinity.
> 
> Also, victims are those who suffered an injury while assisting another endangered victim or when preventing the victimization.
> 
> Colombians can acquire victim status regardless of whether the author is punishable, apprehended, prosecuted, or convicted of the punishable conduct and of the family relationship that may exist between the author and the victim.
> 
> [...] Paragraph 2°. Members of armed groups outside the law are not victims except in cases when removing boys, girls, and/or teenagers from the armed group while still being minors.

This more comprehensive definition of who is a victim aimed to differentiate between perpetrators and victims and survivors of brutalities. The 2011 legislation also promoted the creation of two state divisions for victims' care in January 2012: The Unit for Victims' Assistance and Reparation and the Unit for Land Restitution.

These laws are two turning points to understand the historical memory struggles in Colombia during the second half of the twentieth century, as they encouraged researchers to produce significant data and results about the country's recent violence. In this context, in 2016, after six years of inquiry, the professionals from the CNMH issued the publication *Basta ya! Colombia: Memorias de Guerra y Dignidad*.[24] In this general report, published in English and Spanish, the academics of the institution documented 730 massacres committed by paramilitaries, guerrillas, or the National Army from 1980 to 2014. Furthermore, they found that these insurgent groups disappeared at least 60,630 individuals and forcibly displaced nearly 6,500,000 citizens, mostly women. These numbers, however, are not definitive since they can easily increase as investigations continue. This national report was just the first one of a series of 20 that the CNMH intended to publish. To date, we also have official reports about Granada, Antioquia, the LGBTQ community in the war, and El Salado in the Montes de María region, one of the bloodiest mass killings in recent Colombian history. An updated complete version of the country's internal ravages can be found in the Truth Commission's report of 2022, results that are being socialized in the country as I write this introduction. So far, some of its results show that the warlords recruited between 26,900 and 35,641 boys, girls, and teenagers between 1986 and 2017. According to the Unit for the Victims Assistance and Reparation, also part of the transitional justice Colombian mechanisms, as stated in the noted report, the armed actors have forcibly displaced 32,812 people from their lands and 132,743 have lost everything due to the conflict. Along these lines, the Unit for Land Restitution states that until May 2022, 17,543 people had presented claims to recover their plots and farms for a grand total of 30,331 all over the country.[25] These numbers are just part of the data Colombian citizens are getting to know thanks to the Truth Commission's Report.

Although the massacres, selective killings, kidnappings, disappearances, and forced displacement that marked the 1980s and 1990s have abated, other atrocities still occur. For instance, as RCN News broadcasted in 2020, 25,000 individuals and 8,000 families of the Chocó Department were victims of forced displacement due to confrontations between the Ejército de Liberación Nacional, ELN (National Liberation Army) guerrilla, criminal bands—composed by former paramilitaries—and the Army.[26] Furthermore, since Iván Duque took office as president in August 2018, Colombian violence revived. As an active member of the Democratic Center (Centro Democrático) political party of right-wing president Álvaro Uribe Vélez, Duque removed respected figures and scholars from their positions related to the study and analysis of the armed conflict. For instance, he replaced Gonzalo Sánchez, director of the CNMH since its foundation until 2019, with right-wing historian Darío Acevedo, who negates the existence of an armed conflict in Colombia and resigned due to the recent presidential election results, as noted before. During Duque's first year in office, paramilitaries and criminal bands killed 226 community leaders; during 2019, nearly 100 and 19 by January 14, 2020.[27] A report issued in April 2022 by the Misión de Verificación de la ONU en Colombia (UN Verification Mission in Colombia) found that since the Peace Agreement's signature until March 2022, armed groups assassinated 315 demobilized FARC-EP members and 27 disappeared. On the other hand, the Instituto de estudios para el desarrollo y la paz, Indepaz (Institute for the Study and Development of Peace) states that since 2016, illegal actors have killed 1327 social leaders. The increase reported by the Truth Commission evidences the severe reality local and marginalized communities have endured in Colombia's recent history.

## Colombia's Violent Background

Violent behavior in the country is not a new phenomenon. It goes back to the early nineteenth century, with the battles for Independence in Latin America. Notably, the period known as La Violencia (1948–1958) is a watershed to understand the struggles (1980–2000) of the country, notwithstanding significant differences between the two periods.[28] La Violencia with capital V is a period known for the vicious attacks conservatives and liberals committed against each other. At the core of the conflict was land ownership. Conservative politicians encouraged peasants to seize the lands of liberals. This provoked intense armed confrontations throughout Colombia. Massacres, burning of villages, kidnapping, robbery, rape, and all kinds of atrocities racked the country. People fled to the mountains and formed guerrilla bands to defend themselves. Historian Mary Roldán's *Blood and Fire. La Violencia in Antioquia, Colombia, 1946–1953*, inspired by sociologist Daniel Pecaut's studies about violence in Colombia, states that the brutalities during this time and the confrontations since 1980 are quite different. During La Violencia, the conflict was a rural political confrontation between the liberal and conservative parties for landownership, whereas since the 1980s, violence expanded to the cities, and there were more actors, such as paramilitaries, gangs, the National Army, and drug lords.[29] Researchers from the CNMH divide Colombia's violence during the twentieth century in four stages. First, the period between 1958 and 1982, when the country transitioned from the bipartisan violence between the liberal and conservative parties to one led by guerillas. During these years, the guerrillas grew rapidly. Second, the period from 1982 to 1996 was defined by the political projection, territorial expansion, military buildup of the guerrillas, the emergence of paramilitary groups, the spread of drug trafficking, the end of the Cold War, the Constitution of 1991, and the failed peace processes. In 1986, to complicate the situation, the paramilitaries began to exterminate political leaders whom they considered belonging to the "left." During 1986 and 1987, with complicity and sometimes consent of the National Army, they killed 300 members of the leftist party Patriotic Union (Unión Patriótica, UP). According to Uribe Alarcón and sociologist and geographer Teófilo Vásquez, paramilitaries, guerrillas, and the National Army perpetrated 1,233 brutalities between January 1, 1980, and December 31, 1993. These scholars created a data base which documented statistics on victims, ethnic backgrounds, geographies, and circumstances of these mass killings.[30] In the third phase, from 1996 to 2005, both guerrillas and paramilitary groups expanded. A political radicalization of public opinion advanced a military solution for the armed conflict, as well as a significant increase in drug trafficking. During the fourth phase, between 2005 and 2012, the state proved able to attack and weaken the guerrillas but not to defeat them. At the same time, political negotiations with paramilitaries failed, which meant that these groups restructured themselves, became more involved with drug trafficking, and resulted in criminal organizations that defied state authority.[31]

Historian Marco Palacios, in his book *Between Legitimacy and Violence: A History of Colombia, 1875–2002*, also attempted a periodization for the study of Colombian violence. According to Palacios, during the 1980s, the guerrillas increased their practices of kidnapping and killing, while the National Army of the country started to openly violate civil rights. During that decade, human rights reported 33 special torture centers throughout Colombia. A few months later, the same organization reported 600 of these centers. Although Colombian political violence forms the backdrop of this research, the main goal of *Museums, Exhibitions, and Memories of Violence in Colombia, 2000–2014* is to discuss how the state and local communities victimized by such brutalities represent their experiences.

In addition, the CNMH researchers identified three main sets of actors who perpetrated violent acts from the 1980s, as stared in *Basta ya!*: (1) The guerrillas such as the Fuerzas Armadas Revolucionarias de Colombia-Ejército del Pueblo, FARC-EP (Revolutionary Armed Forces of Colombia-People's Army); Ejército de Liberación Nacional, ELN (National Liberation Army); Ejército Popular de Liberación, EPL (Popular Liberation Army); and Ejército Revolucionario del Pueblo, ERP (People's Revolutionary Army); (2) The paramilitary and drug trafficking organizations such as the Autodefensas Unidas de Colombia, AUC (United Self-Defense Forces of Colombia); (3) The state, involved through the actions of the Ejército Nacional de Colombia (National Army of Colombia). Even though these armed groups had their own signature form of violence, they had similar objectives: control over peasants' land and resources. The guerrillas and paramilitaries associated with drug lords needed strategic corridors for drug commercialization.[32] Related to this, the Truth Commission Report, based on the existing records of the Centro Nacional de Memoria Histórica, CNMH (National Center for Historical Memory), show that paramilitaries have committed 42% of selective killings, followed by 16% perpetrated by guerrillas, and the state with 3%. However, it is worth noting that for 35% of the murders, there are no culprits.[33]

From 1970 to 1990, there was another guerrilla group that gained notoriety: the Movimiento 19 de Abril, M-19 (The 19th of April Movement), due to its defiance against the establishment and the perpetration of spectacular actions. After its demobilization, during the late 1980s, it became a political party, the M-19 Democratic Alliance (Alianza Democrática M-19 or AD/M-19.) By 1985, its active members oscillated between 1500 and 2000, being the second largest guerrilla group in the country after the FARC-EP. Gustavo Petro, Colombian president from 2022 to 2026, was also a member of the M-19 guerrilla; he laid down his arms in 1989 and was one of the founders of the AD/M/19. Chapter 2 of *Museums, Exhibitions, and Memories of Violence in Colombia, 2000–2014*, as previously noted, talks about a commemorative display for one of the M-19 leaders, a comrade of the recently elected Colombian president Gustavo Petro. Parallel to the 1980s, 1990s, and early 2000s situation, drug traffickers created social and political movements to gain the acceptance of the economic ruling class. The threat posed by the permissiveness of the Colombian state toward the drug cartels alarmed the United States, which pressured for the Extradition

Treaty of 1979.[34] This international "war on drugs" ignited a series of targeted killings that started in 1984 and have not stopped.

All the armed actors perpetrated violence in different ways depending on the territory and the period of the conflict. The CNHM team concluded that guerrillas, paramilitaries, and state forces adjusted their violent practices according to their objectives. The paramilitary groups implemented violence based on selective murders, massacres, forced disappearances, torture, threats, massive displacement, and sexual aggression. The guerrillas kidnapped, committed selective murders, damaged civil infrastructure, and attacked, robbed, extorted, forced recruitment, and displaced communities. They also attacked urban areas and planted land mines. The violence perpetrated by the National Army centered on torture, arbitrary detentions, targeted murders, enforced disappearances, and excessive use of force.

By 2006, the paramilitaries and guerrillas could not refute their links to drug trafficking and its leaders, despite their insistence to the contrary. Meanwhile, the guerrillas started to fracture, losing power over territories and even prestige due to their evident relationship with drug traffickers. Since 1983, the US government started to investigate the connections between the Colombian guerrillas, especially the FARC-EP, and the drug cartels and found irrefutable evidence of business links to drug-related organizations. The National Army discovered camps and coca fields near the guerrillas' headquarters.[35] This fact magnified the perception of the FARC-EP as the armed group of the Colombian Communist Party, which tarnished the status of the guerrillas. The relationship existed and government officials exploited it to discredit the rebel groups and justify their persecution and extermination, becoming one of the factors that has contributed to their defeat. Most Colombians did not support the guerrillas, but they feared them. Therefore, every four years, at the time of the presidential election, the country's leaders attempted to reach peace with the armed groups but frequently changed the agreements' conditions or retreated from negotiation, while the insurgents did not fulfill their commitments. Only in 2016, under the mandate of Juan Manuel Santos, the government signed a peace treaty with the FARC-EP in Cartagena. The process started in 2012 and took place in Havana, Cuba.

Scholars of Colombian violence of the twentieth century, such as historians Marco Palacios, Mary Roldán, and Gonzalo Sánchez; sociologist and geographer Teófilo Vásquez; anthropologist and historian María Victoria Uribe; sociologist Alfredo Molano; political scientist Darío Villamizar; and social worker Martha Nubia Abello, among many others, provide insightful descriptions and interpretations of the country's turmoil from 1980 to the early 2000. Palacios is one of Colombian historians whose descriptions and analysis of violence focus on the public perspective, providing a comprehensive picture of this phenomenon. However, sociologist and journalist Alfredo Molano, original member of the Truth Commission, who died in 2019 and was replaced by the anthropologist Alejandro Castillejo, suggested another significant approach to this history, focusing on the Colombian elites and the situation of the ethnic minorities, peasant land struggles, and other situations of injustice. Molano, who lived in exile from 1999 to 2002 due to threats to his life made by paramilitaries and lawsuits from powerful Colombian families, insisted on denouncing the atrocities toward rural communities and was overly critical of the government until his death. Other scholars such as Roldán, Uribe, Villamizar, and Abello have produced significant knowledge about the country's recent violence, calling for greater documentation and analysis of Colombia's internal war to prevent its recurrence and redress the victims and survivors.

## Memory Museums and Exhibitions in Colombia and Latin America

In 1995, the members of the Asociación de Familiares de Víctimas de Trujillo, AFAVI (Association of Trujillo's Relatives Victims), created the first Colombian memory site called Parque Monumento a las Víctimas de Trujillo (Monument Park for the Trujillo Victims). Here, the relatives of the survivors of more than 340 atrocities remember the multiple and successive brutalities endured by them and those departed. From 1988 to 1994, in the municipalities of Trujillo, Bolívar, and Riofrío, Valle del Cauca Department, communities suffered enforced disappearances, torture, and murders. The perpetrators drew on alliances among the Army, Police, local politicians, paramilitaries, and the North Valle drug cartel.[36] The Monument Park opened its doors after the Colombian government recognized its official responsibility for the violence.

Inspired by Trujillo's memory site, since the mid-1990s, associations of victims, community leaders, and survivors of brutalities have come together to choose the remembrances that best sustain their healing processes from the violence they endured from 1980 to 2000. In this context, grass roots memory venues, including halls, murals, photographs, cemeteries, and traveling museums, started to appear in marginal areas. The creation of Colombian memory museums and exhibitions is part of a global trend, and in most cases, these commemorative spaces surged as non-state responses to represent historical violence. Although they are places to mourn, grieve, and remember, they differ from state museums in how they narrate their stories. Most of them are bottom-up initiatives with scarce funding, and they privilege victims' and survivors' voices.

The following chart shows more than 30 examples of memory sites in Colombia. They are part of the Colombian Memory Sites Network, created in 2015. This network is a participatory, community-based, and social organization that aims to promote the production of historical memories of the armed conflict to prevent future atrocities. Until 2022, the Network comprised more than 30 memory sites, the product of compiling local initiatives with, at least, 20 years of experience. The organization is also part of the Red de Sitios de Memoria Latinoamericanos y Caribeños, RESLAC (Latin American and Caribbean Memory Sites Network) (Table 0.1).[37]

**TABLE 0.1** Memory Sites in Colombia, 2022

| Memory Site | Town and Department of Colombia |
|---|---|
| Museo de la memoria Histórica Tras las huellas de El Placer, Memory Museum Tracing El Placer's Tracks | El Placer, Putumayo, 1996 |
| Quiosco de la memoria, Kiosk of Memory | Las Brisas, Bolívar, 2000 |
| Parque Monumento de Trujillo, Monument Park of Trujillo | Trujillo, Valle del Cauca, 1995 |
| La iglesia de Bojayá, Bojaya's Church | Bojayá, Chocó, 2002 |
| Centro integral de formación y fortalecimiento espiritual y cultural Wiwa, Integral Center for Spiritual and Cultural Strength Wiwa | Santa Marta, Bolívar, 2002 |
| Galerías y grupo de teatro El tente, Galleries and Theatre Group El Tente | Villavicencio, Meta, 2003 |
| Movimiento Nacional de Víctimas de Crímenes de Estado, National Movement of State Crime Victims | Cali, Valle del Cauca, 2005 |
| Centro de memoria, paz y reconciliación, Center for Memory, Peace, and Reconciliation | Bogotá, Cundinamarca, 2005 |
| Museo casa de la memoria, Museum-House of Memory | Medellín, Antioquia, 2006 |
| Cementerio gente como uno, Cemetery People Like Us | Riohacha, Guajira, 2007 |
| Galería de la memoria Tiberio Fernández Mafla | Cali, Valle del Cauca, 2007 |
| La piedra de San Lorenzo, San Lorenzo's Stone | Samaniego, Nariño, 2008 |
| Jardines resistentes de vida, Resistant Life Gardens | Medellín, Antioquia, 2008 |
| Bosque de la memoria, Memory Forest | Cartagena del Chairá, Caquetá, 2008 |
| Centro de acercamiento para la reconciliación, Center for Reconciliation | San Carlos, Antioquia, 2008 |
| Lugar de memoria El Lago y la sábana de los sueños, Memory Site El Lago and Sheet of Dreams | San Onofre, Sucre, 2009 |
| Salón del nunca más, Hall of Never Again | Granada, Antioquia, 2009 |
| Capilla de la memoria, Memory Chapel | Buenaventura, Valle del Cauca, 2009 |
| Casa de las mujeres y hombres de Triana, House of Women and Men of Triana | Buenaventura, Valle del Cauca, 2009 |
| Museo Caquetá, Caquetá Museum | Florencia, Caquetá, 2009 |
| Colectivo Sociojurídico Orlando Fals Borda, Social and Legal Collective Orlando Fals Borda | Bogotá, Cundinamarca, 2009 |
| Centro de Memoria del Conflicto, Memory Center for Conflict | Valledupar, Cesar, 2012 |
| La casa de la memoria viva de los hijos del tabaco, coca y yuca dulce, House of Living Memory of the Children of Tobacco, Coca Plant, and Sweet Cassava | La Chorrera, Amazonas, 2012 |

*(Continued)*

| Memory Site | Town and Department of Colombia |
|---|---|
| Centro social y comunitario Remanso de paz, Community and Social Center Refuge of Peace | Pueblo Bello, Antioquia, 2012 |
| Casa de la memoria del Pacífico Nariñense, Memory House of the Nariñense Pacific | Tumaco, Nariño, 2013 |
| Casa de la cultura y la memoria de Las Palmas, House of Culture and Memory of las Palmas | Las Palmas, Bolívar, 2013 |
| Ejes de la memoria, Axes of Memory | Bogotá, Cundinamarca., 2014 |
| Rutas del peregrinaje de la memoria de El Castillo, El Castillo Memory Pilgrimage Route | El Castillo, Meta, 2014 |
| La Casa Arana, The Arana House | La Chorrera, Amazonas, 2015 |
| Casa de la memoria y los derechos humanos de las mujeres-Organización femenina popular, House of Memory and Human Rights of Women-Popular Feminine Organization | Barrancabermeja, Santander, 2018 |
| Museo Itinerante de Memoria y la Identidad de los Montes de María, Traveling Museum of Memory and Identity of Montes de María | Carmen de Bolívar, Bolívar, 2019 |
| Casa de la memoria de El Salado, House of Memory of El Salado | El Salado, Bolívar, under construction |
| Museo nacional de la memoria, National Memory Museum | Bogotá, Cundinamarca, under construction |

The different configurations of the Colombian memory sites shown in the previous chart indicate the cultural decisions behind remembrance initiatives. The emphasis of each site, the layout of their exhibitions, and the spaces selected by their creators to display atrocities confirm memory's diverse character.

Colombian memory sites are not unique to the country nor isolated efforts. On one hand, they respond to the Latin American trend of museum and exhibition studies that started since the nineteenth century with the creation of national museums or of natural history in many countries of the region.[38] For instance, in 1818, the National Museum of Brazil in Rio de Janeiro was an ethnological, archaeological, and natural history venue[39]; in 1823, the National Museum of Colombia opened as an institution dedicated to science[40]; in 1825, the National Museum of Mexico was devoted to the country's archaeological, anthropological, and historical heritage[41]; in 1830, the National Museum of Natural History in Chile focused on biology, geography, and mineral resources[42]; and in 1837, the National Museum of Natural History in Uruguay centered on the country's natural resources. In other countries, such as Peru and Argentina, there have been more than one National Museum since the nineteenth century due to classifications between art, archaeology, history, natural history, and anthropology.

With the arrival of the twentieth century, more museums emerged, but they were much more thematically specific. There was a boom of art museums in Cuba, Costa Rica, Venezuela, Ecuador, Bolivia, and Argentina. In addition, Latin American museums started to specialize in ethnography and archaeology. The region's venues displayed material culture related to their nation's "grand" past, such as the National Museum of Anthropology in Mexico City; the National Museum of Archaeology, Anthropology, and History in Lima; the Gold Museum in Bogotá; the Archaeological Museum of Santiago, Chile; the National Museum of Archaeology in Bolivia; and the archaeological and ethnographic museums of Uruguay and Paraguay. During this time and until the end of the dictatorships of the Southern Cone—from the mid-1980s to the beginning of the 1990s—the approach to museum studies had a "nationalistic flavor," according to museologists Maria Margaret Lopes and Irina Podgorny.[61] Although the authors referred specifically to natural museums, their statement applies to the general scholarship of the topic. Each country has its own rich museological tradition; however, there is a lack of transnational and comparative studies of Latin American museums. *Museums, Exhibitions, and Memories of Violence in Colombia, 2000–2014* not only highlights the need to include Colombia in museum scholarly discussions but also examines the very rethinking of the place of the museum or museums in Latin America.

Challenges to the museum as an institution were notably raised by Italian historian Peter Vergo in *The New Museology* (1989), in which he decried museums as authoritarian entities narrating hegemonic stories supported by objects, frequently taken out of their context, and even purloined. Instead, Vergo called for museums to become inclusive spaces in which underrepresented social groups could advocate for social justice and where the artifacts could speak to their cultural meanings and significance. Vergo's work prompted academic reflections on the role of museums in society.

During the decade of the 1990s and 2000s, memory sites rose in Latin America. As conventional museums, they focus on research, preservation, and display of their collections. They underscored their importance in investigating, guarding, and exhibiting material and immaterial sources related to recent violent events, which still haunt survivors and communities. According to the International Committee of Memorial Museums in Remembrance of the Victims of Public Crimes (ICMEMO), founded during the 31st International Committee of the International Council of Museums in Barcelona on July 3, 2001, a memory museum has:

> [...] the purpose to commemorate victims of state, socially determined and ideologically motivated crimes. The institutions are frequently located at the original historic sites, or at places chosen by survivors of such crimes for the purposes of commemoration. They seek to convey information about historical events in a way which retains a historical perspective while also making strong links to the present.[43]

Although we find memory museums before 2001, this definition categorizes the places and venues that lacked a formal classification. It also makes them visible and gives them social authority.

During the decade of 2000s, sociologist Elizabeth Jelin pioneered the project Collective Memories of Repression, which promoted the research of traumatic memories in Latin America and included archives, memorials, sites, pedagogies, and fieldwork.[44] Jelin's influence, however, was not restricted to the Southern Cone; during the 2000s, her work's impact reached Mexico, Peru, El Salvador, Guatemala, Nicaragua, Brazil, and Colombia. This geographical spread of memory studies in Latin America brought new questions that consider the historical processes of each country. In this context, during this decade, many memory museums arose. Venues such as the Museo de la Palabra y la Imagen (Word and Image Museum) in El Salvador appeared during the late 1990s. In this space, visitors find reports of state and paramilitary violence in the country, which resulted in approximately 75,000 casualties. The museum's objective is to promote historical memory to advance social justice.[45] Another noteworthy institution is Museo de la Memoria y Derechos Humanos (Museum of Memory and Human Rights), inaugurated in 2010 by Chilean President Michelle Bachelet. This venue aims to strengthen Chilean democracy after Augusto Pinochet's dictatorship (1973–1990) to encourage intergenerational exchanges about the violent past and to promote a dialogue between the past and the present. Under the premise *Nunca Más* (Never Again), this Museum is a space for criticism and reflection about the brutalities Chileans endured.[46] In the same year, the Association Memory and Tolerance, composed of Holocaust survivors, created the Museo de Memoria y Tolerancia (Memory and Tolerance Museum) in Mexico City. The purpose of the institution is to highlight the significance of tolerance, non-violence, and human rights and to create awareness of the devastation of genocide. In addition, the Museum advocates against discrimination and indifference.[47] In 2010, the Museo de la Memoria (Memory Museum) in Rosario, Argentina, moved its permanent headquarters, although it has functioned since 1998. This venue pioneered displays of post-genocide memories and brings together artists and communities to reflect about the brutalities committed during the dictatorship (1976–1983).[48] These sites are just some examples of many memory museums that keep emerging in Latin America. For instance, in 2015, in Peru, the Lugar de la Memoria, la Tolerancia y la Inclusión Social, LUM (Place for Memory, Tolerance, and Social Inclusion) opened its doors. Under the Ministry of Culture's wing, the venue offers a space to discuss human rights violations focusing on atrocities perpetrated by rebel groups between 1980 and 2000.[49] In Guatemala, as well, the Museo del Holocausto (Holocaust Museum) was founded by Yahad-In Unum in 2016. Also, in 2019, the Association of April Mothers in Nicaragua created AMA y no olvida. Museo de memoria para la impunidad (Love and Do Not Forget. Memory Museum against Impunity). The mothers of 325 victims of state crimes committed in 2018 created the venue to remember the dead.[50]

In Colombia, the state planned to open the National Memory Museum in 2022 as part of the duties that the aforementioned Law 1448 granted the CNMH.[51] The professional team of this museum is working to find the truth about the brutalities perpetrated since 1980, to promote respect for the diversity of memories about the war, to dignify the victims, to find ways to restore the social fabric destroyed by war, and to strengthen society so violence cannot recur.[52] However, there are several discussions surrounding the institution, its board of directors, and the historical memory policies they intend to promote. Radical changes regarding the nature, interpretation, and representations of the country's armed conflict are occurring. For instance, the recent election results and the quite different approach the new leaders of the country have about historical memories sure will affect the conception and design of the institution. President Duque's appointment of historian Darío Acevedo as the director of the CNMH irked many victims' associations and academics because the latter denied the existence of an internal war. Statements such as "even though the law says that what we lived was an armed conflict, this cannot be the official truth," were widely denounced.[53] Following this logic, the director of the CNHM advanced representations of the war that did not privilege the victims but perpetrators associated with the state, such as paramilitary organizations. In addition, the reports which, under the leadership of Gonzalo Sánchez, gathered significant data about brutalities are not easily available anymore. Another development was Acevedo's initiative to include the conflict narratives and remembrances of big landowners—historically proven to have tight links with paramilitaries—in the National Memory Museum. As a result, some victims' associations have withdrawn their archives from the CNMH and will not have a voice or any representation at the museum. Diana Sánchez, Director of Asociación Minga (Minga Association), stated that this organization removed 31,265 documents from the CNMH. "Colombian memory reconstruction intended by Gonzalo Sánchez to be participatory and include victims and human rights organizations was severely damaged when Darío Acevedo became director of the CNMH. Therefore, we cannot leave our archives there anymore."[54] In addition, Acevedo designated Fabio Enrique Bernal, former curator of the National Army, as the director of the museum until April 22, when the leadership of the institution was assumed by Rosario Rizo Navarro, public administrator. In July 2022, as a major consequence of the last presidential election, Acevedo resigned after being accused of tampering the museum's script to exclude paramilitaries as perpetrators of atrocities. The JEP summoned him to present in a public audience the records of his activities while in office.[55] This occurrence restores hope to the victims' associations, survivors of violence, intellectuals, researchers, and activists who believe in an all-encompassing approach to memory in Colombia.

## Colombia's Cultural Diversity

This country is known for its cultural diversity. In 2018, the country's Ministerio de Salud (Ministry of Health) said that the Indigenous population in the territory is 1,905,617 (4.4%); there are 2,950,072 (6.7%) afro descendants; 25,515 (0.05%) raizales—black communities who live in the islands of San Andrés and Providencia in the Colombian Caribbean; 6,637 (0.01%) palenqueros—communities composed of runaway slaves; and 2,649 (0.006%) ROM.[56] As for the peasant population, the Departamento Administrativo Nacional de Estadística, DANE (National Administrative Department of Statistics), showed that in 2019, 31.8% of Colombians over 18 identified as such. These general data show how challenging it is to create a National Museum of Memory in which all Colombians feel represented. At some point, choices are made, and exclusions happen.

In approaching museum studies, *Museums, Exhibitions, and Memories of Violence in Colombia, 2000–2014* provides detailed accounts of just two peasant communities to find what anthropologist Clifford Geertz means by subtle manifestations of cultural diversity.[57] In bringing together an analysis of political violence, memory, and museum studies, my work underscores how the dynamic of culture shapes representations of the past.[58] Since 1871, when Sir Edward Taylor proposed this definition of culture "[…] that complex whole which includes knowledge, beliefs, arts, morals, law, customs, and any other capabilities and habits acquired by [humans] as a member of society," social scientists and historians have attempted to grapple with the meanings of the term.[59] Two approaches that I find useful to understand how Colombians have determined the place of memory are those developed by Mary Douglas and Clifford Geertz.

In *Risk and Blame: Essays in Cultural Anthropology*, Mary Douglas argues that societies identify distinct kinds of dangers to their collective self-preservation. In the Colombian case, different communities have defended diverse cultural behaviors and norms from perceived social transgressions. Thus, notes Douglas, "We take culture to be the package of values that are cited in the regular normative discussions that shape an institution." In the context of the production of Colombian historical memories in museums and exhibits, Douglas's insights explain why state agents and local communities differ in their representations of the violent past. Chapters 1 and 2 of *Museums, Exhibitions, and Memories of Violence in Colombia, 2000–2014* provide a detailed discussion of the decisions made by specialists at the National Museum of Colombia that reflect both the politics of remembrance and the sensibilities of cultural elites. In Chapters 3 and 4, I explore grass roots endeavors and their logics, contrasting them with interpretations and representations of state agents. In *The Interpretation of Cultures*, Clifford Geertz states that culture informs codes of human behavior. Thus, cross-cultural analysis requires an understanding of meanings ascribed by discrete social groups, organizations, and forms of expression. In the case of *Museums, Exhibitions, and Memories of Violence in Colombia, 2000–2014*, Geertz's discernment paves the way to analyze the array of Colombian historical memories. "Culture is not an entity, something that causally accounts for social occurrences, modes of conduct, institutions, or social processes," and notes moreover, "culture is a context within all these phenomena are described intelligibly."[60]

While Douglas and Geertz's definitions enhance our understanding of cultural diversity, we still face a challenge. Due to the similar kinds of Colombian atrocities committed by paramilitaries, guerrillas, and the National Army throughout the nation—massacres, disappearances, bombings, targeted killings, and forced displacement—it can become hair-splitting to highlight the multiplicity of historical memories and their divergences. Or, as Geertz wryly notes of anthropological analysis, "[…] the good times of cannibalism and witch hunts are over," as cultural diversity often acquires subtle forms.[84] The exhibitions examined in *Museums, Exhibitions, and Memories of Violence in Colombia, 2000–2014* encourage scholars to search for the cultural dynamics that most certainly lie underneath the depictions of violence. Moreover, this text is an invitation for researchers and activists to follow what is happening in Colombia as we speak, perhaps much of the contexts explored here will change in the near future.

## Notes

1 "¿Qué Es La Comisión De La Verdad?" Comisión de la Verdad Colombia, Accessed July 13, 2022, https://web.comisiondelaverdad.co/la-comision/que-es-la-comision-de-la-verdad.
2 SB, teleSUR -, "Fernando Londoño Llama a 'Hacer Trizas' Acuerdo Con FARC-EP," Sitio, teleSUR, May 7, 2017, https://www.telesurtv.net/news/Fernando-Londono-llama-a-acabar-maldito-acuerdo-con-FARC-EP-20170507-0016.html.
3 Amada Carolina Pérez Benavides and Sebastián Vargas Álvarez, "Perspectives on Public History in Colombia," *International Public History* 4, no. 2 (2021): 143–152. https://doi.org/10.1515/iph-2021-2027.
4 Julie Turkewitz, "Why Are Colombians Protesting?" The New York Times (The New York Times, May 18, 2021), https://www.nytimes.com/2021/05/18/world/americas/colombia-protests-what-to-know.html.
5 Jimena Perry and Elizabeth O'Brien, "Opinion: Colombia Is in Crisis, and Vaccine Nationalism Is Making It Worse," Latino Rebels (Latino Rebels, May 20, 2021), https://www.latinorebels.com/2021/05/19/colombiacrisisvaccinenationalism/.
6 Valeria Costa-Kostritsky and Name *, "The Fall of the Conquistadores," Apollo Magazine, August 26, 2021, https://www.apollo-magazine.com/colombia-statues-conquistadores-toppling/#:~:text=On%2016%20September%202020%2C%20members,the%20south%2Dwest%20of%20Colombia
7 Elizabeth Jelin and Wendy Gosselin, *The Struggle for the Past How We Construct Social Memories* (New York: Berghahn, 2021).

8 Gonzalo Sánchez, *Memorias, Subjetividades y Política: Ensayos Sobre Un País Que Se Niega a Dejar La Guerra* (Bogotá: Editorial Planeta Colombiana, Crítica, 2020).
9 Tristan Bravinder, "New Scholarship on the Origins of Latin American Museums," The Iris, Behind the Scenes at the Getty, July 26, 2018, http://blogs.getty.edu/iris/new-scholarship-on-the-origins-of-latin-american-museums/
10 Thomas Cauvin, *Public History: A Textbook of Practice*. 2nd Edition (New York and London: Routledge).
11 Michael J. Lazzara, "The Memory Turn," in *New Approaches to Latin American Studies. Culture and Power*, ed. Juan Poblete (New York: Routledge, 2018), 17.
12 Michael J. Lazzara and Fernando A. Blanco, eds., *Los Futuros de La Memoria En América Latina: Sujetos, Políticas y Epistemologías En Disputa*, University of North Carolina Press, 2022. http://www.jstor.org/stable/10.5149/9781469671994_lazzara.
13 Sharon McDonald, *Difficult Heritage. Negotiating the Nazi Past in Nuremberg and Beyond* (New York: Routledge, 2009).
14 Michael J. Lazzara, "The Memory Turn," in *New Approaches to Latin American Studies. Culture and Power*, ed. Juan Poblete (New York: Routledge, 2018), 14–31.
15 José Gabriel Cristancho Altuzarra, "Gonzalo Sánchez: trayectoria de una experiencia de memoria de la violencia en Colombia," *Revista Colombiana de Educación* (61), no. 73–88 (2011). Retrieved October 16, 2021, from http://www.scielo.org.co/scielo.php?script=sci_arttext&pid=S0120-39162011000200004&lng=en&tlng=es.
16 Paul Ricoeur, *History, Memory, Forgetting*, trans. Kathleen Blamey and David Pellauer (Chicago, IL and London: The University of Chicago Press, 2004), 3.
17 Michael Rothberg, *Multidirectional Memory: Remembering the Holocaust in the Age of Decolonization* (Stanford, CA: Stanford University Press, 2009), 3.
18 Pierre Bourdieu, *Distinction. A Social Critique of the Judgement of Taste*, trans. Richard Nice (Cambridge, MA: Harvard University Press, 1984), 14.
19 Maurice Halbwachs, *On Collective Memory*, trans. Lewis A. Coser (Chicago, IL and London: The University of Chicago Press, 1992), 194–195.
20 Pierre Nora, *Realms of Memory. The Construction of the French Past*, trans. Lawrence D. Kritzman (New York: Columbia University Press, 1996), Vol. I, 6–7.
21 Gonzalo Sánchez, *Guerras, Memoria e Historia* (Medellín: La Carreta Editores, 2006), 25.
22 Pilar Riaño Alcalá and María Victoria Uribe, "Constructing Memory amidst War: The Historical Memory Group of Colombia," *International Journal of Transitional Justice* 10, no. 1 (March 2016): 6–24.
23 "Críticas a Justicia y Paz," February 2014, https://www.elheraldo.co/editorial/criticas-justicia-y-paz-142647
24 Martha Nubia Abello, ed., *BASTA YA! Colombia: Memories of War and Dignity*. General Report by the Historical Memory Group (Bogotá: Centro Nacional de Memoria Histórica, 2016).
25 "Inicio: Informe Final Comisión De La Verdad," Inicio | Informe Final Comisión de la Verdad, accessed July 19, 2022, https://www.comisiondelaverdad.co/.
26 "En 2019 más de 25.000 personas fueron víctimas de desplazamiento forzado," January 3, 2020, https://www.rcnradio.com/colombia/en-2019-mas-de-25000-personas-fueron-victimas-de-desplazamiento-forzado.
27 Adriana Lucía Puentes, "¿Cuántos líderes sociales han sido asesinados durante 2019?" *El Colombiano*, September 18, 2019, https://www.elcolombiano.com/colombia/paz-y-derechos-humanos/lideres-sociales-asesinados-en-colombia-durante-2019-hasta-septiembre-segun-indepaz-PH11611439; "¡Van 18 líderes sociales asesinados en los 14 días de 2020!", January 14, 2020, https://noticias.caracoltv.com/lidera-la-vida/van-18-lideres-sociales-asesinados-en-los-14-dias-de-2020-ie35596.
28 See Gonzalo Sánchez's argument in María Victoria Uribe, *Antropología de la inhumanidad. Un ensayo interpretativo sobre el terror en Colombia* (Bogotá: Editorial Norma, 2004), 112.

29 Daniel Pécaut and Liliana González, "Presente, pasado y futuro de la violencia en Colombia," *Desarrollo Económico* 36, no. 144 (January–March 1997): 891–930.
30 María Victoria Uribe and Teófilo Vásquez, *Enterrar y Callar: Las masacres en Colombia, 1980–1993* (Bogotá: Comité Permanente por la Defensa de los Derechos Humanos 1995), Vol II.
31 Abello, *BASTA YA! Colombia*, 111.
32 Alfredo Molano, *Desterrados. Crónicas del desarraigo* (Bogotá: El Áncora Editores, 2001).
33 "Inicio: Informe Final Comisión De La Verdad," Inicio | Informe Final Comisión de la Verdad, accessed July 19, 2022, https://www.comisiondelaverdad.co/.
34 Marco Palacios. *Between Legitimacy and Violence: A History of Colombia, 1875–2002.* (Durham, NC: Duke University Press, 2007), 281.
35 Darío Villamizar, *Las guerrillas en Colombia: Una historia desde los orígenes hasta los confines* (Bogotá: Penguin Random House Grupo Editorial Colombia, Kindle Edition, 2017), location 7651 of 15707.
36 "Trujillo Massacre," August 7, 2016, https://pbicolombia.org/2016/07/08/trujillo-massacre/
37 ¿Cómo definimos la Red Colombiana de Lugares de Memoria?" http://redmemoriacolombia.org/site/quienes-somos.
38 Irina Podgorny and Maria Margaret Lopes, "Trayectorias y desafíos de la historiografía de los museos de historia natural en América Del Sur," *Anai do Museu Paulista: História e Cultura Material* 21, no. 1 (2013): 15–25.
39 Claudia Rodrigues-Carvalho, Marcelo Carvalho, and Wagner Martins, "From Museu Real to Museu Nacional/UFRJ, Rio de Janeiro, Brazil: Past and Present Fragments," *Revista del Museo Argentino de Ciencias Naturales* 14, no. 2 (2012): 223–228.
40 Martha Segura, *Itinerario del Museo Nacional* (Bogotá: Instituto Colombiano de Cultura, MuseoNacional de Colombia, 1995). Tomo I.
41 Ana Garduño, "Mexico's Museo de Artes Plásticas. The Divergent Discourses of 1934 and 1947," in *Art Museums of Latin America. Structuring Representation*, eds. Michele Greet and Gina McDaniel Tarver (New York: Routledge, 2018), 65–81.
42 Juan David Murillo Sandoval, "De Lo Natural y Lo Nacional. Representaciones De La Naturaleza Explotable en la Exposición Internacional de Chile de 1875," *Historia* 48, no. 1 (2015), 245–276.
43 "What is ICMEMO," http://icmemo.mini.icom.museum/about/what-is-ic-memo/
44 Michael J. Lazzara, "The Memory Turn," in *New Approaches to Latin American Studies. Culture and Power*, ed. Juan Poblete (New York: Routledge, 2018), 14–31.
45 Diana Carolina Sierra Becerra, "Historical Memory at El Salvador's Museo de la Palabra y la Imagen," *Latin American Perspectives* 43, no. 6 (2016): 8–26.
46 Tatiana Wolff Rojas, "Pensamientos sobre la representación de la memoria traumática en el Museo de la Memoria y los Derechos Humanos (mmdh), Santiago de Chile," *Intervención* 7, no. 13 (enero-junio 2016): 61–73.
47 Alejandra Fonseca Barrera y Sebastián Vargas, "Museo Memoria y Tolerancia de la ciudad de México. Aproximación crítica desde contrapesos," *Intervención*, no. 11 (enero-junio 2015): 73–82.https://doi.org/10.30763/Intervencion.2015.11.137
48 Valeria Fabiana Alcino, "Voces de la ausencia/poética de la memoria en la obra *Evidencias* (2010) de Norberto Puzzolo, Museo de la Memoria, Rosario, Argentina. Sonido, silencio e imagen durante la dictadura argentina (1976–1983)," IV Congreso Internacional de investigación en artes visuales: ANIAV 2019.
49 "Quiénes somos," Lugar de la memoria, la tolerancia y la inclusión social, LUM, https://lum.cultura.pe/el-lum/quienes-somos
50 AMA y no olvida. Museo de la memoria contra la impunidad, http://www.museodelamemorianicaragua.org/

51 Michael Andrés Forero Parra, "Colombia's National Memory Museum: Architecture from a Gender Perspective," ICAMT Annual 44th Conference, September 6–8, 2018, Espoo & Helsinki, Finland.
52 "¿Qué es el Museo de Memoria de Colombia?" Museo de Memoria de Colombia, http://museodememoria.gov.co/sobre-el-proyecto/que-es-el-museo-de-memoria-de-colombia/
53 "Dejaré de lado mis opiniones para dirigir el Centro de Memoria Histórica: Darío Acevedo," RCN Radio, February 9, 2019, https://www.rcnradio.com/colombia/dejare-de-lado-mis-opiniones-para-dirigir-el-centro-de-memoria-historica-dario-acevedo
54 "'Retiramos los archivos porque el CNMH está trabajando con victimarios': Asociación Minga," *El Espectador*, March 11, 2020, https://www.elespectador.com/colombia2020/pais/retiramos-los-archivos-porque-el-cnmh-esta-trabajando-con-victimarios-asociacion-minga-articulo-907534
55 Colprensa, "Rubén Darío Acevedo Se Defendió Ante La Jep Por Caso Del Museo Nacional De Memoria," www.elcolombiano.com (ElColombiano.com, July 11, 2022), https://www.elcolombiano.com/colombia/ruben-dario-acevedo-se-defendio-ante-la-jep-por-caso-del-museo-nacional-de-memoria-AI18011706.
56 Ministerio de Salud y Protección Social de Colombia, "Grupos-Etnicos," Inicio, accessed July 19, 2022, https://www.minsalud.gov.co/proteccionsocial/promocion-social/Paginas/grupos-etnicos.aspx.
57 Clifford Geertz, *Conocimiento local. Ensayos sobre la interpretación de las culturas*, trans. Alberto López Bargados (Barcelona, Buenos Aires, Mexico: Ediciones Paidós, 1994).
58 Claude Lévi-Strauss, *Race and History* (Paris: UNESCO, 1952).
59 Edward Burnett Tylor, *Primitive Culture* (London: Dover Publications, [1873] 2016), Vol. I, 13.
60 Clifford Geertz, *La interpretación de las culturas*, trans. Alberto L. Bixio (Barcelona: Editorial Gedisa, 2003), 26.

# 1
# THROWING IN THE TOWEL

Representations of Political Violence in Colombia's National Museum and Their Polemics

In 2001, journalists, politicians, and public opinion accused Elvira Cuervo de Jaramillo, conservative politician, diplomat, and director of the National Museum of Colombia, of being subversive and a guerrilla supporter. She received many disgruntled letters, even death threats, for suggesting that the institution acquire and eventually display a towel belonging to Pedro Antonio Marín, alias "Tirofijo" or Manuel Marulanda Vélez (1930–2008). Marín was the leader of the Fuerzas Armadas Revolucionarias de Colombia-Ejército del Pueblo, FARC-EP (Revolutionary Armed Forces of Colombia-People's Army). His towel had become an icon of the country's armed conflict because when journalists, photographers, and politicians went to the jungle to speak with him, they always saw it draped over his shoulders. Marín never appeared without his towel; he used it to shoo away flies and mosquitoes and wipe the sweat off his neck and face. It was not a single towel but many, which came in different tones: blue, red, and yellow, the colors of the Colombian flag, and sometimes green. It was one of Marín's trademarks (hereafter Tirofijo). He changed its color according to the occasion. For example, during Andrés Pastrana's mandate (1998–2002) and his failed attempt to start a peace process, addressed further in the chapter, Tirofijo carried a red towel. In Colombia, the Conservative Party is associated with blue and the Liberal party with red. "Whenever he [President Andrés Pastrana] arrives with a blue shirt, I wear the red towel," Tirofijo affirmed.[1]

Due to the rag's status as an object that could help represent the recent violent history of the country, Cuervo de Jaramillo insisted that the item should be part of the National Museum of Colombia's collections and even displayed at the venue. She claimed that by acquiring and possibly exhibiting this piece, the museum could tell a more comprehensive history of the country's political violence of the 1980s, 1990s, and early 2000s. Cuervo de Jaramillo claimed that the institution's duty was not only to celebrate official history, glorifying military heroes and battles, but also to present different perspectives and accounts of the country's contemporary civil war. In this context, the towel was a symbol of the 52-year confrontation between the state and FARC-EP guerrilla forces because it accompanied Tirofijo during his entire life. This symbolic object could help to memorialize part of Colombia's internal war.

Cuervo de Jaramillo's proposal, however, received countless criticisms that ultimately doomed the initiative. The disapproval was a sign of many Colombians' unwillingness to move past the atrocities this insurgent group committed from the 1980s to the early 2000s. Politicians, journalists, and segments of the public argued that the National Museum should not glorify the perpetrators of brutalities. Since this failed attempt to include this item in the institution's collection, the museum professionals have made some attempts to display objects related to the FARC-EP at the venue but there has not been a direct reference to the guerrilla group or its history. Still committers of insurrectionary violence would not have a space in this institution.

This chapter, the first of four case studies of museums and memory, advances our understanding of the relationship between the politics of memorialization, silence, and documentation in Colombia's most venerated venue. Considering that remembering is a cultural decision, I examine how Colombians decide not only what to represent in the National Museum but also what to omit from the recent armed conflict of the 1980s to early 2000s. In addition, I explore the interconnection between documenting, which was what Cuervo de Jaramillo attempted to do, and memorializing, which would have been the actual display of the rag. I also analyze the controversy that embroiled journalists, politicians, the public, and the professional team of the National Museum of Colombia over acquiring and possibly displaying Tirofijo's towel, to demonstrate how it was influenced by matters of taste and class.[2] This first chapter of *Museums, Exhibitions, and Memories of Violence in Colombia: Trying to Remember* discusses the perceived role of the storied institution in narrating the recent violent history of the country. Colombian citizens, or at least the outspoken critics, thought of the National Museum as a shrine barred for guerrillas.

During 2001, politicians, journalists, and the public perceived that the attempt to obtain Tirofijo's towel for the institution's collections was to endow the guerrilla fighter with an undeserved honor. By describing which objects the professional team of the National Museum of Colombia selected for, or excluded from, the institution's narratives, I analyze the historical memories and nation-building projects propounded by the institution's scripts. Focusing on barred artifacts and exhibitions, I show how the selections made by curators and other museum professionals sometimes clash with preconceived notions of a museum's social role as a guardian of the past. To acquire and display Tirofijo's towel implied for the venue's professionals to connect the past with the present, to make the museum an active actor in Colombia's recent violent history.

This chapter has three parts. It starts with a historical overview of the National Museum of Colombia and a discussion of Cuervo de Jaramillo's justification for acquiring the towel at the National Museum and the antagonists of the initiative. Next, there is a debate about the significance of the towel controversy at the National Museum of Colombia, the biographies of the director's venue and of Tirofijo, leader of the FARC-EP, and lastly, an account of the guerrilla movement involved in the towel's controversy.

## Remembering and Omitting Violence at the National Museum of Colombia, 2001

In 1992, the conservative politician Elvira Cuervo de Jaramillo became the director of the National Museum of Colombia. Under her leadership, the institution professionals started to display subjects such as forced displacement, peace processes, and others which referred to current violent episodes. Cuervo de Jaramillo envisioned the museum as a critical actor in the ongoing political affairs of the country. As she stated in a column in the newspaper *El Espectador*,

> One challenge for museums is helping to elucidate the problems that concern a society. Amid war, what kind of museum do Colombians want? Can we only conceive a museum of winners, heroes, a sanctuary of past glories? Are we willing to tell a story that represents us all? Are we able to narrate contemporary history while we are alive?[3]

Cuervo de Jaramillo was referring to the strategic plan she wanted the National Museum to implement under her direction, emphasizing the felt need to include recent history in the museum's narrative. She was not encouraging political militancy but using the museum to promote an inclusive history, which includes dark and painful episodes.

With this mindset, the director proposed obtaining Tirofijo's towel to enrich the museum's collections. However, several of the causes for some Colombians to fiercely reject this initiative emanated from cultural conceptions about museums. Historically, curators, directors, museum professionals, and audiences have thought about these institutions as places of certainties, definitions, and authority.[4] Sociologist Tony Bennett, for instance, following Michel Foucault's premises about power and control, states that museums emerged in Britain as a way of "civilizing" or disciplining people's behavior, which is particularly uncanny in the National Museum of Colombia and the history of the building as a panopticon.[5] Cuervo de Jaramillo not only aimed for the venue to house comprehensive collections of the country's history by acquiring diverse objects, but she also wanted to educate people on the current Colombian internal war.

Numerous scholars, such as historian David Cohen, historian Maurice Halbwachs, sociologist Elizabeth Jelin, writer Beatriz Sarlo, professor Michael

Roth, and professor Michael Rothberg, have noted that historical selectivity in remembering and excluding memories of violent events is a core aspect of memory production. In this sense, the National Museum director's failed effort to include certain narratives about the country's armed conflict produced silences that still need attention. By acquiring and eventually displaying Tirofijo's towel, Cuervo de Jaramillo thought, Colombian citizens would be able to have a much more complete perspective of the actors that endured and exerted violence during the recent internal war. However, as noted in this chapter, she was unsuccessful. The kind of censure, such as the one suffered by Cuervo de Jaramillo, appears to reinforce historian Gyan Prakash's directive for museums to tell "inappropriate things," challenging traditional concepts of authority, power, and knowledge production.[6]

Since the 1990s, there has been an explosion of memory venues, such as museums, in Latin America and Africa. These memory venues create tension between their founders, audiences, perpetrators, governments, and violence survivors, but all of them call for reparation and preservation. In Rwanda, for example, Susan E. Cook states that there will always be disagreements between those who advocate for remembering genocide and those who want to forget it, which also leads to conflicts between documentation and memorializing, which seems to be the case with Tirofijo's towel. When talking about the Rwandan genocide of 1994, the scholar notes three activities related to the brutality's remembrance: Preservation, memorialization, and documentation. The first one refers to maintaining something. The second, to redress the victims and survivors in sites such as museums, to write stories, or create monuments. The third one is the endeavor to "establish an authoritative account of particular events based on primary sources."[7] To document, thus, means talking to survivors to gather their testimonies and make them available to the public. Cook states that when well-known public figures or academics carry out this activity it succeeds. Along these lines, Cuervo de Jaramillo attempted to document the Colombian internal war from a different perspective. The director of the museum believed that the institution had to play a central role in the production of historical memories of the country's war. But the adverse responses to the initiative of making the rag part of the National Museum's collections polarized Colombians' public opinion. For many journalists, politicians, and museum professionals, however, it made sense to document the atrocities and history of the FARC-EP and asserted the importance for citizens to know their recent history. This did not mean memorializing Tirofijo in the sense of commemorating him or paying him any kind of respect. To remember is different from documenting and does not necessarily imply celebrating events or personalities.

For critics, however, the museum professionals seemed to equate Tirofijo, a perpetrator of violence, with national heroes such as Simón Bolívar. Traditionally, the National Museum of Colombia had told the history of battles and great men, but in 2001, Cuervo de Jaramillo advocated for more inclusive and all-encompassing narratives. She wanted the museum to have an active role in documenting ongoing Colombian history and valued the incorporation of multiple voices. The director believed that the institution's duty was to document the recent Colombian conflict of the 1980s, 1990s, and early 2000s. In addition, the suggestion of acquiring the towel was unusual in coming from a Conservative politician, since they typically privileged military heroes.

Cuervo de Jaramillo was calling for addressing the past to move forward. Sharon MacDonald has described a similar conflict about the "difficult heritage" of Nazi Germany and the controversies this heritage still sparks in the present. According to MacDonald, the term "difficult heritage" can refer to Nazi buildings and their meanings, but it can also refer to Nazi artifacts. MacDonald defines a difficult heritage as "a past that is recognized as meaningful in the present but that is also contested and awkward for public reconciliation with a positive, self-affirming contemporary identity."[8] She also states that a difficult heritage can be negotiated and acknowledged in the present to look toward the future. In addition, scholar Per B. Rekdal claims that most people are fascinated by war; however, it is challenging to put together an exhibition that combines beauty, war, and violence. Rekdal states that it is impossible to predict how viewers will react; therefore, he encourages museum professionals to take chances. He believes that when difficult heritage is exposed, the public might be grateful for the invitation to think about contentious topics.[9] In this sense, Cuervo de Jaramillo wanted to start a discussion and revision of Colombia's recent violent past; like MacDonald and Rekdal, the director of the National Museum sought an active process of negotiating with the past, including artifacts, spaces, buildings, and narratives. This discussion, however, was challenging, and challenged, due to the connotations of the museum building itself, which was declared a national monument in 2000, and because of its storied history, described later in the chapter. The museum served as a place in which official and government narratives should be kept and revered; consequently, opponents argued, there was no place for criminal groups in it. Including Tirofijo's towel in the museum collections meant the acknowledgment of the FARC-EP as a significant factor in understanding Colombians' identity and state formation project—when, in fact, the guerrillas mocked and aimed to destroy it. At the time of the proposal, the history of the FARC-EP festered as an open wound amid ongoing violent conflict; Tirofijo was very much alive, committing acts of war and defying Colombians' sensibilities with responses like the one he gave to Andrés Felipe's family in 2001, also addressed later on in the chapter.

## The Storied History of the National Museum of Colombia

In December 2021, the National Museum of Colombia closed its temporary exhibition season with one called *Glass Houses: Paul Rivet and Human Diversity*. Its curators decided to go beyond a personal and intimate narrative of a great man and present a national and regional narrative about the significance of understanding and preserving Latin America's cultural diversity. The display gave a historical background of the uses and definitions of diversity and ended with current conceptions of the term. One of the main goals of *Glass Houses* was to promote reflections about inclusion, citizenship, community participation, cultural expressions, and the need to preserve and protect human diversity. Using the figure of the French Ethnologist Paul Rivet, Director of the Museum of Mankind, the display touched upon topics such as racism, fascism, unilinear evolutionism, migration, and violence. *Glass Houses* was significant because it addressed current social phenomena in Colombia and Latin America and the deliberate effort made by the curators to connect the past to the present in critical ways.

This display is only an example of the long journey of the museum since it opened in the nineteenth century. Since then, the institution has undergone several and deep changes that make it what it is today. From the end of the nineteenth to the early twentieth centuries, and after 1881, when there was a reopening of the venue, the Colombian government saw it as a civilizing instrument. Its displays focused on the country's national history with the goal to encourage progress and promote education in official terms. Through the museum, Colombian state officials intended to highlight great characters, especially men, and a glorious past emphasizing the Independence from Spain. The institution was also meant to render citizenship models and exalt a republican tradition, and its natural history collections were meant to produce knowledge leading to the exploitation of resources.[10]

The first Congress of the Republic of Colombia created the National Museum on July 28, 1823, being one of the oldest in the country and Latin America. It started as a natural history institution and mining school, supporting ideas of civilization and progress.[11] The main governmental interest for creating the venue was to continue with the Botanic Expedition of the eighteenth century, which studied New Granada's natural history and created a flora and fauna map of the territory. Thus, the first objects that formed its collections were some minerals imported from Europe, fragments of a meteor, insects, mammals, reptiles, fish, scientific tools, bone fragments, and a mummy. The directors Mariano de Rivero and Jerónimo Torres promoted and established agreements with English and French scholars and institutions with the goal of positioning the mining school and the natural history museum as one of the most significant in Latin America in an attempt to encourage Colombia's economic development. The venue opened to the public on July 4, 1824, when the Colombian vice president and soldier Francisco de Paula Santander made it official.

During the nineteenth century, the National Museum's displays and exhibitions sought to prove, especially to Europe, that Colombia could become a civilized and advanced country. Therefore, Colombian politicians thought that progress could be measured by exploiting natural resources, shown in its creation Decree 117, as shown by historian María Paola Rodríguez:

> [...] natural sciences are [...] absolutely necessary for the advancement of agriculture, arts, and commerce, which are sources for people happiness [...] and that a happy opportunity has presented itself or the Republic to promote the mentioned natural sciences and by this means bring them to light in the same place that nature produces rich metals and many other objects from the mineral kingdom found in our valleys and mountains.

Since the main goals of the institution were research, teaching, and promoting development, the Decree also created 13 teaching seminars and six labs in the Mining School. The venue's emphasis was in science, devoting effort and resources to train students in descriptive geometry, mineralogy, geology, chemistry, metallurgy, zoology, botany, agriculture, anatomy, entomology, drawing, and physics. The Natural History Museum became a science center focusing on training high-quality scientists by selecting highly prepared professionals who could advance scientific knowledge. In addition, the directors of the institution regularly evaluated the performance, advances, and results of both the instructors and students at the Mining School, who were not able to finish their education without significant fieldwork experience documented in some reports addressed to the school's director. Even though during the nineteenth century the Natural History Museum of Colombia was inclined to the sciences, its educational purpose was highly present. Thus, in 1826, this was obvious when the Mining School and the Natural History Museum merged following an educational plan implemented by Vice President Francisco de Paula Santander (1792–1840). Santander's project strengthened the National Museum, which became part of Bogota's Central University. On this occasion, the instruction at the institution included geodesy, topography, landscape drawing, civil and building architecture, and physics oriented to the arts.

As noted by historian María Paola Rodríguez, the National Museum of Colombia's creation took place in a very convoluted nineteenth century in the country. Independence wars affected all Latin American countries, creating a difficult context for consolidating such an institution since all resources were devoted to the armed struggle. Towards the end of the nineteenth century, the museum experienced financial difficulties and deteriorated, but between 1879 and 1900, there was an institutional renewal. The Colombian government bought from the lawyer and politician Nicolás Pereira Gamba a natural history collection which contained minerals, animals, indigenous artifacts, and a herbarium previously exposed in a national exhibition that took place in 1871.[12] The museum director, Gonzalo A. Tavera thought of this as a patriotic gesture because it supposedly equated Colombia with other "cultured capitals." He insisted that the museum should have the same standards as any country with not only bountiful natural resources but also "curios objects," "historical preciousness," "patriotic monuments," and "historical antiquities."[13] Quoting as an example Madrid's cabinet of curiosities, Tavera started a fundraising and item-collecting campaign to recover the glory of the museum and honor what he thought were our Colombian ancestors. Slowly, valuable objects started to enrich the venue's collections, which were mainly composed of archaeological remains, animals, indigenous people's tools and utensils, and other herbariums. What at the beginning of 1880 resembled a cabinet of curiosities, in 1884, under the leadership of curator and director Fidel Pombo, shifted its organization to a natural history, archaeology, and antiquities sections.

With the beginning of the twentieth century and after the Thousand Days War, a civil armed conflict (1899–1902) in the newly created Republic of Colombia, between the Conservative and Liberal Parties, citizens recovered their interest in investigation, which, of course, impacted the museum. In 1911, its director, the archaeologist and historian Ernesto Restrepo Tirado, found appropriate headquarters and enough money to organize collections and publish catalogs. He had the idea that a museum should be a place to study objects and artifacts that belonged to the institution and not only be an exhibition space. In this context, historian Clara Isabel Botero notes, the new museum opened its doors in 1913 with a solid emphasis on archaeological research, ethnohistory, and linguistics. Influenced by European scholars, such as the French ethnographer Paul Rivet, Colombian intellectuals devoted their attention to understanding the processes and development of metallurgy and indigenous technologies. In addition, paintings of independence-era heroes, portraits of distinguished people, and historically significant documents became part of its collections.[14]

During the 1930s, due to the lack of funding the National Museum got from the government, the support received by the institution to enlarge its collections and maintenance came from donations, money transfers, publication of catalogs and pamphlets, and patronage. In this context, one of the most relevant figures to aid the museum was the liberal politician and president Eduardo Santos (1938–1942), who favored education during his mandate. He donated a history collection and money to several cultural entities, such as the National Museum.[15] After the presidency of Alfonso López Pumarejo (1934–1938), also liberal, Santos devoted a lot of time, effort, and resources for the advancement of humanities and social sciences in Colombia. He also promoted the role of women in education and supported his predecessor's educative projects such as the creation of the Escuela Normal Superior and helped to consolidate the National University. Santos's rule was also characterized for being friendly with the exiles of the Second World War. In addition, because of his friendship with Paul Rivet, the French ethnologist found shelter in Colombia from 1941 to 1943, years during which archaeology and anthropology gained a prominent position in the country. Rivet's influence also manifested in the ways in which the National Museum began addressing the territory's cultural diversity. Some local intellectuals, such as Gregorio Hernández de Alba, inspired by the Museum of Mankind in Paris, wanted to emulate the idea of a laboratory—Museum. However, this idea never came to fruition.[16] In 1935, by the National Decree 2148, the museum stopped being an institution devoted to natural sciences and the objects pertaining to these collections were sent to different state agencies such as the National University. Since then, the directors of the museums have made the commitment to document the country's art and history. In 1948, the museum settled in its current building, and until the second half of the twentieth century it was arranged as follows: prehispanic antiquities and ethnographic objects were displayed on the first floor, history was exhibited on the second floor, and fine arts were housed on the third floor. By the end of the 1980s and during the 1990s, a renovation project led by artist Beatriz González and politician Elvira Cuervo de Jaramillo took place. At the beginning, the new exhibition halls present a detailed narration of Colombian history, focusing on great men, battles, and official victories.

It was not until the last half of the twentieth century that museum professionals included other topics, such as the recent Colombian violence, women, indigenous and black communities, and local knowledge. Between 1989 and 2001, there was a significant transformation of the National Museum, which entailed a comprehensive renovation of its collections, narratives, and building. Among the new halls, which aimed to create a chronological account of Colombian history, ethnography, and fine arts, the one called Ideology, Arts, and Industry Hall, played a special role, as discussed in Chapter 2. The architectonic restoration returned some of the stability lost by the building in 1948 and 1980 due to failed interventions. Beside the structural repairs to the institution headquarters, the museum professionals attempted to change the feeling that the decade of the 1980s left in Colombians. The sensation that the country was declining and living in a deep social and political crisis that would only end with a constitutional reform inspired the museum workers to address recent historic events. Episodes such as the Palace of Justice Siege in 1985, the attacks on main newspapers in 1985 and 1998, the systematic extermination of the Patriotic Union leaders, and the assassination of three presidential candidates, discussed in Chapter 2, began to show up in the National Museum narratives. In addition, the National Constituent Assembly that ended in the Political Constitution of 1991 had a definitive influence on the ways the directors of the museum approached the role of the venue, as seen in Elvira Cuervo de Jaramillo's statements regarding what a museum should be, which will be addressed later in the chapter. However, when the National Museum of Colombia opened its doors again in 2001, after a renovation plan, its displays did not totally represent the cultural diversity of the nation, as stated in the 1991 Constitution, but still underscored great men, their battles, and victories.

In 2001, the administration of the museum devised a strategic plan for 2001–2010, which encouraged its script renovation, a process that is ongoing. Since then, the museum professionals have incorporated several topics in the displays and tackled sensitive current issues such as displacement, immigration, inequality, social justice, and the recent armed conflict, just to name a few. These initiatives have promoted and encouraged the acquisition of objects that represent Colombia's recent history, and many of them are part of the new permanent display halls, such as Memory and Nation, Land as Resources, and Strength, Faith, and Substance. The strategic plan 2001–2010 restructured the National Museum in accordance with the 1991 Constitution. It transformed its mission, vision, objectives, and actions to become a reflexive, research, and diffusion space where each Colombian citizen has a place. This period, 2001–2010, was a breaking point with previous decades, and the museum workers made great efforts to include in the institution narratives the concept of citizenship. The mentioned strategic plan focused on three issues: First, the construction of multiple depictions of Colombia's cultural and historical processes; second, audience development; and third, strengthening of the country's museums. The art curatorship endeavored to make the museum a multiethnic and pluricultural identity research dissemination center. Its goal was to enrich the institution's collection to showcase and investigate Colombian cultural diversity. Since this process was meant to be participative, the strategic plan encouraged discussions related to the social function of museums and the ways to represent cultural diversity. Following the 1991 Constitution, the strategic plan of the venue shifted gears. Thus, the museum professionals started to carefully analyze its collections and created tools to support the different curatorships in their gathering procedures and in putting together participative and inclusive exhibitions. By implementing the strategies of the Strategic Plan 2001–2010, the museum professionals created dynamic stories through temporary exhibitions and included citizens to become part of the voices of the institution, an effort which in turn enriched projects such as the one related to the script renewal, 2012–2023. In addition, during the 2000s, the Art and History curators of the museum have encouraged and promoted the enhancement of their collections by incorporating cultural phenomena excluded before, such as poverty, exclusion, racism, and sexual diversity, just to name a few.[17]

Today, from more than 20,000 archaeologic, ethnographic, historic, and artistic objects housed at the museum, curators have only displayed 2,500. Since the Colombian Constitution of 1991, however, the directors of the Museum have emphasized the institution's duty of including violent recent events in its narrative. The Constitution of 1991, which replaced that of 1886, emphasizes the multicultural character of the country and devoted articles 70, 71, and 72 exclusively to the promotion and access to culture for all Colombians. These articles promoted the Law of Culture of 1997, which in turn made possible the existence of a Ministry of Culture. Law 1997, also in its articles 50–56, enhanced the development and enrichment of the country's museums. Article 50 reads,

> **ART. 50.** —Scientific Research and Collections Increase. The Ministry of Culture and the territorial entities will create programs to encourage research and scientific catalogoing of the cultural heritage in all museums of the country through agreements with the universities and institutes devoted to historical, scientific, and artistic research. The Ministry will also promote the acquisition of pieces for the collections by creating and regulating incentives for donations, legacies, and acquisitions.[18]

Both the Constitution of 1991 and the Law of Culture of 1997 opened doors for institutions such as the National Museum to expand their collections and narratives. Considering these legal advances, Cuervo de Jaramillo aimed to document the Colombian armed conflict by recognizing all its protagonists, which included Tirofijo.

## *Headquarters of the National Museum of Colombia*

The institution had several headquarters before settling, in 1946, at the Panopticon. It started in 1823 at the Botanical House (Casa Botánica), in downtown Bogotá, where the mining school operated. It had two halls, one devoted to natural objects and another dedicated to history, arts, and sciences. In 1842, the Botanical House changed proprietors, and the museum moved to a room at the Department of Interior and War until 1845. In 1850, town planners demolished the house.[19] In 1845, the museum moved to the House of Classrooms (Casa de las aulas), headquarters of the National Library of Colombia, founded also in 1823. Also located downtown, this place was built by a Jesuit architect in the seventeenth century to accommodate the Colegio Máximo de la Compañía de Jesús (Society of Jesus Maximum School).[20] Until 1913, the year in which the National Museum moved again to another place, both institutions competed for a space of their own within the same building. While they shared the House of Classrooms, the directors of the museum had to negotiate where to exhibit its collections, sometimes shortening displays and spending exorbitant funds on local repairs.

From 1913 to 1922, the National Museum operated at the Rufino Cuervo Passage. Throughout the first three decades of the twentieth century, Bogotá still had a colonial urban structure of city blocks, with spaces for commerce or offices on the periphery and dead zones in the center. Urban planners, therefore, wanted to use the empty spaces and designate "commercial passages" for profit.[21] Here, the museum seemed dismembered and dispersed since the passage had several premises. There was not enough room for its collections and exhibitions. In 1922, the National Museum moved to the Pedro A. López building. The museum's deposits were housed at the National Capitol, the Rufino Cuervo Passage, the National Library, and its minor collections were sent to diverse institutions, such as the National University of Colombia, the Ministry of Education, and the Presidential Palace.[22] In 1946, the museum's permanent headquarters became the Panopticon, and Teresa Cuervo was placed in charge of the institution.

In March of the same year, 1946, the IX Pan-American Conference was held in Bogotá; therefore, the Ministry of Education and the organizers of event decided to move permanently the National Museum of Colombia to the Cundinamarca's Central Penitentiary, the Panopticon, notorious for its cruelty and inhumane conditions where prisoners stayed from 1874 to 1946,[23] before moving to the Picota Jail.[24] The project of reorganizing the National Museum was to integrate the separate Archaeological, Natural Sciences, and Fine Arts Museums into a single institution. Thus, the government supported the renovation of the Panopticon to meet the National Museum's needs, but the government cancelled its inauguration, originally planned for April 9, 1948, because of the assassination of Jorge Eliécer Gaitán.

Elvira Cuervo de Jaramillo grew up at the National Museum. She spent her afternoons there with her aunt Teresa Cuerva, also director of the venue during this time, and remembers vividly the *Bogotazo* or April 9 in an interview she gave me on February 9, 2017:

> Teresa was getting ready for reopening the museum. I did not have school, so I went there with two friends to help clean. While doing this, I saw my father running towards us and the museum workers and yelling, "Gaitán has been killed!" Approximately 300 workers that were at the museum disappeared, and some police officers also vanished. Only between twelve and fourteen people stayed, including me, Teresa, and my father. I remember fire, looting, and people running. Some rioters came towards the museum to liberate the prisoners they thought were still there, but Teresa and my father confronted them and told them that the building was not a prison anymore, but a historic place that deserves respect. The agitators only took the flagpoles displayed at the entrances and burned them. They did not enter. Teresa, my father, and I stayed at the museum until midnight. That memory has never left me. Teresa was the director of the institution until 1984, and she worked there for 28 years. She took care of it, cataloged every single object, and I witnessed all that.

The National Museum opened at its new headquarters on May 2, 1948. Its first floor was dedicated to archaeology and ethnography, the second story devoted to history, and its third level to fine arts. One of Cuervo de Jaramillo's first recollections of the museum is "being a bunch of boxes in a basement. Teresa had to direct that." [25]

## Reactions to Elvira Cuervo de Jaramillo Towel Initiative

In 2001, when the director of the National Museum of Colombia made her proposal public, some researchers and journalists backed it. Scholars Carlos del Cairo and Jefferson Jaramillo analyzed Cuervo de Jaramillo's initiative in their article, "Los dilemas de la museificación. Reflexiones en torno a dos iniciativas estatales de construcción" ("The Dilemmas of Museification. Reflections on Two State Building Initiatives"). They argued in her defense that her proposal conformed to the institution's function as the country's keeper of memory, preserving artifacts of cultural value for future exhibitions.[26] Consistent with its mission, the National Museum aimed to compile significant pieces of Colombia's contemporary history; however, this did not necessarily imply that the collected items would be displayed. Cuervo de Jaramillo knew that not enough time had passed to present these artifacts of war in public exhibitions. The Museum's director acknowledged that the institution could not show recent history yet, but she insisted on Tirofijo donating the towel for the institution's collections.[27]

Concurrently, some journalists throughout the country endorsed Cuervo de Jaramillo's initiative. Jotamario Arbeláez from *El Espectador* wrote,

> I think that Elvira's proposal of enthroning the towel at the museum due to its originality directs our attention to this important historical relic… and it encompasses certain subtle institutional mischief. It implies Tirofijo throwing in the towel even if it is for hanging the piece as a symbol of some reached peace, in the place that consecrates it as a cult object.[28]

The Spanish translation for "To throw in the towel," is "Tirar la toalla." In the quote above, it symbolized a possible surrendering of Tirofijo and his wars.

Journalist José Jaramillo Mejía, from the regional newspaper *La Patria,* also agreed with the director of the National Museum. He acknowledged Tirofijo's importance in the country's recent history and believed that the rag belonged in the museum with other personal artifacts of notable Colombian historical figures. He even stated that the towel should convey its use, therefore, washing or cleaning it was against Cuervo de Jaramillo's original intention of narrating the conflict through the artifact. Mejía also stated that excluding Tirofijo's presence at the museum did not diminish his importance; as painful as his actions were, his influence was undeniable in Colombians' lives.[29]

Journalist Héctor Rincón, amid the controversy about the towel's potential presence in the museum, reflected on questions raised by Cuervo de Jaramillo's initiative. He suggested that Colombians' rage at the thought of the towel's preservation in the museum's collection derived from their understanding of the social role of such institutions. What is the purpose of a museum? Which kind of memory should a museum create and convey? Rincón criticized the extreme reactions against the proposal and emphasized that museums are sites to document history, "not a place for ladies to attend cocktails and show off their dresses."[30] The journalist argued that Colombians had no memory, that forgetting was what they did best, and that this oblivion did not help in the necessary healing processes. Rincón also called readers' attention to the words and context in which Cuervo de Jaramillo intended to make the towel a collection piece: she did not want to perpetuate the policy of silence that surrounded other historical events such as The Banana Massacre of 1929 and the Revolt of the Commoners of 1781, both violent and bloody Colombian episodes. Both were bloody and violent historic episodes in which many Colombians died. One of Cuervo de Jaramillo's arguments for acquiring Tirofijo's towel was precisely related to remembrance, as noted by Rincón. The National Museum director and the journalist agreed that Colombians tend to forget rapidly, giving the sense that there is no historical memory in the country. They also noted that recollections of violent events past usually occur when the main protagonists are dead, making it difficult, if not impossible, to collect artifacts that belonged to them.

Nevertheless, conservative politicians and journalists told Cuervo de Jaramillo to let Tirofijo die before she could acquire or display the towel.[31] In 2001, Colombians were highly polarized due to the failed peace process of El Caguán, mentioned later in the chapter. The government felt the FARC-EP leader had mocked the president, and as a state institution, the National Museum should not have the towel in its inventory. Cuervo de Jaramillo, however, envisioned a broader role of the National Museum as a place in which a group of professionals decide what is important for viewers to remember. As she stated:

> The main concern for a museum, in a country without memory, is how to tell Colombian history. It is hard to display historical events relying on artifacts because they must tell what happened and many of them have disappeared. Museums must make sure this does not keep happening and make collections which account for Colombian recent history. We always do things backwards in Colombia. We get out to seek for events that happened forty years ago. We need to collect history while it is happening.[32]

Cuervo de Jaramillo, in other words, was concerned with the kinds of memories that museum professionals conveyed and safeguarding the institution's prerogative to have an engaged participation in representing ongoing events.

During 2001, Cuervo de Jaramillo's goal was to make the National Museum a more inclusive institution. She was aware of the need to tell the last 15 years of the history of Colombia, including actors such as drug traffickers, paramilitary fighters, and guerillas. The museum's director also rejected the institution's perceived role of telling stories full of "green ribbons and white doves."[33] She wanted a museum in which Colombians could find references to an all-encompassing history, not fractured or biased stories. Further, the museum held and displayed items of other persons considered unheroic in Colombian national consensus, such as paintings and documents that belonged to Pablo Morillo, mentioned before, a fearsome soldier sent by the Spanish Crown to reconquer New Granada in 1815–1816.[34] The director of the National Museum also supported her position by relying on a survey the institution conducted among 100,000 people, which concluded that one of the artifacts people wanted to see at the museum was the towel.[35]

Agreeing with historian Steve Stern, I suggest that excluding some memories from the museum's narrative can be understood as a way of "forgetting the uncomfortable," a way of avoiding what is painful or ignoring artifacts that trigger glorification of violent events.[36] In this context, Tirofijo's towel became contentious because it represented a man who inflicted too much pain on Colombians' lives. In the end, despite Cuervo de Jaramillo's intentions, the rag never arrived at the National Museum and currently does not belong to any collection in any Colombian museum.

The controversy raised by the possibility of the towel's acquisition by a state institution is also reflective of sociologist Elizabeth Jelin's insights into the historicization of painful remembrances. Memory of violence is polemical, she argues, because it is the source and result of political disputes. In the towel's case, the controversy became too heated because it aroused anger and pain. In this sense, Cuervo de Jaramillo tried to memorialize Colombia's armed conflict through the towel, but she failed in this endeavor.[37] The disagreement was so vast that she had to abandon the idea. If the artifact had arrived at the National Museum, perhaps it would have suffered the same destiny as other contentious pieces in the Museum's collections, which have still not been exhibited and, therefore, have not been officialized either. Such pieces include the shirt that Jorge Eliécer Gaitán wore when he was murdered on April 9, 1948, an event that triggered the riots of *El Bogotazo*. In addition, the museum holds the bloodied suit worn by Luis Carlos Galán, Liberal presidential candidate, murdered by order of Pablo Escobar, in 1989. His wife donated it to the museum in 1999.[38] The museum collections also hold the dress coat of Marshal José Antonio Sucre, who assumed Simón Bolívar's mantle of leadership and was shot at point-blank range in the back in 1830.

The non-exhibited artifacts of the National Museum of Colombia reflect that to exhibit an artifact is not enough for it to belong to a historical character. It also needs to adjust to the aesthetics, class, and taste fostered by the venue, and to convey the sense that the museumgoers will enrich their cultural capital. According to Pierre Bourdieu, people gain cultural capital from the individual's family and inheritance system, formal education, and skills acquired outside official schooling. This accumulation of knowledge dictates what members of a society consider adequate to see in a National Museum. In Colombia's case, citizens did not expect to find at the institution Tirofijo's towel, not only because it was a war symbol but also because it was old and dirty. Per Bourdieu, it would be seen as untasteful for the professionals of the institution to exhibit a vulgar item because its aesthetic did not befit a place considered a high-cultured place. This sense is also a marker of class.

Exhibiting Tirofijo's towel implied that the National Museum could lose its character of solemnity associated with a high level of education and status. This meant, for some Colombians, reducing "things of art to things of life."[39] Tirofijo's towel was never a work of art but a piece to narrate the country's recent violence. Its display among artistic masterpieces irritated some politicians and journalists. In addition, presenting the rag implied blurring deeply rooted and accentuated Colombian social hierarchies. This aligns with sociologist Stuart Hall's assertion about how culture is expressed in language and signals and maintains the identities and differences between social groups. Along these lines, the towel at the museum meant incorporating another "language" at the institution, one that disrupted representational systems in Colombia.[40] Following Hall, displaying this item ignored "the severe lines of division within our system of education, the identification between 'culture' and 'class,' and the question of distinct cultural climates in different sections of our stratified society."[41]

The furor surrounding the presence of the towel at the National Museum was evident in the results of a survey conducted by the professionals of the institution. The answer to the question of which historic personalities should be present at the institution, Simón Bolívar was the first option. Figures such as journalist Jaime Garzón, politician Luis Carlos Galán, and painter Fernando Botero also came up frequently. Guerrillas, paramilitary fighters, and drug lords were conspicuously absent. However, some museum professionals think that images of Pablo Escobar, for instance, belong in museum's displays to remind Colombians who they should not want to resemble.[42]

Elizabeth Jelin identifies different ways of dismissing painful remembrances from the individual mind and official memory. She says that in cases when hurtful memories surface, sometimes silence offers the best strategy to cope and maintain a certain social order. Jelin calls this evasive memory, and it seems that Cuervo de Jaramillo's idea of acquiring the towel caused great discomfort by opposing a chosen quietness. Evasive memory, following Jelin, "prevails in historical periods following large social catastrophes, massacres, and genocides, which may engender among those who suffered them directly and survived them the desire to not know, to avoid painful remembrances as a means to continue living." Certainly, for Cuervo de Jaramillo, the memories about the Colombian ongoing armed conflict were nothing like survivors' reminiscences nor the same as the social actors who opposed the presence of the towel in the museum, because they had not lived the horrors of the war directly.

The adverse reactions of journalists, politicians, and the public opinion to Cuervo de Jaramillo's proposal outnumbered the ones in favor. Reactions of museum visitors, such as the following one published in *El Tiempo* newspaper, convey the public displeasure with Cuervo de Jaramillo's proposal:

> A history of blood, sweat, and tears which have us about to throw in the towel. Not even mister Manuel feels flattered about giving away his cloth because he knows it is not to exalt him. It does not matter if he donates the yellow one that he uses now, or the red one that he washed, or the blue one, which he wears to complete our flag's colors; people are going to see it as a black and stained cloth just as the history we live.[43]

In addition, a public survey carried out by El Tiempo newspaper asked Colombians whether they supported Cuervo de Jaramillo's initiative. Of 1,074 people interviewed in Bogotá, Cali, Medellín, Barranquilla, and Bucaramanga (main Colombian cities), 73% opposed the initiative and 22% thought it was not such a bad idea. In addition, the newspaper's website received 2,138 votes. Of these, 88.1% opposed bringing the towel into the museum, and only 11.8% supported this effort. The online survey was open for 24 hours.[44]

Similar reactions appeared on radio, television, and printed media, criticizing the Museum, Colombia's emblematic patrician institution, for a proposal that would glorify criminals. As journalist Adriana Mejía wrote:

> Mrs. Cuervo is right about the institution she leads collecting artifacts that are part of the country's history. But she lacks common sense because she is offending recent sensibilities. When we talk about history, we refer to people or events which we can look back at. This is not the case... the common citizen does not want Tirofijo's rag at the National Museum. This is logical because the common citizen is the first victim of a history written by too many hands with fears, pains, and uncertainties... and too much blood.[45]

Writer Víctor Paz Otero also manifested his discontent with the towel in a sardonic column published in *El Espectador* newspaper. His text, which initially appears to support Cuervo de Jaramillo's initiative, turns into a sarcastic critique of the FARC-EP's actions and argues that it would be wrong to include the towel in the museum's collections. He criticized

> this dispassionate praise of Mr. Manuel Marulanda, when somebody tells me that the FARC killed an outstanding family, mother, son, bodyguard, and dogs. That the FARC for nine thousand pesos massacred seven hikers... That the FARC—who were not going to use gas cylinders anymore—just wiped out a whole peasant population, et etcetera. And that the FARC are behind an attempt at killing a journalist.[46]

Reactions like this were common. Colombians had no sympathy whatsoever for the FARC-EP and their actions against civilians.

The hate mail and threats Cuervo de Jaramillo received demonstrated that many Colombians refused to look back dispassionately upon violent episodes; it was too soon. Although her position aimed to look beyond the moment to thinking about the kind of knowledge of the past the museum might convey to future generations, the present generation was unremitting. With the following post in the *El Espectador* newspaper, the director of the National Museum of Colombia directed the matter to the National Government.

## Historic Artifacts

> As you know, the National Museum of Colombia is part of the Ministry of Culture; therefore, its actions are framed by the policies established by the National Government. The recent polemic promoted by the mass media, surrounding the trivialization about the legal mission of the museum of collecting artifacts of the country's recent history to be exhibited in the right moment and within an appropriate context, has taken on nuances that go beyond the cultural sphere. In consequence, the National Museum of Colombia has decided to leave this matter in hands of the National Government, due to the sensibilities it has awakened in Colombian society.
> 
> Elvira Cuervo de Jaramillo. National Museum of Colombia.[47]

With this publication, Cuervo de Jaramillo withdrew the museum from the controversy and ended her intentions of enriching the institution's collections with contentious artifacts.

The idea of acquiring Tirofijo's towel and perhaps exhibiting it at the National Museum, nevertheless, raises several questions, such as who decides which memorialization belongs at the venue. To defend her position, Cuervo de Jaramillo stated that the matter of how to display the towel should become the central issue. "It depends on how it is placed in the display case."[48] This statement has several meanings. One is Cuervo de Jaramillo's insistence on incorporating multiple narratives of the violence in the museum's scripts. Others relate to the aesthetic and context of the towel in the glass case.

Museum professionals know that most, if not all, exhibitions and displays take artifacts out of their cultural contexts of production and consumption and endow them with other meanings. As anthropologist Johannes Fabian notes, the terms employed to designate material culture influence museum professionals in their item classification. The author, therefore, differentiates between objects and artifacts. An artifact usually refers to ethnographic studies or a cultural context that implies ethnological concepts. It is something that tells the history of its production; therefore, it belongs to culture rather than nature.[49]

The term object belongs more to the natural sciences. In Tirofijo's towel case, Cuervo de Jaramillo imbued the rag with cultural and symbolic significance to tell Colombia's recent violent history from a non-conventional perspective. Thus, following Fabian, the towel was to become a cultural artifact. Fabian's differentiation also speaks to the conventional meaning of the National Museum of Colombia.

Created in 1823 as a mining and science school, the venue's tradition, until the 1990s, was to display objects. So, the towel became an artifact due to the cultural context—aesthetics, politics, and class—in which Cuervo de Jaramillo imbued it. When detractors portrayed Tirofijo's towel as just a dirty old rag, they signaled an agent of pollution, a disruptive agent of the established order—something that defiled a hallowed environment, such as a museum. Dirt goes against order, and the Colombian society of the 2000s believed that getting rid of turmoil was a way of trying to make sense of the heated political climate of the country. According to anthropologist Mary Douglas, these perceptions of uncleanliness also lead to ideas about contagion and danger, which alter the given order of a society. Tirofijo's towel was a threat, a transgression of the beliefs about what a good citizen had to be—patriotic, loyal to the state, and respectful of the law—and what an upstanding institution should display. It was an insult to refined taste.[50] Even though Douglas' discussion about purity and danger refers to primitive religions, it can apply to museum settings, which are considered contemplative and sacred spaces in need of protection from defilement.

> Shoes are not dirty in themselves, but it is dirty to place them on the dining-table; food is not dirty in itself, but it is dirty to leave cooking utensils in the bedroom, or food bespattered on clothing; similarly, bathroom equipment in the drawing room; clothing lying on chairs; out-door things in-doors; upstairs things downstairs; under-clothing appearing where over-clothing should be, and so on. In short, our pollution behavior is the reaction which condemns any object or idea likely to confuse or contradict cherished classifications.[51]

Of course, aesthetics, like "culture," is highly subjective. Choices and tastes about what is beautiful/ugly, clean/dirty, orderly/disorderly vary in the eyes of the beholder and their own cultural background. People revere a blood-stained depiction of Jesus rather than repudiate it. In our context, aesthetics, defined by class and taste, also dictated which artifacts or objects were worthy to include in an institution such as the National Museum of Colombia. This was one more reason the Museum's acquisition of Tirofijo's towel was an anathema.

Some scholars, like semiologist Eduardo Utrera, said that the rag was a trivial object, and perhaps the museum professionals should have acquired Tirofijo's weapons. He was referring to a collective memory represented by arms, which most Colombians can agree upon.[52] Perhaps the towel was also problematic because it was a personal object, an item that could somehow awaken feelings of empathy toward Tirofijo. Scholars Robert Ehrenreich and Jane Klinger claim that to exhibit personal artifacts from the victims of the Holocaust, for example, could call the public's attention to the humanity of the dead. They believe this is a way to fight against indifference toward victims of violence and give some dignity to the casualties and survivors of the Holocaust.[53] By viewing personal items, perhaps the visitors to an exhibition could put themselves, at least for a moment, in others' shoes.

This trend started with anthropologist Franz Boas (1858–1942) and his arrangements at the American Museum of Natural History, in which he displayed the everyday life of the Kwaikiutl, known today as a First Nation tribe. Boas believed that context was definitive for understanding the artifacts displayed. It made the public aware of what they were seeing because the items exhibited were significantly different from what the US citizens of the time had seen or were expecting.[54] Similarly, the significance of displaying Tirofijo's towel depended much on the context and narratives that would surround it due to the unexpected and novel nature of the artifact. Perhaps some of the fears regarding Tirofijo's presence at the National Museum were related to Boas's objective of bridging the gap between displays and viewers, creating some sense of familiarity.

Although Tirofijo's towel was a personal object, Cuervo de Jaramillo's proposal to display this artifact was not meant to promote the guerrilla leader's humanity or compassion. Nor was Cuervo de Jaramillo's intention to side with Colombian perpetrators of violence. Instead, her aim was to tell part of the country's recent history through the towel. Ehrenreich and Klinger argue that presenting personal artifacts can help to tell the horrors of war and counterbalance displays which glorify battles and wars; this was Cuervo de Jaramillo's purpose.[55]

José Roca, Colombian curator and Artistic Director of FLORA ars+natura, an independent space for contemporary art in Bogotá, and Curator of the Latin American Roaming Art (LARA), however, had another position that ultimately supported Cuervo de Jaramillo's initiative. He referred to the changing meaning and nature of museum artifacts. Roca argued that there are examples of museums in which slave shackles were kept from the public for a long time, and when they were displayed, their meaning shifted precisely due to their exhibition. Roca concurred with Sharon MacDonald regarding her argument about the value of displaying a difficult past and the ways in which people reacted to exhibitions about violent events. He stated that depending on their background, age, social status, and political views, observers will have different impressions of what they are seeing. Instead of horrifying the viewers, perhaps showing difficult heritage can spark criticisms and innovative thoughts about identity.

MacDonald, in her article "Is Difficult Heritage Still Difficult," discusses the turn toward difficult heritage, which started in Germany after the Second World War and extended worldwide. Although she notes general acceptance for exposing difficult heritage, she also considers that it is disturbing. MacDonald admits that these displays are sometimes regarded as a way of reconciling with historical atrocities, as an act of absolution—as if exhibiting and acknowledging atrocities in the present cleans up the past and helps prevent brutal acts from happening again in the future. However, she also clarifies that even though exposing difficult heritage has become more accepted, it is still not universally done, particularly if it involves a recent historical development. In these cases, it requires careful follow-up and attention to answer the severity of tough pasts and their duration as problematic; the answer to this depends partly on how "difficult" is understood. Both Roca and MacDonald suggest that a community's perception of its own difficult heritage shifts as time passes because viewers change. The Association of Colombian Victims, for instance, currently claims that displaying brutalities no longer disrupts their processes of identity formation and, on the contrary, they want people to know what they endured. Those who opposed Cuervo de Jaramillo's proposal related to the idea that Tirofijo's towel thought this would encourage Colombians to glorify perpetrators, something inimical to national identity formation. But as Roca and MacDonald have demonstrated, that is rarely the case. In addition, since 2000 non-governmental organizations and victims' movements stated that displaying outlaw's voices might help build trust and honesty, which is positive for contemporary community building.[56]

## *The Director's Public Life*

Elvira Cuervo de Jaramillo was born in Bogotá in 1941. She belongs to a well-known Colombian family involved in politics for 200 years, so it is no surprise that she decided to be a politician and public servant. Besides being the director of the National Museum of the country, she was a congresswoman in 1986 and served as the vice president of the International Constitutional Commission. She has also been the vice president of the Departmental Assembly of Cundinamarca, the national coordinator of the presidential campaign of conservative politician Álvaro Gómez Hurtado, the Colombian representative to the United Nations, secretary of the Education Secretary of Cundinamarca, Director of the District Social Welfare Institute, and Minister of Culture. But she recalls her appointment at the National Museum of Colombia with special affection. Despite her commitment to politics, she did not hesitate when offered to lead the institution, stating, "My relationship with the museum is very intimate."[57]

Motherless at the age of three, Elvira lived with her father and three aunts; one of them, Teresa Cuervo, was director of the National Museum of

Colombia from 1946 to 1974, as previously mentioned. She was a definitive influence for Elvira because of her interest in public service and museums. Cuervo was the Director of the Exhibit Section and Museums of the Ministry of Education, being the first person in the country to hold this position. In 1946, she was also the founder of the Museum of Colonial Art until appointed director of the National Museum of Colombia, a position she held until 1974.

Elvira Cuervo married Eduardo Jaramillo when she was 18 years old and went to live in a town near Bogotá for four years. Her first two children were born there, and then the family came back to Bogotá, where she joined a gardeners' club and organized the first flower international exhibition in 1972, inaugurated by the Conservative president Misael Pastrana Borrero (1970–1974). After this achievement, Elvira left for Cartagena with her four children. While she was living in this Caribbean city, the Mayor of Bogotá, Aníbal Fernández de Soto (1973–1974), appointed her Director of Social Welfare. This was her pathway to the political arena. After Pastrana's term, the Liberal Alfonso López Michelsen took office (1974–1978) and appointed Cuervo de Jaramillo as Education Secretary of the Calera Municipality. Cuervo de Jaramillo won three times the elections to be part of the Assembly of Cundinamarca, winning the votes of the Movimiento Obrero Independiente y Revolucionario, MOIR (Revolutionary Independent Labor Movement), despite being a Conservative. Cuervo de Jaramillo belonged to the Conservative wing led by Álvaro Gómez Hurtado, mentioned before.

Following her political path, Elvira made it to the Colombian House of Representatives, where she realized her presence "was an inconvenience." She arrived in the House in 1986, when the Liberal Virgilio Barco Vargas was president. There, she was in close contact with politicians such as Luis Carlos Galán and a representative of Pablo Escobar—the drug lord—elected representative to the House in 1983. President Barco, to counteract Escobar's power, promoted a constitutional reform that aimed to make the extradition a real possibility for imprisoning Colombian delinquents, such as narco-traffickers. The final vote to approve this project occurred on December 21, 1989. "I was so naive," claims Elvira. "One night, one of the doormen of the House told me that somebody requested me at the door. I found myself in front of a guy with a very pronounced scar on his face who said to me:

> Mrs. Elvira, I want to tell you that we already have most of the First Commission voting against the extradition article, but we are still missing your vote, and we want to make sure we can count on you.
> Who wants that? – Elvira asked.
> The boss sends me to tell you that some members of the First Commission have received twenty million pesos, but he is willing to give you fifty for your campaign next year."

At this moment, the man became very specific and gave Elvira intimate details about her and her family, to which she answered:

> Look, sir, I belong to a family that has served this country for more than 200 years. I serve the country, and I am the last member of the family who carries the surname Cuervo. I would rather be dead than threatened by your boss. Tell him that you gave me the message, but I did not receive it.

Cuervo de Jaramillo resigned immediately from the House and from politics, "not for me but for my kids." For the next two years, she devoted herself to writing. After her career in politics and social service, she was appointed director of the National Museum of Colombia in 1992. When Cuervo de Jaramillo went to see the museum's building, however, she had some concerns, as she expressed in an interview she gave me:

> The place was in bad shape. The wastewater of a nearby school was stagnant at the main entrance lobby, it was humid, dirty, and very neglected. Kids had to enter with rubber boots to avoid getting infected with the sewage waters.

So, in 1992, a restoration process started. Simultaneously, Cuervo de Jaramillo and a well-known Colombian painter, Beatriz González, designed a new script. Elvira retired from the National Museum in 2005, leaving the institution well-positioned, functioning, and with an acknowledged reputation.

The path to Cuervo de Jaramillo's professional crisis began nearly a decade earlier, in 1992, when Ramiro Osorio, Director of Colcultura, nowadays the Ministry of Culture, appointed her Director of the National Museum of Colombia, a position she held until 2005. When taking office, Cuervo de Jaramillo had two major objectives. The first one was for the institution to gain international recognition. For that purpose, she organized significant exhibitions such as the sample of Henry Moore's monumental bronze sculptures (1997); 45 Pablo Picasso paintings (2000); the Gustav Rau collection, composed of approximately 800 paintings by famous European artists (2002); 73 pieces, including sculptures, of the Terracotta Army of Qin Shi Huang, Emperor of China (2006); and 100 artifacts of The Lord of Sipán, a Moche mummy found at Huaca Rajada, Peru (2007). Cuervo de Jaramillo also arranged for preservation specialists from the Louvre Museum to train the Colombian museum staff.

For her second objective, Cuervo de Jaramillo wanted the institution's narratives and exhibitions to include timely topics such as forced displacement, attempts at peace treaties in Colombia, and historic armed conflicts. Therefore, she created the annual public history lectureship, Ernesto Restrepo Tirado, in which academics and specialists gather to analyze current cultural and social affairs. This event paved the way for including topics such as the recent

Colombian violence in the museum's narratives. Cuervo de Jaramillo's proposal of displaying the towel also aimed to serve this purpose.

The aversion the inhabitants of the country felt toward Tirofijo intensified when Conservative President Andrés Pastrana initiated a peace process with the FARC-EP in 1998. He aimed to resume dialogue with this guerrilla group after talks had been suspended during César Gaviria's administration (1990–1994).[58] At the beginning of Gaviria's mandate, there was a conducive atmosphere for negotiating with the guerrillas that were part of the Coordinadora Guerrillera Simón Bolívar, CGSB, (Simón Bolívar Guerrilla Coordinating Board): FARC-EP, Ejército de Liberación Nacional, ELN (National Liberation Army), Movimiento 19 de Abril, M-19 (19th of April Movement), Ejército Popular de Liberación, EPL (Popular Liberation Army), Partido Revolucionario de los Trabajadores, PRT (Workers Revolutionary Party), Movimiento Armado Quintín Lame, MAQL (Quintín Lame Armed Movement), and Corriente de Renovación Socialista, CRS (Current of Socialist Renewal). In 1990, however, the CGSB attacked two rural towns, an action rejected by the government. Towards the end of 1990, state forces fired upon the main headquarters of the FARC-EP. This meant the end of the peace negotiations. In 1991, there was another attempt to resume the conversations, which ended in an exploratory meeting in the Arauca Department. César Gaviria won the election of 1990 because Colombians associated him with Luis Carlos Galán, the presidential candidate killed by drug-lord Pablo Escobar in 1989, and who was committed to fighting drug trafficking and publicly denounced the drug lord on several occasions. After Galán's assassination, Escobar targeted Gaviria, but the politician survived the attack. Since then, Gaviria and Escobar confronted each other constantly. In 1991, the president and Escobar agreed on the non-extradition of the drug dealer to the United States. Instead, he could remain in Colombia in a special prison, called La Catedral (The Cathedral). In 1992, one year before the Colombian Military with the help of the US Special Forces shot him dead, Escobar escaped The Cathedral. During his stay in the arranged prison, Escobar had loud parties, kept his business, and came and went as he pleased. The Cathedral episode is one of the most embarrassing moments in Colombia's judicial history. In 1998, Pastrana and the FARC-EP agreed to create a demilitarized zone of approximately 40,000 km$^2$, located in the El Caguán river basin, a jungle region in south central Colombia, between the Departments of Meta and Caquetá. During Pastrana's peace process, images of Tirofijo draped in his towel became very popular. The peace attempt, however, turned into a resounding failure. In 1999, when everything was set for Pastrana and Marulanda Vélez to sit down and talk at El Caguán, the guerrilla leader did not appear; he stood up to the president. Tirofijo said that he did not show up, as agreed, because he felt Colombians were not ready for achieving peace in the face of gaping inequality. In addition, he claimed there were snipers waiting to kill him. The authorities have never proven this.[59]

Cuervo de Jaramillo's search for Tirofijo's towel had nothing to do with political affiliations; she just wanted the piece to be part of a documentation process. The towel was supposed to enrich the reserves of the museum, which also include, among other artifacts, the suit that presidential candidate Luis Carlos Galán was wearing when he was murdered in 1989.[60] Cuervo de Jaramillo suggested the acquisition of Tirofijo's towel because the object could be easily connected to the FARC-EP and Colombia's violence of the 1980s, 1990s, and early 2000s, but she said that the museum would also be open to acquiring one of his hats or even one of his weapons.[61]

The proposal of making Tirofijo's figure more mainstream was not unique to Cuervo de Jaramillo. In 1999, the painter Fernando Botero—an artist from Medellín famous for satirical depictions of political figures in large, exaggerated proportions—had depicted the rag as well as Marulanda Vélez. This piece is in the Botero Museum in Medellín, Colombia. This indicates that artists, as well as politicians such as Cuervo de Jaramillo, were concerned about representing the country's armed conflict. They viewed guerrilla leaders as figures that recent Colombian historical narratives needed to address, which does not imply paying them homage.[62]

The initiative to incorporate Tirofijo's towel into the National Museum collections was also understood in a global context. Even though journalists and politicians were shocked, Uruguayan writer Horacio Buscaglia contextualized the idea. He looked beyond the proposal and found other museums which had non-traditional narratives to humorously temper the adverse reactions to Cuervo de Jaramillo's initiative. Buscaglia found a museum in Japan devoted to socks and one in Georgia, USA, for exhibiting ticks—both as iconoclastic as the towel in aesthetic terms. There is also the Parasite Museum in Tokyo, the Devil's Museum in Lithuania, the Match Museum in Sweden, the Museum of Exotic Chickens in England, and the Museum for Animal Droppings.[63] As funny as the former institutions might seem, they demonstrate that artifacts vary, tell different stories, and value different notions of aesthetics.

## The Founding Father of the FARC-EP, Tirofijo, and His Victims

There is no definitive number for the fatalities of the Colombian armed conflict of the 1980s, 1990s, and early 2000s. One reason is that authorities are still finding bodies and mass graves, which makes it difficult to have an accurate record. The state agency Unidad para la atención y reparación integral a las Víctimas (Unit for the Victims Assistance and Reparation), created in 2016 during the presidency of Juan Manuel Santos, has registered 9,278,531 victims until June 1, 2022, but there might be more. The Colombian government distinguishes victims by genre, ethnic group, age, and disability, providing the following results (Tables 1.1–1.4).

**TABLE 1.1** Genre

| | |
|---|---|
| Men | 4,737,891 |
| Women | 4,535,688 |
| LGBTI | 4,290 |
| Not specified | 298 |
| Intersexual | 364 |

**TABLE 1.2** Ethnic Group

| | |
|---|---|
| None | 7,543,543 |
| Black or Afrocolombian | 1,165,671 |
| Indigenous People | 249,699 |
| Gypsy ROM | 9,077 |
| Gypsy (RROM) | 710 |
| Palenquero | 5,805 |
| Raizal of the San Andres and Providencia Archipelago | 11,272 |

**TABLE 1.3** Age

| | |
|---|---|
| Between 0 and 5 | 207,704 |
| Between 6 and 11 | 776,276 |
| Between 12 and 17 | 1,056,048 |
| Between 18 and 28 | 2,103,600 |
| Between 29 and 60 | 3,736,289 |
| Between 61 and 100 | 1,142,982 |
| ND | 255,632 |

**TABLE 1.4** Disability

| | |
|---|---|
| Multiple | 66,750 |
| Auditive | 24,515 |
| Physical | 108,254 |
| Intellectual | 21,750 |
| Psychosocial (Mental) | 5,525 |
| Visual | 33,003 |
| Not established | 142,272 |
| None | 8,876,462 |

These numbers come from the Registro Único de Víctimas (Unique Victim Registry), where people who fit into one of the previous categories can register to receive financial compensation for the damages suffered during the recent violence. However, in a poor country like Colombia, many are potentially victims, and the database risks assigning resources to individuals not directly affected by the internal war. Therefore, the figure of eight million is debatable. The Unit of Victims' agents claim that the government has compensated 7,206,144 Colombians.[64]

On the other hand, the Centro Nacional de Memoria Histórica (National Center of Historical Memory) published a comprehensive report in 2013, *¡Basta Ya! Colombia: Memorias de guerra y dignidad (¡Basta Ya! Colombia: Memories of War and Dignity)*. In this account, historians and specialists in violence, after many years of research and fieldwork, came up with the number of 220,000 Colombians who died as a result of the civil war between 1985 and 2012.[65] The researchers who compiled the data were more aware of the different kinds of victims; hence, the numbers for the Unique Victim Registry and the National Center for Historical Memory diverge. The *¡Basta Ya!* account also considers the kinds of atrocities inflicted by the main actors of the conflict: guerrillas, paramilitaries, and the National Army. The numbers for the brutalities perpetrated by guerrillas, according to the investigation for the *¡Basta Ya!* report, are: 24,482 kidnappings, 3,900 assassinations, more than 700 civilian victims in warlike actions, 854 attacks on populations, 77 terrorist assaults, 343 massacres, more than 4,323 raids on civil goods, nearly 800,000 acres of land dispossessed, and almost 4,000 children recruited.[66] The report states that 238 massacres were perpetrated by the FARC-EP; 56 by the Ejército de Liberación Nacional, ELN (National Liberation Army); 18 by the Ejército Popular de Liberación, EPL (Popular Liberation Army); three by the Movimiento Quintín Lame (Quintín Lame Movement); seven by two or more guerrillas together; 18 by unidentified guerrillas; and three by dissidents or factions of the EPL or ELN.

Since the FARC-EP was the guerrilla group that committed most of the recorded atrocities known to date, the idea of acquiring and eventually displaying Tirofijo's rag was problematic for many Colombians. The item became a contentious object because it appeared to grant official status to the FARC-EP and its presence in the country. Tirofijo's marksmanship made him famous. He commanded the FARC-EP for more than 30 years and was the only guerrilla fighter to die at a ripe old age: 78. He came to be known for his cold-bloodedness, strategic planning, resistance to the establishment, and his towel. He was born in the Colombian coffee region, Department of Quindío, although there is disagreement on whether he was born in 1928 or 1930.[67] From a very young age, Tirofijo started working to help in his household. He came from a humble peasant liberal family, was the oldest of five siblings, and worked in a lumber mill in 1948, when the so-called *Bogotazo* erupted. The trigger of this uprising was the assassination of the liberal politician Jorge Eliécer Gaitán, whose murder is still under investigation. The *Bogotazo* represented the violent peak of rivalries between the Liberal and Conservative parties during the first half of the twentieth century. Gaitán's homicide led to a political mass movement in Bogotá and other cities such as Barrancabermeja, Bucaramanga, Cali, Ibagué, and some towns of Tolima and Cundinamarca. Other riots took place on the

Atlantic Coast, and in the Departments of Antioquia, Boyacá, and Nariño. The *Bogotazo* initiated the ten years of La Violencia (1948–1958).[68]

One year after the *Bogotazo*, 19-year-old Tirofijo, who identified ideologically with the Liberal Party, organized an armed group with 14 of his cousins to defend himself and his family from Conservative attacks. In an interview with the Chilean newspaper *El Mercurio*, Tirofijo said: "In that time, to rise up in arms was the only way to survive."[69] It seems that the country's situation encouraged him to become a guerrilla fighter. Until that moment, he was a peasant and worker, a businessman who had a store, played violin, and knew how to be a farmer. Soon after embracing the armed struggle, Tirofijo demonstrated leadership, despite his origins. Uneducated, not handsome, unglamorous, he did not belong to a prestigious family, and did not follow the pattern of the idealized young and attractive leftist fighters such as the Argentinian Ernesto "Che" Guevara and the Cuban Fidel Castro. Mistrustful and astute, his recourse to violence was unapologetic. Thus, he is incomparable to the above revolutionaries because his representations, including the towel, have not yet become something to commodify.[70] For some Colombian journalists, such as Arturo Alape, Tirofijo was not a terrorist but a revolutionary.[71] For others, such as Roberto Pombo, he was just a guerrilla fighter.[72] In 2001, when Cuervo de Jaramillo proposed acquiring Tirofijo's towel, most citizens were against any kind of presence or representation of the FARC-EP at the museum. Colombians must not acknowledge Tirofijo in any manner. Due to the extreme acts of cruelty and violence the FARC-EP committed under Tirofijo's leadership, his personal items did not have the significance of other historic artifacts such as the swords, weapons, or clothes of Colombian great men or founding fathers, such as Simón Bolívar or past presidents. Conservative politicians and journalists argued that Tirofijo's towel only exacerbated painful memories, and, in 2001, they did not want to soft-pedal the horrors of the war. In addition, the rag did not have the potential to generate any profit—not only in monetary returns but also in social terms, because its display would have been highly contested. Journalists and politicians revealed a tendency explored by Ksenija Bilbija and Leigh Payne for museums to make atrocities only part of a more distant history, safely distanced from the present, perhaps as a way of aiding a grieving process or avoiding public controversy.[73]

The Colombian Intelligence Service gave Tirofijo the name Manuel Marulanda Vélez in 1950. The real Marulanda Vélez was a very critical union member of Laureano Gómez, an extremely conservative politician, president of Colombia (1950–1953) until forced into exile by a coalition of Liberals and Conservatives. He died in 1965. The real Manuel Marulanda also lambasted the Conservative Party, the National Army, and the Colombian high class. He died due to a beating in 1953. After this, his union member colleagues looked for Tirofijo and requested him to take Manuel Marulanda's name to honor the union member's assassination and keep alive the Marxist-Leninist ideals he espoused.[74] Tirofijo, therefore, used Manuel Marulanda Vélez as his *nom de guerre*. From the 1950s until 1964, Tirofijo served in secrecy. He founded the FARC-EP during the National Front (1958–1974), a time when a bipartisan coalition between the Liberal and Conservative parties governed the country. These political forces came to the agreement of alternating their time in power every four years. The first president of the National Front was the Liberal Alberto Lleras Camargo (1958–1962), and the last one was the Conservative Misael Pastrana Borrero (1970–1974). The National Front attempted to end La Violencia. The decade of 1960 started with many expectations of peace and coexistence, but by the 1970s, this social experiment collapsed. According to historian Marco Palacios, the National Front failed due to political leaders' inability to fulfill the promises they had made, such as agrarian, administrative, fiscal, and labor reforms.[75]

The foundation of the FARC-EP by Tirofijo in 1964 was also a consequence of the "War of Villarrica" (1955) and the "War of Marquetalia" (1964), two armed confrontations between groups led by Tirofijo and the National Army. The Colombian government felt threatened by the influence of Liberal guerrillas and Communist armed groups in these parts of the country because these working-class uprisings and riots jeopardized the official establishment.[76] Other conflicts occurred in Colombia as well, such as those in Riochiquito, the Department of Cundinamarca, and in the Sumapaz region near Bogotá. The government sought complete military and political control of these territories; hence, the policy aimed to exterminate the armed opposition.

To counteract the guerrillas, the National Army launched the "Sovereignty Operation," designed to pacify Marquetalia. This military maneuver occurred from May 18, 1964, until May 27 of the same year. The National Army was heavily armed and even offered money to the people who gave away weapons and their colleagues' locations, but no one talked. Due to the Marquetalia population's refusal to speak, the government sent two fighter planes equipped with bacterial weapons. As a result, 15 children died, and the confrontation hurt many people. During "Sovereignty Operation," the Colombian National Army displaced 2,000 peasants and tortured and imprisoned another 2,000. When the operation finished, 16,000 soldiers had still not defeated 48 peasant fighters. Women, children, and elderly people were hiding in the forest. Those remaining after the military offensive became the Fuerzas Armadas Revolucionarias de Colombia—Ejército del Pueblo, FARC-EP.[77] Its main leaders were Tirofijo and Luis Alberto Morantes Jaimes, alias Jacobo Arenas (1924–1990), another ideological commander.

After this confrontation with the National Army, Tirofijo became a legend. Before Marquetalia, there were just a few testimonies about Marulanda Vélez's abilities. One of his friends, however, describes a very meticulous and fearless warrior. The rumor was that when Tirofijo was in combat, it was very hard for the National Army to win. The guerrilla fighter became such a feared and popular figure that people reported seeing him at the same time in different places, and several chronicles of his death surfaced, even with pictures.

Beginning in 1948, Colombian media issued reports of Tirofijo's death in the Quindío Department. The first time the media reported him dead, Tirofijo was 18 years old and had fled his parents' home due to the confrontations between Conservatives and Liberals. The second time the news announced Tirofijo's death occurred during the Marquetalia confrontations with the National Army. The media and the government reported his death five more times. The members of the FARC-EP laughed every time their leader died, and so did Tirofijo himself. The seventh time he died, in 2008—this time for real—there were some doubts, but finally the guerrilla group confirmed his demise.

Tirofijo's skillfulness, the influence of communism in the guerrilla forces, and the abandonment of the countryside by the Colombian state enabled the rapid and noticeable growth of the FARC-EP. Until his death in 2008, Tirofijo always served as the military leader in chief and the coordinator of peasant activities in the FARC-EP zones.[78] He and the FARC-EP had a not-so-bad reputation in the Colombian countryside until 1980, when they began using kidnapping to fund their cause. This practice terrorized the population and was heavily condemned.[79] However, the first abduction this guerrilla group conducted was in 1965, when Tirofijo ordered the kidnap and murder of the ex-Chancellor Harold Eder.[80] After Marquetalia, the FARC-EP made great efforts to regain popular support. During the confrontations with the National Army in a town called Inzá, near Marquetalia, the guerrilla fighters planned to attack a bus carrying police officers. Tirofijo commanded the attack; however, tactical mistakes triggered a violent guerrilla shooting of the bus. Two nuns and civilians were among the casualties, in addition to the policemen. Jacobo Arenas, co-leader of the FARC-EP, acknowledged this tragedy, which greatly discredited the guerrilla group. After the decade of the 1980s, Tirofijo decided not to participate personally in any more direct violent confrontations. As he told the journalist Arturo Alape, "We thought that our participation in battles was not important but how those battles were commanded politically and militarily. [...] I will help guiding but not shooting. I do not do that anymore."[81]

During the 1980s, the FARC-EP allied with drug traffickers to fund its cause. This also deeply hurt the guerrillas' image. Tirofijo founded the group to fight for peasants' rights, battle against injustice, and fight for a more inclusive country. Drug trafficking was not about those ideals but about making money quickly and illegally. The FARC-EP betrayed their ideals, and this disappointed their supporters. In a meeting the leaders of the rebel group had with Carlos Ossa Escobar, advisor during the mandate of Virgilio Barco Vargas (1986–1990), the guerrillas admitted having connections to drug lords and coca plantations. When the meeting finished, Tirofijo approached Ossa and confirmed the FARC-EP links with these activities. He was worried and thought the guerrilla group had made a mistake.[82]

In addition, Colombians despaired when a ten-year-old boy, Andrés Felipe Pérez, died of incurable cancer in 2001, and Tirofijo refused to let him see his kidnapped father for the last time. In 2000, by taking the boy's father, the FARC-EP prevented Andrés Felipe from having the only possible suitable transplant donor. Instead, the guerrilla leaders told the family to take him to the FARC-EP headquarters, where one of the guerrilla doctors could see him. Many Colombians even offered to trade places with the father so he could see his son, but Tirofijo was intractable. Andrés Felipe's death greatly tarnished the FARC-EP and Tirofijo's image.[83] That same year, the director of the National Museum of Colombia proposed to acquire the guerrilla leader's towel to enrich the institution's collections.

As scholars such as Eduardo Pizarro Leongómez (2001) and Arturo Alape (1998) note, Tirofijo only understood the logic of war. Due to his upbringing and background, he felt that taking up arms was the only way to fight against a state that had abandoned or mistreated poor communities. The FARC-EP's methods of war were controversial. This guerrilla group claimed to fight for people's rights, but at the same time they bombed entire towns, leaving blood, anger, and death. One of the most widely condemned war techniques used by the FARC-EP was the use of gas cylinders filled with explosive powder. Other guerilla tactics included kidnapping, selective killings, threats to civilians, bombings, antipersonnel mines, forced recruitment, and forced displacement. The FARC-EP assailed the basic liberties and goods of Colombians, kidnapping more people and causing more infrastructure damage than paramilitaries or the National Army.

The FARC-EP's reputation drove away popular support. The repulsion Colombians felt toward this guerrilla force reflected in the government's inflexible policies toward them. When Tirofijo died on March 26, 2008, Colombian state representatives viewed a new chance for reaching a peace process with the FARC-EP.[84] For the government and the conservative media, however, Tirofijo was a terrorist and an outlaw, an obstacle to achieving peace.[85] An editorial published in *El Espectador* newspaper demonstrates commentators' reactions to his death:

> Today, when [the FARC-EP]'s founder is dead, many reforms in Colombia have not been made, and the FARC-EP has become a true drug trafficker army which systematically violates the population's human rights—undergoing practices questioned by Humanitarian International Law, such as kidnapping as a financing method, and executing massacres and forced displacement as deterrence. They have children in their ranks, and paradoxically, they are one of the worst enemies that peasant movements have.[86]

In 2001, when Cuervo de Jaramillo attempted to acquire and eventually display one of Tirofijo's towels at the National Museum of Colombia, her intention was far from honoring or exalting the FARC-EP leader's actions. As she affirmed,

> [...] the museum must register the personal objects of those who have a major role in the country's life, no matter their political affiliation. Just as we have items that belonged to "The Pacifier" Pablo Morillo, who was no angel, we must have Manuel Marulanda's towel.[87]

Cuervo de Jaramillo, Congresswoman for the Conservative Party and the director of the museum, deplored the harm guerillas had inflicted on the country's residents, like most Colombian politicians. Her goal was for the National Museum to document, register, and bear witness of the recent Colombian violence from as many perspectives as possible.

## Conclusions

The virulent reactions to Elvira Cuervo de Jaramillo's proposal to exhibit Tirofijo's towel raised fundamental questions related to the production of historical memories: How and when to include the voices of the perpetrators in official state remembrances of violence? Should state museum professionals incorporate the narratives of those who committed atrocities into the institution's exhibitions?

The United States Holocaust Memorial Museum, opened in 1993, provides an example of how curators use offenders' testimonies to underscore the victims' suffering. In its main exhibit, viewers can see images of the Nazis displaying their hatred toward Jews and can read excerpts of fascist texts. However, after visiting the venue, the message conveyed by the depictions of the Holocaust is quite clear: Perpetrators must be held accountable for their actions and not praised or equated with the martyrs and survivors. According to scholar Micaela Dixon, venues such as the Holocaust Museum, which address the Holocaust and German violence, privilege victims' voices, leaving perpetrators' narratives impugned. This assertion can easily apply to most venues in Latin America that memorialize political violence. Dixon, nevertheless, highlights the relevance of devoting some attention to perpetrators' perspectives because they provide an encompassing visitor experience. She suggests, and I concur, that testimonies of those responsible for committing brutalities provide the sociopolitical contexts in which it is possible to understand the occurrence of violent episodes. Therefore, their relevance in memory venues is increasing. The question that remains is how to present accounts of atrocities without re-victimizing survivors. There are several ways to do this. One example, analyzed by Dixon, employs a combination of textual, visual, and experiential perpetrator focalization, which means being in the latter's shoes at least for a moment: "The temporary alignment of perception between perpetrator and visitor permits the latter to actively experience the past by assuming the role of the [perpetrator] as s/he moves through the exhibition space and engages with the exhibits and displays." [88] This strategy is used in some German museums precisely to provide the visitors with a sense of the cultural context in which perpetrators committed their actions. It is by no means a glorification or exaltation of crimes, war, or torture.

Along these lines, in 2005, historian and filmmaker Laurence Rees commemorated 60 years of the Auschwitz Camp liberation through the television series *Auschwitz 1940–1945: Inside the Nazi State*, which privileged narratives of the perpetrators. When asked why he devoted his show to Nazis instead of victims of the Holocaust, Rees stated that it was important to him for people to know that there is usually much more to understand beyond the binary distinction between "good" and "bad." To achieve his goal, Rees spent more than ten years to obtain first-hand testimony from perpetrators, since most did not want to talk about their participation in the Nazi regime. He also compared their oral histories with original SS records. The historian stated that he wanted people to better understand the perpetrators. They were not "crazy"; many did not believe their actions were even wrong or claimed that they were just doing their job. When asked why they committed violent acts, one stated that it was because he learned to hate Jews, and he believed that. These raw testimonies, according to Rees, can enrich the representation of historical memories because they provide a sociocultural context that enlightens our understanding of why individuals and groups commit brutalities.[89]

The previous examples frame the initiative of acquiring Tirofijo's towel for the National Museum of Colombia by Elvira Cuervo de Jaramillo. She wanted the museum to become an active political interlocutor in the country's conflict, a place to represent as many voices as possible and to demonstrate that all histories are part of complex contexts. She strongly stated that her intention was not to glorify the Colombian guerrillas, but she was also aware of their relevance to the twentieth-century history of the country. Perhaps the timing of her proposal was not right because Tirofijo was still alive and defying the state.

Ten years later, in 2011, the National Museum organized an exhibition about a guerrilla leader. Named *Hacer la paz en Colombia: 'Ya vuelvo', Carlos Pizarro* (*Peacemaking in Colombia: 'I Will Be Right Back,' Carlos Pizarro*), this exhibit featured the demobilized guerrilla fighter and presidential candidate, Carlos Pizarro Leongómez, which begs the question of why he was worth remembering at the storied venue and Tirofijo was not.

## Notes

1 Pilar Lozano, "El oficio de ser Tirofijo," *El País*, May 31, 2008, National Museum of Colombia Archive.

2  Pierre Bourdieu, *Distinction. A Social Critique of the Judgment of Taste*, trans. Richard Nice (Cambridge, MA: Harvard University Press, 1984).
3  Elvira Cuervo de Jaramillo, "Qué mostramos, qué escondemos," *El Espectador*, March 1, 2001, National Museum of Colombia Archive.
4  Karsten Schubert, *The Curator's Egg: The Evolution of the Museum Concept from the French Revolution to the Present Day* (London: Ridling House, 2009), 15.
5  Tony Bennett, *The Birth of the Museum. History, Theory, Politics* (London and New York: Routledge, 1995).
6  Gyan Prakash, "Museum Matters," in *Museum Studies. An Anthology of Contexts*, ed. Bettina Messias Carbonell (Malden: Blackwell Publishing, 2004), 317–324.
7  Susan E. Cook, "The Politics of Preservation in Rwanda," in *Genocide in Cambodia and Rwanda*, ed. Susan E. Cook (Piscataway, NJ: Transaction Publishers, 2006), 281–299.
8  Sharon MacDonald, *Difficult Heritage. Negotiating the Nazi Past in Nuremberg and Beyond* (New York: Routledge, 2009), 55.
9  Per B. Rekdal, "About the Beauty of War and the Attractivity of Violence," in *Does War Belong in Museums? The Representation of Violence in Exhibitions*, ed. W. Muchitsch (Bielefeld: Museumsakademie Joanneum, 2013), 130.
10 Santiago Robledo, "Las colecciones industriales del Museo Nacional de Colombia," in *Cuadernos de Curaduría. Aproximaciones a la historia del Museo Nacional*, No. 17 (Bogotá: Museo Nacional de Colombia, 2020),23.
11 María Paola Rodríguez Prada, "Origen de la institución museal en Colombia: entidad científica para el desarrollo y progreso," in *Cuadernos de Curaduría. Aproximaciones a la historia del Museo Nacional*, No. 14 (Bogotá: Museo Nacional de Colombia, 2008),2.
12 Clara Isabel Botero, *El redescubrimiento del pasado prehispánico de Colombia: viajeros, arqueólogos y coleccionistas, 1820–1945* (Bogotá: Instituto Colombiano de Antropología e Historia, Universidad de Los Andes, 2012), 116.
13 Gonzalo A. Tavera, "Informe del bibliotecario nacional," en Anales de la Universidad Nacional de los Estados Unidos de Colombia, no. 89, Bogotá, febrero de 1879, 47.
14 Martha Segura, *Itinerario del Museo Nacional. Itinerario del Museo Nacional. Tomo I* (Bogotá: Instituto Colombiano de Cultura, Museo Nacional de Colombia, 1995.
15 Naila Katherine Flor Ortega, "Eduardo Santos y el mecenazgo cultural: la donación al Museo Nacional de Colombia," in *Cuadernos de Curaduría. Aproximaciones a la historia del Museo Nacional*, No. 14 (Bogotá: Museo Nacional de Colombia, 2008),116.
16 Jimena Perry, *Caminos de la antropología en Colombia: Gregorio Hernández de Alba*, (Bogotá: Universidad de los Andes, 2006).
17 Camila Martínez Velasco, "La cultura popular entra al museo: curaduría participativa en el Museo Nacional de Colombia (2005–2011)," in *Cuadernos de Curaduría. Aproximaciones a la historia del Museo Nacional*, No. 18 (Bogotá: Museo Nacional de Colombia, 2021),11.
18 Ley 397 de 1997 (Ley General de Cultura), Accessed September 25, 2019, https://www.culturarecreacionydeporte.gov.co/es/ley-397-de-1997-ley-general-de-cultura
19 Segura, *Itinerario del Museo Nacional*.
20 Teresa Morales de Gómez, "La Casa de las aulas. Sede del Museo de Arte Colonial en Bogotá," *Credencial Historia*, 138 (June 2001).https://www.banrepcultural.org/biblioteca-virtual/credencial-historia/numero-138/la-casa-de-las-aulas-museo-de-arte-colonial-en-bogota
21 Germán Téllez Castañeda, "La arquitectura y el urbanismo en la época republicana, 1830–40/1930- 35," in *Nueva Historia de Colombia*, ed. Álvaro Tirado Mejía (Bogotá: Editorial Planeta, 1989), 280.
22 Segura, *Itinerario del Museo Nacional*. Tomo II, 57–65.

23 Adolfo León Gómez, *Los Secretos del Panóptico* (Bogotá: Imprenta de M. Rivas & Cía, 1905).
24 "El Museo Nacional, el panóptico que cumple 140 años de historia," *El Tiempo*, October 3, 2014, National Museum of Colombia Archive.
25 Elvira Cuervo de Jaramillo, interview by Jimena Perry. February 9, 2017.
26 Jefferson Jaramillo and Carlos del Cairo, "Los dilemas de la museificación. Reflexiones en torno a dos iniciativas estatales de construcción," *Memoria y Sociedad* 17, no. 35 (2013): 76–92.
27 "Continúa debate sobre la toalla de Tirofijo," *El Tiempo*, March 4, 2001, National Museum of Colombia Archive.
28 Jotamario Arbeláez, "La toalla en el Museo," *El Espectador*, February 19, 2001, National Museum of Colombia Archive.
29 José Jaramillo Mejía, "Piezas de museo," *La Patria*, February 26, 2001, National Museum of Colombia Archive.
30 Héctor Rincón, "Memoria," *Cambio*, February 26, 2001, National Museum of Colombia Archive.
31 Elvira Cuervo de Jaramillo, "La toalla en el museo," *Museo. La Revista del Museo de Antioquia*, March 2001, National Museum of Colombia Archive.
32 Arbeláez, "La toalla en el Museo."
33 Víctor Paz Otero, "Éste es otro paseo," *El Espectador*, March 3, 2001, National Museum of Colombia Archive.
34 "El Museo de Colombia quiere exhibir la toalla de Tirofijo," *El Nuevo Herald*, February 15, 2001, National Museum of Colombia Archive.
35 "Polémica por exhibición de Toalla de Tirofijo en Museo Nacional," *El Tiempo*, October 2, 2001, National Museum of Colombia Archive.
36 Steve Stern, *Reckoning with Pinochet. The Memory Question in Democratic Chile, 1989–2006* (Durham, NC: Duke University Press, 2010).
37 Elizabeth Jelin, *State Repression and the Labors of Memory*, trans. Judy Rein and Marcial Godoy- Anativia (Minneapolis: The University of Minnesota Press, 2003), XV.
38 Fernando Salamanca, "Lo que el Museo Nacional no ha podido exhibir," *Kienyke*, October 6, 2013. National Museum of Colombia Archive.
39 Pierre Bourdieu, *Distinction. A Social Critique of the Judgement of Taste*, trans. Richard Nice (Cambridge, MA: Harvard University Press, 1984), 3, 14, 34.
40 Stuart Hall, *Representation: Cultural Representations and Signifying Practices* (London: Sage Publications, 1997), 3, 5.
41 Stuart Hall and Paddy Whannel, *The Popular Arts* (Durham, NC and London: Duke University Press, 2018), 74.
42 Paola Villamarín, "La Colombia de colección," *El Tiempo*, 2001, National Museum of Colombia Archive.
43 "La toalla de la discordia," *El Tiempo*, February 17, 2001, National Museum of Colombia Archive.
44 "Los colombianos no quieren la toalla en el museo," *El Tiempo*, February 19, 2001, National Museum of Colombia Archive.
45 Adriana Mejía, "La Percha Vacía," *Cromos*, February 26, 2001, National Museum of Colombia Archive.
46 Víctor Paz Otero, "Éste es otro paseo," *El Espectador*, March 3, 2001, National Museum of Colombia Archive.
47 Elvira Cuervo de Jaramillo, "Objetos Históricos," *El Espectador*, March 9, 2001, National Museum of Colombia Archive. My translation.
48 "Polémica por exhibición de Toalla de Tirofijo en Museo Nacional," *El Tiempo*, October 2, 2001, National Museum of Colombia Archive.
49 Johannes Fabian, "On Recognizing Things. The '"Ethnic Artefact' and the 'Ethnographic Object,'" *L'Homme*, no. 170, (April/June 2004): 47–60,49.

50 Mary Douglas, *Purity and Danger. An Analysis of Concepts of Pollution and Taboo* (New York: Routledge, 1966), 2.
51 Carol Duncan and Alan Wallach, "The Universal Survey Museum," in *Museum Studies: An Anthology of Contexts*, ed. Bettina Messias Carbonell (Malden, MA: Blackwell Publishing, 2004), 51–71.
52 "El de la toallita roja," *El Espectador*, March 2, 2001, National Museum of Colombia Archive.
53 Robert Ehrenreich and Jane Klinger, "War in Context: Let the Artifacts Speak," in *Does War Belong in Museums? The Representation of Violence in Exhibitions*, ed. W. Muchitsch (Bielefeld: Museumsakademie Joanneum, 2013), 146.
54 Ira Jackins, "Franz Boas and Exhibits: On the Limitations of the Museum Method in Anthropology," in *Objects and Others. Essays on Museums and Material Culture*, ed. W. G. Stocking (Madison: University of Wisconsin Press, 1995), 75–112.
55 Robert Ehrenreich and Jane Klinger, "War in Context: Let the Artefacts Speak," in *Does War Belong in Museums? The Representation of Violence in Exhibitions*, ed. W. Muchitsch (Bielefeld: Museumsakademie Joanneum, 2013) 154.
56 Sharon MacDonald, "Is Difficult Heritage Still Difficult? Why Public Acknowledgement of Past Perpetration May No Longer be so Unsettling to Collective Identities," *Museum International* 67, no. 1–4, 6–22 (2015): 12–13, 16.
57 Elvira Cuervo de Jaramillo, interview by Jimena Perry, Bogotá, February 9, 2017.
58 Timothy Ross, "Escobar Escape Humiliates Colombian Leaders," *The Guardian*, July 24, 1992.
59 "El fracaso de los diálogos de paz en El Caguán. El Gobierno despeja una zona para dialogar con las Farc, pero el intento no resulta y aumentan las acciones guerrilleras," *El Tiempo*, November 23, 2010.
60 "Toalla de Tirofijo, de Museo." El Tiempo, February 15, 2001. National Museum of Colombia Archive.
61 "El Museo de Colombia quiere exhibir la toalla de 'Tirofijo'," *El Nuevo Herald*, February 15, 2001, National Museum of Colombia Archive.
62 Isabel Fernández Suárez, "La Toalla de Tirofijo, Pieza de Museo," *ABC*, February 16, 2001, http://www.abc.es/hemeroteca/historico-16-02-2001/abc/Gente/la-toalla-de-tirofijo-pieza-de-museo_12880.html.
63 Horacio Buscaglia, "El Mundo En Que Vivimos," *Noticias Uruguay LARED21*, February 22, 2001, National Museum of Colombia Archive.
64 "Víctimas conflicto armado," *Unidad para la atención y reparación integral a las víctimas*, https://www.unidadvictimas.gov.co/es.
65 Martha Nubia Abello, *¡Basta Ya! Colombia. Memories of War and Dignity* (Bogotá: General Report of the Historical Memory Group, 2013), 20.
66 Álvaro Sierra, "La escala de la violencia y sus responsables," *Semana*, Julio 2013, https://especiales.semana.com/especiales/escala-violencia-colombia/quienes-asesinaron-220000-colombianos.html.
67 "El Museo de Colombia Quiere Exhibir La Toalla de 'Tirofijo,'" *El Nuevo Herald*, February 15, 2001, National Museum of Colombia Archive.
68 "José Antonio Ocampo López, Gobierno de Mariano Ospina Pérez," *Historia* 2, 1976, http://www.banrepcultural.org/blaavirtual/biografias/ospimari.htm.
69 "Tirofijo, el retrato de la violencia en Colombia," *El Mercurio*, January 25, 2002, National Museum of Colombia Archive.
70 Ksenija Bilbija and Leigh A. Payne, eds. *Accounting for Violence. Marketing Memory in Latin America* (Durham, NC: Duke University Press, 2010).
71 Arturo Alape, *Manuel Marulanda, Tirofijo. Colombia: 40 años de lucha guerrillera* (Argentina- México: Editorial Txalaparta, 2000), 231.
72 Roberto Pombo, "El guerrillero más viejo del mundo," *El Tiempo*, September 6, 1998, http://www.eltiempo.com/archivo/documento/MAM-795619.

73 Bilbija and Payne, eds. *Accounting for Violence. Marketing Memory in Latin America*, 1, 18.
74 Fernando Araújo Vélez, "El Verdadero Manuel Marulanda," *El Espectador*, January 4, 2017, http://www.elespectador.com/noticias/cultura/el-verdadero-manuel-marulanda-articulo-673162.
75 Marco Palacios, *Between Legitimacy and Violence: A History of Colombia*, 1875–2002 (Durham, NC: Duke University Press, 2006), 69.
76 Eduardo Pizarro Leongómez, *Las Farc (1949–2011). De guerrilla campesina a máquina de guerra* (Bogotá: Grupo Editorial, Norma, 2001), 97.
77 Paola Nancy Moreno, "Operación Marquetalia, 53 Años de Un Mito Fundacional," *El Espectador*, May 28, 2017, http://www.elespectador.com/noticias/cultura/operacion-marquetalia-53-anos-de-un-mito-fundacional-articulo-695965.
78 Daniel Samper Pizano, "La Última Muerte de Tirofijo," *El País*, August 11, 2002, http://elpais.com/diario/2002/08/11/domingo/1029037960_850215.html.
79 "Cronología de Secuestros de Las Farc," *El Tiempo*, July 2, 2008, http://www.eltiempo.com/archivo/documento/CMS-4357994.
80 Valeria Sáenz, "80 años de la infamia del primer secuestro," *El Tiempo*, May 8, 2013, http://www.eltiempo.com/archivo/documento/CMS-12785385.
81 Arturo Alape, *Manuel Marulanda, Tirofijo. Colombia: 40 años de lucha guerrillera* (Argentina- México: Editorial Txalaparta, 2000), 35.
82 Arturo Alape, *Manuel Marulanda, Tirofijo. Colombia: 40 años de lucha guerrillera* (Argentina- México: Editorial Txalaparta, 2000), 233.
83 "El silencio de un inocente," *La Nación*, December 9, 2001, http://wvw.nacion.com/dominical/2001/diciembre/09/dominical7.html
84 Maité Rico, "Las FARC confirman la muerte de Tirofijo," *El país*, May 26, 2008, http://elpais.com/diario/2008/05/26/internacional/1211752801_850215.html.
85 "Las FARC confirman la muerte de Tirofijo por un infarto," *El País*, May 25, 2008, https://elpais.com/internacional/2008/05/25/actualidad/1211666401_850215.html.
86 "La Muerte de Manuel Marulanda Vélez," *El Espectador*, May 25, 2008, https://www.elespectador.com/opinion/editorial/articulo-muerte-de-manuel-marulanda-velez.
87 "El Museo de Colombia quiere exhibir la toalla de Tirofijo," *El Nuevo Herald*, February 15, 2001, National Museum of Colombia Archive.
88 Micaela Dixon, "The Unreliable Perpetrator: Negotiating Narrative Perspective at Museums of The Third Reich and the Gdr. P," *German Life and Letters* 70, no. 2 (April 2017): 241–261.
89 Interview with Laurence Rees. PBS, N.D., https://www.pbs.org/auschwitz/about/.

# 2
# LIVES ENDED IN THEIR PRIME
Political Violence at the National Museum of Colombia

Ten years after Elvira Cuervo de Jaramillo's failed proposal to acquire Tirofijo's towel for the National Museum collections, her successor as director of the institution, María Victoria de Angulo de Robayo, and the venue's team of professionals decided to exhibit *Hacer la paz en Colombia: 'Ya vuelvo', Carlos Pizarro (Peacemaking in Colombia: 'I Will Be Right Back,' Carlos Pizarro)*. They reached this decision in 2010 after one year of negotiations with María José Pizarro, one of the daughters of Carlos Pizarro Leongómez, a demobilized guerrilla fighter and former presidential candidate murdered by a cartel-hired gunman in 1990.

The inaugural version of the exhibition took place in 2009 at Casa América Catalunya, Barcelona, Spain, under the name "*Ya vuelvo. Carlos Pizarro, una vida por la paz.*" ("*I will be right back. Carlos Pizarro, a life for peace.*") According to newspaper accounts, then presidential candidate Juan Manuel Santos saw the display in Barcelona and endorsed its presentation at the National Museum of Colombia. Santos, who was about to start his first executive term (2010–2014), praised the moderation with which the exhibition narrated a highly convoluted period of Colombia's history.[1] So, from September 2010 to March 2011, the institution housed *Ya vuelvo*, a display that reflected on the personal and political life of Carlos Pizarro Leongómez. However, there are significant differences between the Spanish and Colombian versions of *Ya vuelvo*. The Spanish original edition was the result of María José Pizarro's personal endeavor to reconcile with her absent father. The moderation Santos referred to was related to the fact that Spain's *Ya vuelvo* was an intimate family account. As María José stated during the opening in Barcelona, "I do not have any remembrances of my father, the memories I had died with him in 1990."[2] The Barcelona display was meant to help María José and the Pizarro family to make sense of Carlos's murder and to ponder his absence. The Colombian version, as developed in

DOI: 10.4324/9781003283997-3

this chapter, became a national account due to the vision of the curators of the National Museum, who foresaw a broader significance of the display.

The name of the exhibition, *Ya vuelvo* (*I will be right back*), alluded to Pizarro's renunciation of the FARC-EP, in which he served from 1968 to 1973. On September 11 of the latter year, Pizarro left a note over his folded uniform beside his service gun with those words.[3] The exhibit also addressed the ex-guerrilla fighter's participation in the foundation of the Movimiento 19 de Abril, M-19 (April 19th Movement), along with other renowned leftist activists; the Movement's Palace of Justice Siege in 1985; Pizarro's decision to lay down his arms in 1989; his reintegration into civilian life, followed by his short presidential campaign; and his death.

*Ya vuelvo* commemorated 20 years since the politician's tragic death in 1990. A hired assassin shot Carlos Pizarro Leongómez in a commercial airplane en route from Bogotá to the coastal city of Barranquilla, 45 days into his presidential campaign. One of his bodyguards returned fire and downed the killer, but Pizarro had taken fifteen gunshots. When the aircraft returned to Bogotá, it was too late to save him. He died two hours after the attack. Before Pizarro's death, two other candidates were murdered between 1989 and 1990, over an eight-month period: Luis Carlos Galán Sarmiento, liberal (August 1989); Bernardo Jaramillo Ossa (March 1990), leader of the leftist party Unión Patriótica, UP (Patriotic Union); and Carlos Pizarro Leongómez (April 1990), from the Alianza Democrática M-19 (Democratic Alliance M-19). These killings overwhelmed Colombians, who saw in these politicians some hope to achieve peace in the country; therefore, they attained the aura of martyrs, and in the minds of the curators became worthy of a place at the National Museum of Colombia.

This chapter, the second case study of four, also explores the question of which historical events connected to the nation's political violence journalists, politicians, and the public consider worthy of remembering at Colombia's pantheon of memory, the National Museum. In this section, I analyze *Ya vuelvo's* narratives and display, devoting attention to class and aesthetics as determinant factors that ensured *Ya vuelvo's* success. I examine how the Spanish and Colombian versions of the exhibition differed to demonstrate how the curators decided to transform a personal account into a national, inclusive narrative. I claim that the fact that Carlos Pizarro belonged to a well-known Colombian family, had formal education, was handsome, and changed his belligerent stance for a peaceful one influenced the positive reception of his display. In addition, I extend this reasoning to the *Galán vive* (Galan Lives) exhibition done before *Ya vuelvo,* commemorating the murder of Luis Carlos Galán Sarmiento, other of the presidential candidates shot between 1989 and 1990. Bernardo Jaramillo Ossa was the only one of the three who did not earn a remembrance space at the National Museum of Colombia.

Drawing on the catalog and objects of the *Ya vuelvo* exhibition, interviews (with one curator of the display and two of the directors of the National

Museum), documents of the National Museum's Archive, newspapers, and magazines, I argue that the political context of the country during 2010 and 2011 facilitated both *Galán vive* and *Ya vuelvo's* displays at the national venue. At the time, the right-wing President Álvaro Uribe Vélez's second term (2006–2010) ended, along with his war against the guerrillas of the country. Colombians were uncertain if the new chief of state, Juan Manuel Santos, would continue with Uribe's militarized policies against the insurgent groups. Santos advocated for peace and reconciliation and began his mandate by opening pathways for dialogue. Thus, I suggest that these exhibits would not have thrived at any other time. Santos's efforts resulted in the signing of a peace accord with the FARC-EP in 2006. The Colombian President also won the Nobel Peace Prize the same year. By focusing on *Ya vuelvo's* narrative and the fact that the Colombian curators had the skillfulness to confront military and guerrilla voices related to the 1985 Palace of Justice assault in this exhibition, for instance, and to convert an intimate account into a national story, this chapter provides a deeper understanding of the dynamic nature of historical memory production in Colombia. It also explains why Carlos Pizarro, guerrilla leader, deserved a place in Colombians' memory and Tirofijo did not.

## The National Museum of Colombia Innovative Pathways

The changes started by the director of the National Museum of Colombia, Elvira Cuervo de Jaramillo, during the 1990s paved the way for the curators to set up *Galán vive* and *Ya vuelvo* in the following decade. With this exhibition about Pizarro's political and personal life, the team of professionals at the venue conveyed a message of reconciliation with the purpose of creating new memories about Carlos Pizarro and the demobilized M-19. María Victoria de Angulo de Robayo, director of the institution (2005–2014), knew that the exhibit offered the museum the opportunity to become an active participant in the documentation process of Colombia's recent history: "I went for it because in that moment the National Museum faced the challenge of being a real national museum, which meant to include as much people as possible and all kinds of thinking."[4] In addition, to confront radically different perspectives about violent episodes such as the Palace of Justice Siege in 1985, the team of professionals at the venue actively encouraged a critical view of the historical memories only validated by official government actors.

The museum experts, in this sense, upheld historian Michael Rothberg's concept of multidirectional memory as "a subject of ongoing negotiation, cross-referencing, and borrowing; as productive and not privative." Pitting the versions of the military and the guerrilla about the Palace of Justice Siege against each other, the curators of *Ya vuelvo* experimented with one of Rothberg's questions: What happens when different stories confront each other in the public sphere? More broadly, the Museum's decision embraced what anthropologist

Sharon MacDonald has called "difficult heritage." She argues that a nation's patrimony includes not only victories, achievements, great men, and successes but also events that are traumatic and hard to accept. Failures, battles, and wars are all part of a people's identity.[5] In a 2015 article titled "Is Difficult Heritage Still Difficult? Why Public Acknowledgement of Past Perpetration May no Longer be so Unsettling to Collective Identities," MacDonald revisits this concept and confirms that to recognize and accept difficult heritage or painful past events is essential in official institutions; she also claims that this recognition is a positive development for contemporary identity, despite the changes and different ideas about the heritage that communities might have.

In the Colombian case, *Ya vuelvo* made clear the tension between the views of the military and guerrilla groups about some significant national events, such as the Palace of Justice Siege in 1985, the failed peace processes between the government and the M-19 guerrilla, and the group's demobilization. In fact, various Colombian social actors—such as military officials, extreme right-wing politicians, and the conservative media—resisted the museum's effort to give prominence to the M-19 due to the feelings of anger, pain, and sadness that particularly the 1985 attack still sparked.

The opposition to displaying stories at the National Museum associated with guerrilla leaders also relates to issues of class and aesthetics. Unlike Tirofijo, Pizarro belonged to a prominent Colombian family, had formal education, was handsome and charismatic, and, more significantly, he demobilized from the guerrilla and adopted a reconciliation and peace discourse. Tirofijo, as noted in Chapter 1, never abandoned his armed struggle. Politicians and journalists also differentiated between Tirofijo and Pizarro because, following Pierre Bourdieu, the towel, for instance, blurred the distinction between vulgarity, coarseness, and the refinement people expect to find at the National Museum.[6] The institution, as well as its objects and exhibitions, conventionally corresponds to what Stuart Hall refers to as high culture. For Hall, the opposition between high and low culture determines matters of status and superiority. In this context, Tirofijo's towel was an object pertaining to low culture, but Pizarro's exhibition showed a sophistication associated with preeminence.

The Ideology, Arts, and Industry Hall housed *Ya vuelvo*. The National Museum's professionals mounted this exhibition as part of the strategic plan that sought "to contribute effectively to the country's development and to overcome national conflicts."[7] The curators followed the renovation project guidelines that started in the 1990s to promote a space that allowed people to remember violent acts that occurred during the late twentieth century in a critical way. The Colombian Constitution of 1991 inspired Elvira Cuervo de Jaramillo to remake, strengthen, and position the museum as a venue in agreement with the social and political developments of the country. Thus, she and the painter Beatriz González proceeded with scripts with that vision. Since then, the institution has undergone several remodeling and restoration processes of its building, and Elvira's successors have implemented gradual changes in its narratives and spaces. The first phase of the project ended in 2001, and thereafter, the museum professionals introduced new exhibition themes to make the venue a place for all Colombians.

The chronological and linear narratives are no longer predominant at the National Museum of Colombia, and the directors that followed Elvira Cuervo de Jaramillo (1992–2005), such as the already mentioned María Victoria de Angulo de Robayo (2005–2015), Daniel Castro (2015–2021), and Juliana Restrepo Tirado (2021–), plan to open several thematic exhibition spaces by 2023.[8] Under the names Memoria y nación (Memory and Nation) in 2014 and La tierra como recurso (Land as Resource) in 2016, Castro inaugurated two new halls. "To celebrate the museum's bicentennial, in 2023, we will open seventeen new exhibition spaces, eleven big ones and six small ones."[9] The renovation of the National Museum is a collaborative endeavor between state agents and consultants to keep the institution as a national resource. Other display rooms launched are Tiempo sin olvido: Diálogos desde el mundo prehispánico (Time without Forgetting: Dialogues since the Prehispanic World), 2018; Mirada panóptica al arte (Panoptic Art Perspectives), 2018; Hacer Sociedad (Make Society), 2019; Ser territorio (Be Territory), 2019; El museo en la historia y la historia del museo (The Museum in History and the History of the Museum), 2020; Ser y hacer (Be and Do), 2020; and Historia del panóptico (The Panopticon History), 2020.[10] Juliana Restrepo, the director of the institution, also faced the challenge caused by Covid-19 when museums, like every other public venue, had to close. For her, the mission of the National Museum must continue to be the narration of Colombian diversity through the collections it houses. "The goal is that every person that enters the museum feels represented because they can identify with the histories displayed."[11] Since the pandemic struck, Restrepo realized that museumgoers needed another way to relate to the displays and encouraged the institution's virtualization. Many exhibitions were available online, as well as openings and several activities such as talks, workshops, and concerts. This made her more aware of one of the main goals of the museum, which is to inform. Thus, she devoted efforts and resources to ensure the public to keep having access to the contents provided by its exhibitions. In addition, due to the pandemic, Restrepo emphasized the significance of reaching territories other than Bogotá, the country's capital. A pandemic silver lining was for the museum professionals to access remote places and make them part of the project of nation-building the institution proclaimed. For her, the question "why a museum" is "when in the space provided by the venue so many different people gather to dialogue, exchange ideas, be surprised, dream, discover. Museums are places where everybody can exercise their cultural rights."[12]

As expressed by Cuervo de Jaramillo since 2001, the museum's agenda should include little-known personalities and local processes of survival and focus on themes such as memory, land, diversity, inclusion, participation, violence, everyday life, minorities, and reconciliation.[13] Therefore, the institution's specialists aimed to answer a significant question: How to avoid traditional stories of winners and heroes? In this chapter, I analyze that interrogation, focusing on the "success" of *Ya vuelvo* and asking why Pizarro and Galán were worthy of having commemorative exhibitions but not Bernardo Jaramillo, murdered during the same period, and a presidential candidate. Highlighting the significance of *Ya vuelvo*, the Minister of Culture stated that it was the "first time that a display about an ex-revolutionary has taken place in an official institution," portraying various aspects of Pizarro's story "his clandestine life; his ingenuity, creativity, and motivations;" and "his demobilization."[14]

This chapter is divided into three parts. I start with a biographical perspective of Carlos Pizarro Leongómez and a historical background of the M-19 guerrilla. Next, I present and analyze the positions in favor and against *Ya Vuelvo* and *Galán vive* and the reasons for leaving the leader of the UP out of the National Museum of Colombia; finally, I discuss the significance of the exhibitions.

## Carlos Pizarro Leogngómez: From Elite to Commander of the M-19

Pizarro has been not only a controversial figure but also an endearing character for many Colombians. He was born in Cartagena, Department of Bolívar, on June 6, 1951, and assassinated in Bogotá on April 26, 1990, the third presidential candidate killed in an eight-month period.[15] Due to his resemblance to Ernesto "Che" Guevara—Argentine revolutionary and hero of the Cuban revolution— during his 1990 presidential campaign, Pizarro Leongómez's staff nicknamed him "Comandante Papito," which in Colombian slang means handsome. To this day, Colombian authorities have not brought the perpetrators of his murder to justice.

Born into a renowned Colombian family, Carlos Pizarro Leongómez was the third of five children. His father, Juan Antonio Pizarro, was a high-ranking active member of the Colombian Navy. Due to his father's job, Carlos and his family lived in Cartagena, Cali; Bogotá; and Washington, DC. When Juan Antonio Pizarro retired from the Navy in 1959, they settled down in the city of Cali. Due to his rebellious character, Carlos's parents sent him to a boarding school, and he also had a brief stint in a seminary. In 1969, he went to Bogotá to study law at the Pontificia Universidad Javeriana, as did his two older brothers, Juan Antonio and Eduardo. However, the three siblings were expelled from the institution because they did not adapt well, according to the university directors.[16] Some of the pictures displayed in *Ya vuelvo* hinted at Carlos' defiant nature: "I reacted against poverty, I reacted against social climbing, against the lack of respect towards humble men, to the humiliation of those who are less fortunate in life, with less luck. I felt that this society demanded rebels."

The display showed a young Pizarro, his family, and his first contacts with philosophers such as Herbert Marcuse and Karl Marx, who were influential figures in the university life of the 1960s and 1970s in Bogotá. Pizarro's words also appeared on one of the panels of *Ya vuelvo*, providing a window into his first years at college: "I encountered a world of university agitation. With Marcuse, the young Marx, the utopian socialists, the encyclopedists, and the French Revolution." In 1969, Pizarro became an active member of the FARC-EP because of his deep concern with poverty and social inequality; he later left this guerilla group in 1973. In one of the panels of the exhibition, the public could read this Pizarro's statement: "I retired from the FARC-EP because they did not provide the political, ideological, doctrinaire, or human space that I needed." This statement is definitive to understand why *Ya vuelvo* was accepted by journalists, politicians, and the public. Pizarro distanced himself from the FARC-EP action, which implied that he had profound disagreements with Tirofijo and his struggles. After Pizarro left the FARC-EP, he and other leftists consolidated the M-19. In 1971, he went to the National University of Colombia and joined the Juventud Comunista Colombiana, JUCO (Colombian Communist Youth), a youth Marxist organization created on May 1, 1951. It is closely related to the Colombian Communist Party (Partido Comunista Colombiano). His reasons for becoming a guerrilla fighter, as presented in *Ya vuelvo*, were:

> I believe that is why I joined the guerrilla group. Because there are no political spaces in Colombia. There are no political spaces with a transformative perspective. And if they do not exist, we need to create them. And if you cannot create them within legality, you create them from what we in the M-19 have called: 'Democracy in arms.'

The M-19 was a guerrilla movement that devoted considerable energy and resources to prove to the public that it was possible to besiege the government and humiliate political elites without causing bloodshed. Thus, the media broadcasted and advertised almost all their attacks. The first public act perpetrated by the M-19 was the theft of Simón Bolívar's sword in 1974 from the Quinta de Bolívar (Villa of Bolívar), which is currently a museum. Álvaro Fayad, the cofounder of the M-19, stated that they took the weapon and did not plan to return it until the government fulfilled its promises of peace, democracy, and liberty.[17] After this attack, the members of the M-19 carried out other assaults, such as the "Operación Ballena Azul" (Operation Blue Whale), during 1978 and 1979, in which they managed to steal more than 5,000 weapons from one of the installations of the National Army in Bogotá. The M-19 also seized milk and chocolates to distribute in low-income neighborhoods; transported weapons by ship from Northern Africa; and occupied the facilities of a newspaper named *El Bogotano*, where the members of the guerrilla group replaced the journal's content and printed 80,000 copies the same day. Another sensational operation was the Siege of the Dominican Republic embassy in 1980. From February 27 to April 25 of the mentioned year, Rosemberg Pabón, "Comandante Uno" (Commander One), one of the M-19 guerrilla leaders, directed the siege of the Dominican Republic embassy. Planned by "Commander Pablo" or "el flaco" (skinny), nicknames for Jaime Bateman, the Siege was meant to be a surprise attack during the commemoration of the Dominican Republic's independence (February 27, 1844). Among the guests were the ambassadors of Colombia, the United States, Costa Rica, Mexico, Brazil, Uruguay, Switzerland, Peru, Venezuela, and the Papal Nuncio. The Siege was supposed to last for a week but lasted 61 days. The M-19 demanded 50 million dollars from the government of Julio Cesar Turbay Ayala (1978–1982) to release more than 300 political prisoners. The M-19 called the Siege Operation Democracy and Liberty and ended when the M-19 fighters boarded a plane provided by the Cuban government. During the episode, the M-19 denounced the role of the Colombian military, the state's inability to take care of its citizens, and the reasons why regular Colombians dissented from the government. Their declarations gained them popular support and made Colombians remember the event as a successful one. This act was very significant due to its media coverage, which resulted in publicity for the M-19 and its ideals. According to journalist Patricia Lara, in 1982, Jaime Bateman, a top leader of the M-19 and intellectual leader of the attack, had 82% popularity in the country and had the same support for his political views. Bateman fought against corruption, advocated for social equality, encouraged the participation of the people in democracy, and wanted to eliminate poverty.

From 1979 to 1982, the M-19 leaders continued with their assaults against the state. During these years, Pizarro and 150 other members of the guerrilla groups went to prison to serve a 26-year sentence behind bars. However, they were set free in December of 1982 due to the Amnesty Law issued under the presidency of Belisario Betancur (1982–1986). Between 1984 and 1985, the government and the M-19 signed a peace treaty that seemed successful but ended in a resounding failure. Amid the truce, two hitmen on a motorcycle killed the M-19 leader Carlos Toledo Plata and the National Army wounded Pizarro, circumstances that generated considerable mistrust toward the state. By the end of 1984, some National Army strikes on the M-19 preceded the 1985 Palace of Justice Siege, scuttling the peace initiative. Moreover, the M-19's rising popularity generated fear in some parts of society. In *Ya vuelvo*, critical guerrillas' voices against the government were displayed in a glass case with documents such as images that accounted for the government's bad faith and a handwritten letter from Pizarro, claiming:

> Thus, it was necessary to take the M-19 out of the peace process and annihilate the revolutionary movement. They harassed us, they attacked us, they took us out. I think that the only problem was that we did not

have a complete and clear comprehension of the strategy organized by the oligarchy to frustrate the peace process.

This part was also meant to highlight the M-19 and Pizarro's struggle to reach peace. One of the major daring accomplishments of *Ya vuelvo* was the treatment museum professionals gave to the Palace of Justice Siege. It was the first time curators included in the same exhibition both the government and the guerrilla's perspective.

### *The Palace of Justice Siege in* Ya vuelvo: *A Multi-Sided History*

On November 6, 1985, late morning in downtown Bogotá, 28 M-19 guerrilla fighters stormed the Palace of Justice's basement. They entered in three vehicles, killing the security guards and the building administrator. Another seven guerrilla members waited inside and outside, another 28 insurgents had to wait because they did not arrive on time. Thus began the Antonio Nariño Operation, an armed action designed to delegitimize President Belisario Betancur. He had violated Law 35 of 1982 and a ceasefire agreement signed between guerrillas and the government on August 24, 1984.[18] When President Betancur took office, he sought to achieve peace in the country. For the first time in Colombia's history, the state recognized the political and social character of the armed conflict and encouraged dialogue.[19] Therefore, Betancur created a Peace Commission, and Congress issued Amnesty Law 35 of 1982, which aimed to pardon some actions of the guerrillas so they could demobilize and rejoin society. However, the National Army considered the law too lenient on the rebel group. In October 1982, Minister of Defense Fernando Landazábal Reyes stated, "Let's hope this is the last amnesty."[20] The M-19 and the National Army agreed to a ceasefire on August 24, 1984, which irked the military. The displeasure of the Army with the government generated tensions and even rumors of a *coup d'état*. The Army provoked the guerrillas and attacked them on several occasions. Colonel Luis Alfonso Plazas Vega was the commander responsible for securing and recovering the Palace of Justice in 1985. He also deplored the 1982 amnesty and pressured the government to break any truce with the guerrillas.

The exact number of casualties of the Palace of Justice Siege is still uncertain. Newspaper articles and audiovisual archives cannot agree on a fixed number due to several versions propagated by the Army. However, the Truth Commission, created in 2005 (but published in 2010) by magistrates of the Colombian Supreme Court to investigate the attack, confirms 94 bodies were taken to the National Institute of Legal Medicine and Forensic Sciences. Still, the state of the corpses made identification nearly impossible and generated serious doubts about the existence of a greater number of victims. The Truth Commission highlighted the fact that in the days after the Siege, the National Institute of

**78** Lives Ended in Their Prime

Legal Medicine also received human remains that were not directly related to the attack but that were also classified as victims, like a man found shot dead in a nearby street. The number of disappeared people during the Siege is also a controversial matter. Until 2001, 11 families kept going to the Office of the Attorney General to insist that their relatives were still missing. In addition, the forensic team misidentified some of the cadavers, which dismayed surviving relatives.[21] For the families of the disappeared, the search continues, and new generations still demand justice and truth.[22]

Journalist Ana Carrigan analyzed the details of the attack, which included President Betancur's broken promises and other provocations of the M-19 guerrillas. Some victims and perpetrators died due to fire and smoke ignited inside the Palace by crossfire between guerrillas and the Army, as well as the intrusion of National Army tanks, which rushed violently into the building, despite magistrates' pleas.[23] After 28 hours of fierce combat, the Colombian army defeated the guerrillas.

When the Palace of Justice Siege took place, the leaders of the rebel group were Álvaro Fayad, who made the decision to carry out the attack; Carlos Pizarro Leongómez; Gustavo Arias Londoño; and Antonio Navarro Wolff. However, due to a combat injury, Wolff was recovering in Cuba, and the Siege took him by surprise. In 2015, four years after *Ya vuelvo* took place and 30 years after the assault, Navarro Wolff made the following statement:

> It was a terrible mistake, and we can never repent enough due to the victims the Siege caused and for its effects on Colombian history of that time. I highlight that the sons and daughters of the dead magistrates have forgiven us. The children of our comrades have forgiven those who killed their parents, even outside of combat. That demonstrates reconciliation among Colombians is possible. That demonstrates we can look forward. Forgiveness is a personal decision. It does not follow rules. What I have learned during these years is that forgiveness produces relief. That is why so many times it is unilateral, gratuitous, not an answer to a request, but an autonomous decision of who forgives. When it happens, the life of the one who forgives improves, he or she gets rid of a heavy and painful bitterness. Forgiveness makes life lighter, less bitter, without resentments or hate. Therefore, truth is so important for the victims. To know the truth helps to forgive.[24]

The sixth section of the Colombian version of *Ya vuelvo* addressed the Siege. It included a cabinet with some objects that survived the attack, such as a complete list with the names of the people who died and an audio file of Colonel Alfonso Plazas Vega, who had the task of recovering the Palace even if it meant "blood and fire."[25] Next to this showcase, there was an audio file with the voice of the resident of the Supreme Court, Alfonso Reyes Echandía, one of

Lives Ended in Their Prime  **79**

the magistrates killed during the crossfire between the M-19 fighters and the National Army. Visitors could hear his pleas for help:

> Please, we need help, stop the fire. The situation is dramatic. You must tell the government to stop the fire. Beg the Army and the Police to stop… They do not understand. They are pointing at us with their guns. I beg you to stop because they are capable of anything. We are magistrates, employees, we are innocent. I have tried to speak to the authorities. I have tried to communicate with the president, but he is not there. I have tried to talk to him…

Near the audio boxes with Reyes Echandía's cries for help, and between the two cabinets, there was a beheaded sculpture, a burnt typewriter, and the helmet of Coronel Plazas Vega, as seen in Figure 2.1.[26]

At the end of this section of *Ya vuelvo*, there was a panel with Pizarro's words related to the Palace of Justice Siege and M-19's accountability:

> Of course, we are responsible, and when we arrive at a democratic place, we must discuss the Palace of Justice, as we must also discuss all the parts involved in the attack, including those who did not prevent it from happening. We all must be accountable. That is my historical judgment, which needs to keep unfolding so we do not avoid showing ourselves to the nation to answer for the actions we have done and provoked.

**FIGURE 2.1** Picture by Catalina Ruíz, Curator of *Ya vuelvo*. Bogotá, 2011.

To end this section with the above words was suggestive and intentional since the main purpose of *Ya vuelvo* was to emphasize Pizarro's commitment to reach peace in Colombia. The quotation portrayed a repentant guerrilla fighter who had renounced armed struggle as a solution. Pizarro accepted responsibility and was willing to talk about the violent attacks committed by the M-19, which reinforced his eagerness to reach a national agreement. This narrative merited inclusion in the National Museum of Colombia because his personal and political trajectory led him to privilege a conciliatory discourse, as opposed to Tirofijo, for instance, who never backed out of his war logic.

In 1989, the M-19 leaders, Pizarro among them, decided to demobilize. After 20 years of armed confrontations and of being part of two significant guerrilla movements, he realized that the war would not take him or any Colombian anywhere. Pizarro, in that period, started to advocate peace through dialogue. To address this issue, which was the core of *Ya vuelvo*, the National Museum's curators created four chronological sections, which began in 1982. They called them: Amnesty, In Search of Peace, Laying Down Arms, and 45 Days of Political Campaign. Curators designed these segments to walk the audience through Pizarro's thought process, to underscore his idealistic character, his commitment to peace, and his advocacy for social movements that encouraged reconciliation and forgiveness.

These parts of *Ya vuelvo* were composed of audiovisuals, photographs, and newspaper quotations selected by the museum's professional team to highlight the M-19's efforts to end their armed confrontation in Colombia. The panels in these parts also presented fragments of speeches in which Pizarro talked about peace, such as:

> Weapons have made a lot of damage, the government's weapons have done a lot of damage, weapons in general make a lot of damage. Thus, let's have that in common, to tell Colombians that it is good to say goodbye to weapons.

In another panel, visitors could read, "I think that we can live in an underdeveloped and poor society, but we cannot accept that, besides poverty, we have to endure the humiliation and castration of the possibility of getting out of this situation someday."

In 1990, five years after the Palace of Justice Siege, the M-19 guerrilla force demobilized and began to take part in Colombia's public and political life, but they were unable to succeed because a fierce persecution and extermination of leftist parties took place in the country. In March of that year, Colombians witnessed one of the most brutal massacres of the twentieth century. This policide made no distinction between members of the leftist party Unión Patriótica (UP), created in 1985 by former FARC-EP guerrillas, and the demobilized fighters of M-19. More than 1,598 UP affiliates were either murdered or disappeared. Until 2017, Colombian authorities had only issued 137 sentences against perpetrators, but 91% of these crimes remained unpunished.[27] As for the M-19, which became the political party Alianza Democrática M-19 (Democratic Alliance M-19), Pizarro's slaying started its decline, which ended in its dissolution. The decimation of the UP and Pizarro's murder were a way to counteract the left in Colombia. On March 11, 1990, two days after the M-19 laid down its weapons, Carlos Pizarro Leongómez ran for Mayor of Bogotá. He obtained 70,901 votes and came in second to Liberal politician Juan Martín Caicedo Ferrer. Vera Grabe, cofounder of the M-19, received 31,147 votes and became a representative for the Congress. In addition, the M-19 Alliance won in some municipalities and managed to win the Cauca governorship.[28]

## *"Ya Vuelvo* Should Stay": Positive Reactions to the Exhibition

When the Colombian version of *Ya vuelvo* opened to the public in 2010, it was mostly well-received by the public, journalists, and politicians. The media wrote a considerable number of reviews of the display, mostly laudatory, or at least neutral. The articles emphasized the exhibition's commemoration of the twentieth anniversary of the death of Pizarro and his life cut short while pursuing a peaceful political solution.

In *Ya vuelvo*, María José Pizarro, the main curator of the display, decided to redeem her father's reputation as a peace promoter. For this reason, one of the focal points of the exhibit was Pizarro's departure from the FARC-EP and then the amnesty with the M-19. For the inauguration of the exhibit, politicians like liberal president Ernesto Samper (1994–1998) said:

> More than idealizing him, [this display] makes him real, because he was a big romantic, an idealist, a revolutionary, and this brings us back to who he was as a person. In each object and each phrase, we recognize the Pizarro we knew.[29]

The Minister of Culture agreed with Samper and stated that Pizarro was a symbol of dialogue and negotiation for conflict resolution. Other former M-19 combatants also remembered Pizarro's past commitment to social justice and equality by pointing out that: "It is important to not forget because we do not have a shameful past."

Painter Lucas Ospina also highlighted the transcendence of *Ya vuelvo* and lamented that the Minister of Culture and the National Museum of Colombia's director did not make the display permanent. Ospina praised the efforts of the curators to make the institution more like:

> [...] a lab where symbols become changing signs according to their configuration. Therefore, this kind of displays are feared: If the meaning

of the objects changes, do we change as well? Symbols can be useful to encourage social engineering and maintain people's identity, but they also defy and challenge, and make us grow, not as a national herd but as individuals that inhabit a place in the world. *Ya vuelvo* is the name of the exhibition, but Pizarro is never coming back. The museum should not let go of this display.

The artist also pointed out that, regardless of the public's possible discomfort with the presence of a guerrilla fighter at the National Museum, more than 50,000 Colombians visited the exhibition.[30] Ospina correctly asserted that *Ya vuelvo* positioned the museum as a visible actor regarding Colombia's history of violence. He saw the display as a sign of change within the institution: both curators and directors sought to tell stories from vantage points that differed from the official state perspective.

Another section of the Colombian version of *Ya vuelvo* that had a deep impact on journalists, politicians, and the public was the last one, which addressed the assassination of the three presidential candidates, Luis Carlos Galán, Bernardo Jaramillo, and Carlos Pizarro, between 1989 and 1990. Designed especially for the Bogotá display as well, this section featured their pictures to impact viewers with a narrative that highlighted the country's political violence and absence of justice. Its name was Impunity in Colombia: The Magnicide of Three Candidates. However, this section of *Ya vuelvo* reinforced the stigma against the Colombian leftist party. Of the three murdered candidates, two had commemorative single exhibitions at the National Museum: Pizarro and Galán. The leader of the UP, Bernardo Jaramillo, was only part of the last section of *Ya vuelvo*. Regarding this difference, the director of the institution, María Victoria de Robayo, stated in an interview with me:

> [...] I would have approved an exhibition about Bernardo Jaramillo and Jaime Pardo Leal, despite journalists taking everything out of context, like they did with Tirofijo's towel... I said to the Minister of Culture: "If we did an exhibit for Galán, how come we do not do the same for Pizarro?" And I would have done one about the UP. It was not about making a series of state crimes, but I did not understand how the specialists of the National Museum could deny the possibility of curating these kinds of displays. I inquired, "But we did one for Galán..." But the Minister of Culture stated it was different with the UP and I still think it is not. They were guys [the UP leaders] trying to change and improve the country. But nothing happened.

Jaime Pardo Leal (March 28, 1941–October 11, 1987), mentioned in the quote above, was a Colombian lawyer, union leader, and politician who ran as candidate of the UP for the Presidency of Colombia in 1986. The drug dealer Gonzalo

Rodríguez Gacha ordered his assassination. In 2014, the office of the Attorney General of the Nation declared his murder as a crime against humanity.[31]

One of the reasons why Bernardo Jaramillo Ossa did not gain a space at the National Museum of Colombia, as his peers did, was the fact that he represented a leftist party, which in Colombia is associated with lower social classes. Neither the New Liberalism nor the Democratic Alliance M-19 were associated with the left, as their names clearly state. Also, Jaramillo was one of the survivors of the UP policide mentioned before and still carried the stigma of being associated with the FARC-EP. Despite the willingness of some curators and the director of the museum, the Colombian Ministry of Culture did not approve an exhibition about the assassination of one of the UP's most recognized and cherished leaders. In an interview on September 16, 2010, María José Pizarro deplored that the International Criminal Court had recognized the assassinations of the three candidates as crimes against humanity only six months before *Ya vuelvo* opened, after systematically ignoring them over the previous 20 years.[32]

This section ended Pizarro's exhibition, which conveyed an aura of martyrdom for the politicians. As modern-day saints, they deserved, therefore, their place in Colombia's national shrine: The National Museum. The final excerpt from Pizarro read:

> People always mobilize, bleed, and never achieve anything. In one hundred and fifty years there has been no social reform that breaks archaic privileges of the political power, the land, the capital... Gaitán, Rafael Uribe Uribe, Sucre, etc., incorruptible men murdered (preventive assassination). Magnicides have been constant towards the few honest [leaders] in our history.

In 2019, as part of the renovation plan of the museum, its team of professionals opened the hall Hacer Sociedad (Make Society), mentioned before, which used some of the panels related to the magnicide of the three candidates. In this hall, the curators made a clear statement about including significant voices in the country's recent violent history. Daniel Castro, Director at the time, stated: "[This hall presents] our historic social and political ways of living together through our social fabric and an array of voices that compose our territory and its confrontations."[33]

## *Two Other Candidates Killed in 1989: Luis Carlos Galán Lives, Bernardo Jaramillo Does Not*

Like Carlos Pizarro Leongómez, Luis Carlos Galán (1943–1989) was a beloved Colombian politician and similarly belonged to a well-known family. Pablo Escobar, the same drug lord who threatened Elvira Cuervo de Jaramillo, gave the order to kill him, and his father was a liberal who suffered persecution after the assassination of Jorge Eliécer Gaitán in 1948.

The exhibition *Galán vive* ran from August 12 until December 12, 2009, before the opening of *Ya vuelvo*. The National Museum of Colombia professionals assembled a display to commemorate that 20 years had passed since his shooting. In agreement with the Pontificia Universidad Javeriana and the Foundation Luis Carlos Galán Sarmiento, director María Victoria de Angulo de Robayo fully supported the initiative. Since the year 1989 was so hard on Colombians, the museum intended to remember those who represented hope.

*Galán vive* presented a timeline of Galán's public life along with photographs and artifacts given to the Museum by his family. Visitors were able to see clothing, such as a shirt Galán wore in political meetings, his senator of the Republic card, his Colombian ID, and the card he used while being the assistant director of *El Tiempo* newspaper. As a highlight, the display showcased the appointment book in which he had scheduled the event where he got shot.[34] However, the suit he was wearing the day of the shooting, donated by his wife to the Museum in 1999, was not presented and has become part of the objects or pieces that the National Museum of Colombia has yet to exhibit.

Colombians recognized Luis Carlos Galán as an honest politician who lived and died fighting against drug trafficking and corruption.[35] Journalists and politicians have compared his assassination to Jorge Eliécer Gaitán's. The most significant parallels are the feelings of despair, emptiness, sadness, and anger they inspired in Colombians due to their impunity. The two presidential candidates represented a new hope, reconciliation, honesty, and a channel to achieve peace in the country, but as they were about to come to power, they got killed.

Luis Carlos Galán was born in Bucaramanga, Department of Santander, and was 45 years old when Pablo Escobar ordered his death. Media all over the world reported his murder.[36] Galán committed his political career to fight against the corruption and drug trafficking that severely affect the country's institutions. Since 1950, Galán lived in Bogotá, where he attended middle and high school and then pursued his undergraduate degree in law at the Pontificia Universidad Javeriana. In 1963, he founded *Vértice*, a liberal magazine, which was his first journalistic experience. He was the assistant director of the newspaper in 1965, and in 1970 he took office as Minister of Education under the conservative president Misael Pastrana Borrero (1970–1974). In 1972, he served as Ambassador of Colombia to Italy, in 1974 as the Colombian representative to the Food and Agriculture Organization of the United Nations, and in 1976, he ran for council member in a small town of the Santander Department. In 1977, Galán was elected Senator from the same department.

It was also during 1977 that Galán became an active contributor to the liberal weekly magazine *Nueva Frontera*, where he authored an article denouncing the existence of drug trafficking cartels in Colombia and their corrupting influence on politics. In 1979, Luis Carlos Galán and Rodrigo Lara Bonilla created the political party, Nuevo Liberalismo (New Liberalism), which was a breakaway from the traditional Liberal party, which slowly dissolved after Galán's murder.[37] Lara Bonilla (1946–1984) was a Colombian lawyer and politician, Minister of Justice under President Belisario Betancur. He was also assassinated by Pablo Escobar due to his prosecution of drug traffickers belonging to the Medellin Cartel.

When New Liberalism started, Pablo Escobar identified with the ideas the movement promoted, "[…] national Independence, national and regional cultural identity, organic democracy—a revitalized democracy including all tiers of society—and a new concept of state linked to cultural and economic decentralization and social equality."[38] Galán's criticism of the Colombian state also appealed to Escobar: "Colombian society is dominated by a political oligarchy that controls the public corporation and has profited from administering the state; they distribute their bounty after each election."[39] Thus, the drug dealer contacted Galán and Lara and offered them economic support in order to become a member of the party. The two politicians rejected Escobar in front of thousands of people in Antioquia at a public event, action that infuriated him. In response, Escobar vowed to exterminate the party and its members. In 1984, one of Escobar's hitmen felled Rodrigo Lara. Further investigations have demonstrated that Galán had several enemies such as Liberal politician Alberto Santofimio Botero, whom the Colombian Supreme Court of Justice ordered to detain in 2011. He was a Liberal politician accused of receiving money from drug trafficking. After years of investigations, authorities had proven he was an influential part in Galán's killing. In addition, some state security agencies, like the Director of the Administrative Department of Security (Departamento Administrativo de Seguridad, DAS) and its director, Miguel Maza Márquez, were involved in the magnicide.

Since Lara's murder, Galán took precautions regarding his safety and left the country to teach in Oxford, but in 1988, he made his comeback to Colombian politics. The politician returned even more determined to fight the cartels led by Pablo Escobar and Gonzalo Rodríguez Gacha, which made him again a target.[40] On July 6, 1989, the Liberal Party appointed Galán as their presidential candidate for the 1990 elections, and the death threats against him and his family started. He confirmed his life was in danger on August 14, 1989. He was attending a public event at the University of Antioquia when the National Police of Colombia frustrated an attack. Subsequent analyses showed that Pablo Escobar planned the crime since July of the same year.[41] Galán, however, ignored the threats and kept going with his presidential campaign. Among the candidate's most renowned phrases, sparking the cartels' fury, was this one: "the drug trafficking phenomenon is one of the most terrible threats against liberty and justice in the world."[42] To which the cartels answered:

> We declare total and absolute war on the Government, on the industrialists and the oligarchy, on the journalists that have attacked and ravaged us,

on the judges that have sold out to the Government, on the extraditing magistrates, on the presidents of the unions and all those who persecuted and attacked us. We will not respect the families of those who have not respected our families.[43]

The group called The Extraditables (Los Extraditables) made the threat. The association was composed by the heads of the Medellín drug cartel in Colombia: Pablo Escobar, chief of the cartel; Gonzalo Rodríguez Gacha and Fabio Ochoa Vásquez, two of the main leaders of the same organization. Their slogan was, "We prefer a grave in Colombia to prison in the United States." Its purpose was to intimidate the Colombian government into banning extradition at the constitutional level. Luis Carlos Galán and Rodrigo Lara were ardent supporters of extradition.

The first threats Galán received were phone calls to his home landline followed by pamphlets in his mailbox in which the Extraditables warned the politician about his children's safety. Galán's response was increasing his security measures, but he did not stop his political endeavors. By 1989, he was an enormous success and was ahead of his competitors by more than 60%, according to the polls.[44]

Luis Carlos Galán was very aware of the danger he faced and started to use a bulletproof vest, which he had rejected in the past. The politician had scheduled a public appearance in Soacha, a borough of Bogotá. He was to deliver a speech on a platform built for the occasion in the town's main square. On August 18, 1989, Galán wore his vest and left for Soacha, despite his family's fears. He traveled in a car with only one bodyguard, while the other ones left ahead. Of the seven bodyguards Galán had that day, two were sent to another town following orders of his security chief, who later was brought to justice due to his lack of experience.[45] When Galán and his bodyguard arrived at Soacha's square, there was a large crowd. There were no controls, the other bodyguards were not nearby, and the area had no protection. At 8:45 pm, Galán took the stage, and when he raised his arms to say hello, he dropped. A hitman was hiding underneath the platform and fired five times his gun from below, where the vest did not protect him. He died on his way to the nearest hospital.[46]

Galán's murder astonished the country. Feelings of despair and disbelief spread through the country; Colombians overwhelmed with shock and grief stopped their activities, and the whole nation shut down. Because of Galán's assassination, President Virgilio Barco Vargas (1986–1990) ordered an unprecedented military offensive against the Medellín Cartel. As a result, the Colombian elite police killed Gonzalo Rodríguez Gacha in 1989. The drug lords' power, however, did not diminish. Galán's family, following the initiative of his 17-year-old son, Juan Manuel Galán, decided that César Gaviria Trujillo should continue with Luis Carlos Galán's ideas and promote his legacy. The appointment enabled his election as the next Colombian president (1990–1994) but also made him Escobar's next target: "tell those who are by Gaviria's side that they are with a cadaver." Gaviria knew the threats against his life were serious, so his campaign did not have any public events. In December 1989, Gaviria was supposed to board a plane to travel to Cali but did not end up on the flight. After taking off, the plane exploded, leaving more than 100 casualties—a crime ordered by Escobar. Gaviria took office as President of Colombia in 1990. He claims to have governed as Galán would have, but the former members of the New Liberalism complain that Gaviria got rid of Galán's allies, sending them to diplomatic representations overseas.[47] That was the real end of New Liberalism and of the many hopes Colombians had for achieving peace and a country with less corruption. However, Galán's memory is ever present in newspapers and magazine articles published since his death and in two books. One written by the lawyer Hernando Roa Suárez in 2009, titled *Luis Carlos Galán. Un demócrata comprometido* (*Luis Carlos Galán. A Committed Democrat*); and another by his brother Gabriel Galán Sarmiento, 2014, called *Luis Carlos Galán. Íntimo y público. Mi hermano* (*Luis Carlos Galán. Intimate and Public. My Brother*).

Along with Pizarro and Galán, the third presidential candidate murdered was Bernardo Jaramillo Ossa, leader of the leftist Unión Patriótica, UP (Patriotic Union). Jaramillo, aware and worried due to what criminal organizations were doing to him and his peers, met with Pablo Escobar in Medellín to reach a truce, but the drug lord said that although he did not bear any animus toward him, Rodríguez Gacha, significant member of the Medellin Cartel, did, as Carlos Castaño, the paramilitary chief. Escobar warned the UP politician about the danger he was in and about his bodyguard, who apparently was infiltrated by both crime organizations. After this meeting, Jaramillo left the country only to return when he knew about Rodríguez Gacha's death. Nevertheless, drug lords' hitmen shot Jaramillo on March 22, 1990. He and his wife were traveling for vacation to the Colombian coast when they arrived at the airport with their bodyguards, where many people wanted to greet him. In the midst, Jaramillo fell on the floor. Although his wife threw herself over him to protect him, it was too late. His last words were, "Hug me, Mariela, these sons of a bitch killed me."[48]

Members of the Medellín Carter murdered Luis Carlos Galán Sarmiento and Bernardo Jaramillo Ossa within five months, and to add insult to injury, Carlos Pizarro Leongómez suffered the same fate three months later. The three politicians died in tragic ways, plunging Colombians into sadness, fear, and anger. The exhibition *Galán vive* was short lived, had no catalog, and went unnoticed by the media. For an exhibit that lasted five months, the scarcity of sources is surprising. In the Archive of the National Museum, there is only one press release published in different national newspapers.

Although Galán and Pizarro earned a space at the National Museum of Colombia, Bernardo Jaramillo Ossa did not. Following Bourdieu and Hall, I argue that the UP leader's exclusion from the National Museum of Colombia is related to the fact that he represented the fear of communism so deeply embedded in Colombian society. In addition, the UP politician did not belong to a well-known family. Instead, he had a working-class background, advocated for equality of rights for every citizen, condemned the FARC-EP and their tactics, and was always an active member of the leftist movements of the country.[49] Other institutions, such as the Centro de Memoria Paz y Reconciliación del Distrito, did an exhibition and a podcast to commemorate his murder.[50] The fact that Jaramillo was the only candidate without an exhibition at the National Museum demonstrates that change is slow. Although at the hall Hacer Sociedad (Make Society), the UP candidate is mentioned, and in other exhibitions such as *Glass Houses: Paul Rivet and Human Diversity*, that ran from December 2021 until March 2022, there were objects related to the leftist political party, there is still some reluctance to be associated with leftist movements in Colombia. As María Victoria de Angulo de Robayo clearly confirmed, "It was not about making a series of state crimes." The good news is that the current team of professionals from the institution recognizes the importance of making the venue as inclusive and comprehensive as possible.

## The Military Outrage: *Ya vuelvo* Does Not Belong in the National Museum of Colombia

Although the reception of Pizarro's exhibition, *Ya vuelvo*, was mostly positive, one sector of society reacted angrily: the military. In 2000, Coronel Plazas Vega, who oversaw the recovery of the Palace of Justice, published *La Batalla del Palacio de Justicia* (*The Battle of the Palace of Justice*), in which he told his side of the story and gave details of the government's decision to enter the Palace by force. In the book, he justifies President Betancur's orders. Also included in the introduction is a testimony of a survivor who thanks the general for his service:

> The fierce guerrilla attack, of unimaginable proportions, which touched our national soul, started the building's fire and led to the sacrifice of prominent magistrates, and official employees, Army officers, Police Officers, and civilians, who lost their life in that stormy nightmare [...]
>
> [...] the President had no alternative -after consulting with ministers, advisors, former presidents, etc., when he had the solid support of the sensible public opinion- but to give the order to the public force to recover the Palace of Justice [...]
>
> Finally, I want to thank Colonel Luis Alfonso Plazas Vega for choosing me to comment on this book. As a survivor of the Siege, I am very interested in the topic. Therefore, I have read passionately, although full of sadness and pain, these pages that I highly recommend to all Colombians.

This quotation by the former president of the Council of State, Samuel Buitrago Hurtado, which opens Plazas Vega's book, sets the tone of the text, in which the reader encounters explanations and justifications for the President's decision. However, *Ya vuelvo* excluded this text because the survivors and the M-19 guerrilla fighters deemed the government's show of excessive force.

Historian Catalina Ruiz, co-curator of the exhibition, remembers the letters she and other colleagues received related to *Ya vuelvo* and its portrayal of the Palace of Justice Siege. She noted in an interview held in 2017:

> The reactions to the exhibition were both positive and negative. We got letters from an organization that defends the actions of Colonel Luis Alfonso Plazas Vega. Several people signed a letter that the curators had to answer. These protesters of *Ya vuelvo*, mainly affiliated with the military, stated their outrage at the presence of a guerrilla fighter at the National Museum of Colombia, the temple of our national heroes. In addition, there were about twenty-one emails complaining about the display. The curators, however, achieved certain changes in people's perspective. We encouraged polemic, discussion, and the sense that the museum needed to be a space to tell our own recent history.

Luis Alfonso Plazas Vega was born on June 21, 1944. He is a retired Colombian Colonel. In 1985, he commanded the recovery of the Palace of Justice seized by the M-19. On August 22, 2001, the families of eleven missing victims condemned him for using excessive force during the operation. They also denounced him for causing the disappearances of people who were inside the Palace of Justice during the siege. A criminal investigation began on August 16, 2006, and a judge placed Plazas Vega under preventive arrest on July 12, 2007. On February 11, 2008, authorities found enough evidence to sentence him for being a co-perpetrator in the crimes of aggravated forced disappearances and aggravated kidnapping, but justice failed to punish him.

In 2010, a Colombian judge sentenced Colonel Luis Alfonso Plazas Vega to 35 years in prison for his actions during the Palace of Justice Siege in 1985, particularly his responsibility for the disappearance of civilians and guerrilla fighters. The judge reported threats and harassment after issuing her decision. In 2015, the Colombian Supreme Court of Justice acquitted Plazas Vega based on a supposed lack of evidence for his sentence. [51]

## Representations and Remembrances of Carlos Pizarro Leongómez and His Struggles to Achieve Colombian Peace in *Ya vuelvo*

The year 2010 was pivotal in Colombia's recent history. It marked a long-awaited change of the country's head of state. In August, President Juan Manuel Santos replaced former President Álvaro Uribe Vélez, who served as president for two consecutive terms, from 2002 to 2010. Under his mandate, the Congress approved the Law of Peace and Justice (2005) to facilitate the paramilitaries' demobilization; eventually, this law would also apply for the disarmament of guerrilla groups. This law purported to provide truth, reparations, and a measure of justice to victims of the armed conflict, but it did not. Although more than 30,000 paramilitary fighters have demobilized since 2002, fewer than 10% of them fall within the purview of the Justice and Peace Law; the rest qualify for a more liberal amnesty. Further, the law was subject to harsh criticism when it failed to provide adequate incentives for truth-telling and reparations. The Colombian Constitutional Court revised some portions of the law to address this concern; however, its promises of both peace and justice have so far remained elusive.[52]

During Uribe's presidency, the armed conflict with all its atrocities escalated alongside illegal national intelligence surveillance of human rights defenders, journalists, opposition politicians, and Supreme Court justices. Thus, when President Santos won the presidential elections, Colombians felt a respite due to his attempts to promote legislation that could restore land to displaced persons and compensate victims of abuses by state agents. Although Santos was involved in the extrajudicial killings scandal while being Minister of Defense, during his presidential campaign he voiced respect for an independent judiciary and denounced threats against human rights defenders.[53] Santos wanted to promote peace in Colombia, and he was awarded the Nobel Peace Prize in 2016 in recognition of this effort. However, his peace initiatives came under serious threat since the return to power of the right-wing party, led by Álvaro Uribe. Iván Duque, a member of Uribe's political group, won the 2018 presidential elections. However, two presidential candidates, not from Uribe's party, ran for the 2022 elections. One of them, Gustavo Petro, a demobilized member of the M-19 guerrilla and Carlos Pizarro's friend, won the presidency and will take office on August 7, 2022.

In this context, the end of Uribe's administration and the beginning of Santos's proved propitious for an exhibition such as *Ya vuelvo*. The political climate of the country allowed alternative voices to be part of national narratives, and professionals of the National Museum took the opportunity to display *Ya vuelvo* at the Colombian venue. The curators also saw the chance to include in the museum some narratives associated with lay people or popular culture to appeal to the common people Pizarro fought for. Furthermore, this version incorporated additional information regarding Pizarro's political life and its impact on the country's recent history. One of the curators of *Ya vuelvo* in Colombia, Catalina Ruíz, remembers the negotiations with María José Pizarro about the exhibition's presentation at the National Museum. For the Colombian curators, Pizarro was much more than a father and a husband; he was a significant political figure that required analysis from a historical memory perspective. Ruíz meant that the curators suspected that *Ya vuelvo's* narrative extended beyond an intimate account. The institution professionals claimed that Pizarro's influence in Colombian political life deserved the attention of all citizens. In addition, María José's story is a common one in Colombia because most citizens have lost loved ones during the war; thus, many visitors could identify with her experience.

> However, I understood María José. She had a conflict, and this display was her opportunity to reappropriate her surname, reconcile with her past and her father's, and come out of a life of secrecy. But at the same time the exhibition was significant for the leftist movements [Patriotic Union, UP, for instance] in the country. Here I understood that memory processes are alive.[54]

Ruíz words have a twofold meaning. First, her perspective about how to display Pizarro's life in the Colombian context by turning a personal account into a social one illustrates the negotiations and compromises that take place during the creation of historical memories from all the parties involved. Second, she emphasized the decision-making that takes place when victims and museum professionals refer to historical memories. Since the opening of the display in Barcelona in 2009, María José stated that she wanted the audience to remember her father as a peacemaker, which implied a conscious selection of artifacts and other materials presented in *Ya vuelvo*.

In addition, the political context of the country—Uribe's last term in office and Santos's first one—was an auspicious moment to redefine the National Museum's role in regard to how to display recent violence. It allowed the institution to be part of the creation of historical memories about the country's armed conflict. These changes also align with museological trends that privilege memory museums over history museums.[55] Even though the National Museum of Colombia is not mainly a memory venue, its curators valued spaces to narrate the recent violent episodes of the country. Thus, the venue's team aimed to widen the institution's scope to include diverse and marginal voices in its exhibitions. In this sense, they were critically interrogating conventional historical claims related to official history. They also knew that *Ya vuelvo* could tell a complex political history of the country. It provided a chance to embrace topics such as the history of the M-19 guerrilla, the laying down of their weapons, and its demobilization process. For the Colombian version of *Ya vuelvo*, ten sections addressed the political climate of the country from the 1960s until the 1990s.

The part of the display that started the tour was called "Pizarro's deaths"—pluralized because the items that opened the exhibition, a photo collage of his face and a panel, referred to the symbolic moments in which he gave up his weapon. The first time was in 1973, when he left the FARC-EP; second, in 1989, when the members of the M-19 demobilized; and third, in 1990,

**92** Lives Ended in Their Prime

when Pizzaro's assassination occurred. *Ya Vuelvo* included quotes from Pizarro's public statements, like the last one he made as a presidential candidate in 1990: "We offer something elementary, simple, and plain: that life should not be taken in its prime."

Even though *Ya vuelvo* opened with references to the end of Pizarro's life, the section sought to make sense of what was incomprehensible not only for María José and her family but also for many Colombians: Why are some lives cruelly and inexplicably cut short?[56] The opening of the exhibition used artifacts, such as pictures, that were also the segue into the segment about Pizarro's hat. The use of personal items in *Ya vuelvo* helped María José and her family to transition from grief to forgiveness. It was, according to sociologist Michael Brennan, what historical memories are supposed to do: "Help people to grieve, to confront, and create other realities." At the entrance of the exhibition, the viewers could see an image of Pizarro's face composed of many other pictures. Through the collage, the curators wanted to convey that Pizarro devoted his life to Colombians (Figure 2.2).

The second section of the exhibition presented Pizarro's emblematic hat. His headwear, white and clean, contrasted dramatically with Tirofijo's towel, old, sweaty, and dirty. The hat became a defining symbol of peace and the M-19 demobilization efforts, and it resembled the white dove's common use.[57] In 1990, when the M-19 laid down its weapons during the administration of Virgilio Barco, not only the guerrilla fighters but also the state representatives

**FIGURE 2.2** View of the opening of Ya vuelvo. Picture by Catalina Ruíz. Bogotá, 2011.

wore white hats.[58] For the exhibition, the artifact was donated by María José Pizarro, and it became a central piece of the narrative's display.

The arrangement of the hat included a video, where visitors could hear Pizarro's speeches and see him wearing the accessory, like in January 1989 in the Tolima Department, during the first meeting between M-19 leaders and state representatives. The layout of the hat brings us back to Elvira Cuervo de Jaramillo's words, when she claimed that the display of the towel depended on how curators placed it in the glass case.

A panel of the same section also featured a penned part of a speech Pizarro gave to his men on March 8, 1990, in which he referred to the object: "We understand the hat as a peace symbol, but it is better not to assume that everybody thinks in the same way." The hat also became the logo of the Fundación Carlos Pizarro Leongómez (Carlos Pizarro Leongómez Foundation). According to paperwork from Casa América Catalunya, which granted authorization to the National Museum of Colombia to display the *Ya vuelvo* materials, the hat was the most distinctive and valued artifact in the exhibit.

The third part of the exhibition, Retrato de Carlos (Portrait of Carlos), had no changes for the Colombian version. This space entailed a series of glass boxes that enabled the viewers to see pictures and writings of Pizarro. The fourth section of the exhibition, Historical Context of the M-19, consisted of a video produced only for the Colombian museums. The film included testimony from journalists, historians, M-19 members, and politicians about the 1970 presidential elections and the context in which the M-19 appeared in the public sphere. The movie also explained the differences between the various guerrilla groups: The M-19, Ejército Popular de Liberación, EPL (Popular Liberation Army), Ejército Nacional de Liberación, ELN (National Liberation Army), and FARC-EP.

The next part of the exhibition concentrated on the portrayal of the M-19 by the Colombian media. One week before the M-19 committed their first public act, snatching Bolívar's sword, its members paid to advertise the act in the most important newspapers of the country. They conducted a publicity campaign with eye-catching newspaper ads. After the heist, *El Tiempo* and *El Espectador* newspapers published the news, "In an unprecedented action in Colombia, members of an urban guerilla group took Simón Bolívar's sword, and other items, from the museum housing them. The historic venue was wallpapered with political material that belonged to a movement called M-19."[59] Subsequently, the M-19 stopped their newspaper ads and stated how they were different from other guerrilla organizations such as the ELN, FARC-EP, or the EPL. The leaders of the M-19 claimed that "We accomplish what we promise" and that they stood out from the other guerrilla groups because they did not attack civilians or cause bloodbaths. That was the birth of the M-19 guerrilla group.

This section of *Ya vuelvo,* called the M-19 in Headlines, displayed newspaper clippings and served two purposes: first, to show how the guerrilla movement developed over time, and second, to illustrate how Colombian journalists depicted M-19. One of the most significant images was one in which Pizarro appears with a blue t-shirt and his white hat. This appeared on the cover of the journal *Cromos* on April 30, 1990, which published it after the politician's murder. The words that accompany it are: "I did it for you, Colombia, and I got killed." This remark was not Pizarro's but Jaime Bateman's, the top commander of M-19.

The seventh section, the Second Peace Process (1989–1990), was perhaps one of the most significant of *Ya vuelvo* because it addressed Pizarro's demobilization and reincorporation into civilian life. During the mandate of Virgilio Barco, Pizarro realized that the armed struggle was no longer viable. Influenced by the fall of the Berlin Wall and the increasing presence of drug trafficking in the country, his speeches began to contain words such as reconciliation, hope, agreement, and accord as he pursued the legal channels of politics to combat corruption and drug dealers, as shown in excerpts of a speech he gave on Christmas 1988 and included in the museum exhibit:

> And it is within this reconciliation panorama where we can find our national soul, near the edge, again, hope. The last chance for Colombians to reunite palpitates in our hands and calls for a dignified and certain execution, one that allows us to build, at last, a political solution to the national conflict, a victory for all Colombians… Mr. President, just tell us when and where we have that appointment with history, and we will immediately go.

The message conveyed to the public stressed the importance of national unity against drug trafficking and rebel armed groups. These parts of *Ya vuelvo* showed an individual in favor of change for the common good.

Another addendum for the Colombian version of *Ya vuelvo* was the eighth part, titled Laying Down Arms. It emphasized the M-19 guerrillas' demobilization and their reincorporation into civilian life. On March 8, 1990, Pizarro left his 9-mm gun and placed it on top of a Colombian flag (like what he had done in 1973). That day, in Santo Domingo, Cauca Department, the M-19 gave up their uniforms, military and communication equipment, weapons, and campaign boots, thereby signifying that they had given up their commitment to seize power through armed conflict. From that day on, the M-19 was to participate legally in the elections of May 27, 1990, reorganized as the Democratic Alliance M-19, which later became the Independent Democratic Pole and finally the Alternative Democratic Pole.[60]

The ninth part of *Ya vuelvo*, titled Forty-five Days of Presidential Campaign, consisted of pictures, videos, and a panel with some of Pizarro's speeches while he ran for office. In March 1990, he started to tour the country as part of his electoral campaign. According to the exhibition's narrative, his candidacy represented an alternative to the traditional political power in the country because it explicitly involved calls for social justice. Three days before his murder, on April 23, 1990, Pizarro gave a public speech in Valledupar, with these words included in one of *Ya vuelvo's* panels:

> We arrived here and found your sympathy, honest affection, open affection of people who have been with us from afar and that today know that can count on the M-19. We earned the right to walk with our foreheads up through the streets and rural areas of our country.

In addition, the Bogotá display included a section about the National Constituent Assembly that promulgated the Constitution of 1991. On January 31 of the same year, the demobilized M-19 fighters returned Bolívar's sword to the government in a ceremony that took place at the Quinta de San Pedro Alejandrino, the museum from which they had taken the item in 1974. The idea of the ninth part of *Ya vuelvo* was to highlight the contributions of the M-19 and Pizarro to this political process of democratization. The curators aimed to show Colombians that the Constitution of 1991 resulted from an inclusionary process advocated by the M-19 since its origins and in which Pizarro served as a protagonist.

The artifacts displayed in this section included the Constitution of 1886, the M-19 flag, and the pen used to sign the Constitution of 1991. The museum exhibition noted that on April 20, 1990, Pizarro said on television, "We succeeded to bring the country closer to peace, which today has three main components: The ability to build a strong nation, a democratic economy, and an inclusive constituent, which represents us all." The tenth and final section of *Ya vuelvo* at the National Museum of Colombia was Impunity in Colombia: The Magnicide of Three Candidates.

## Auspicious Historical Memories: *Ya vuelvo's* Sensible Reception

Besides the favorable political and cultural context of 2010 in Colombia to remember diverse voices from the recent armed conflict, *Ya vuelvo* appealed to other public sensibilities. Among the reasons that the exhibition achieved a good reception among journalists, politicians, and the public was the fact that one of Pizarro's daughters was the main curator of the display. In addition, *Ya vuelvo's* appeal to secondary witnessing, to make visitors part of the story, assured its positive response from Colombians. To achieve this goal, the curators of *Ya vuelvo* used devices such as the recordings of the voices of magistrate Reyes Echandía in which he pleaded for help. *Ya vuelvo's* emphasis on Pizarro's devotion to the people, the nostalgia it evoked, and its bold critique of the Colombian state also accounted for the exhibit's popularity.

*Ya vuelvo* originated as an idea of Pizarro's daughter, María José. She yearned to know her father better and to fill in the silences from her childhood. María

José was 12 years old when her father died, and she grew up committed to recovering his documents, papers, and memory, which became the exhibition's artifacts.[61] Currently, she is a peace activist and part of the leftist party that came to power on June 19, 2022. She is also a survivor of Colombian violence, spent long periods apart from her parents because of the conflict, and was always afraid for the safety of her father. When she decided to curate *Ya vuelvo*, she assumed her role as victim, and she said as much, which touched the public and gained her much sympathy from Colombian citizens. The following is an excerpt from a 2015 interview, in which she talks about her parents:

> Yes, for so many years I blamed her, especially when I was a teenager. My mom had to endure all the reproaches, the ones for her and my father, because she was the one left alive. One refuses to understand that their absence was not an abandonment, because it is stuck in your mind that they left, and one wonders why they are not coming back. Then, I start this process and to digest things in a different way. I begin to understand, to process, not to judge. I began to comprehend why they made those decisions, and even though I always knew the truth —they never told me cowboy stories— I had to accept it was their life choice. In time, I have come to be grateful to have been born in that nucleus and in those circumstances. I feel that, even though that took away my childhood and with so many people dying around me, it gave me liberties and certainties, a clear path, despite the pain and recriminations.[62]

María José Pizarro gave several interviews on radio, television, and printed media, and even made some documentaries in which she spoke about her father as a peacemaker. As she noted in an interview given to a journalist of *El Espectador*:

> We cannot condemn ourselves as a nation. War is not the only way, and we must not repeat the past. We are living an exceptional moment that requires all our strength for a new mobilization.
> This country has touched rock bottom. I hope we are up to this challenging moment, so we can reflect on what Jaime Bateman used to say: "Whoever keeps the peace flag wins the war." We must defend our country and lives for the years to come.[63]

To create a positive memory of her father, María José decided to include in *Ya vuelvo* a touching letter Pizarro wrote to his own dying father while in prison. During 1979 in a confrontation between state forces and the M-19, the National Army captured and tortured Pizarro and other guerrilla fighters. When President Betancur decided to amnesty these prisoners in 1982, Pizarro's father, Admiral Juan Antonio Pizarro, had already died. The following are some excerpts from the letter, which visitors of *Ya vuelvo* could read:

> [...] Today, I say I am proud to be a political prisoner and an M-19 fighter because the M-19 is a new political force that has proved its political justice and its operational audacity. [...] Because the M-19 has maintained its doors open for a dialogue with all political sectors if they are interested in the national well-being -in conquering democracy. [...] Because the M-19 is willing, as demonstrated, to be part of the national current that believes that it is possible to defeat the oligarchic civil minority that dishonors or violates the most traditional national values and monopolizes wealth. [...] I have always wanted the public opinion to judge my life for my own merits and independently from yours. I do not avoid the responsibilities that carrying your blood implies. I recognize with pride that the solid moral base that illuminates my life is your work. I will never stop seeing in you my most important agent. I will render perennial worship to your public honesty and your impeccable private life. I will maintain my conviction that your life does not need improvised defenders, even if one of them is your son. I am certain that, from your dying bed, you are watching wisely over me. I know you will be relentless towards my actions, and you will keep trusting me. I cannot be by your side when you leave us, but I have never been away. Receive my message of eternal gratitude and love. Your Son, Carlos.[64]

Despite his strong commitment to the M-19, this letter allows people to see Pizarro as a loving son and family member, which María José wanted to emphasize from the very beginning of the exhibition. This item, cherished by the curators, aimed to move the audience deeply. María José also echoed President Juan Manuel Santos's peace endeavors when she stated: "The Colombian version of the display conveys the message that war destroys us and that peace is a necessity."[65] In addition, another of her goals, perhaps the most important for her and Pizarro's family, was to pressure the authorities to bring her father's murderers to justice.

A further reason why *Ya vuelvo* impacted Colombians in a positive way was its appeal to secondary witnessing. Concurring with museum scholar Silke Arnold de Simine, curators of displays that deal with traumatic events aim to touch the public to make them feel part of history, even if they did not experience it directly. De Simine, who takes this concept from historian Dominick LaCapra, emphasizes that to be a secondary witness is to listen—and in the case of this exhibition, to watch—and develop empathy not only with the survivors but also with the dead. When curators or other museum professionals represent violence in museums and promote mediated memories, they resort to empathy because that attracts people to the exhibits.[66] However, this entails the risk of promoting what historian Virginia Garrard has called the "pornography of violence," which transforms viewers into voyeurs of atrocities.[67] Thus, part of the responsibility of museum professionals is to decide how to exhibit violence. Empathy also implies that the viewers of the information presented will experience fear, outrage, and emotions that produce memories of the victims.[68]

The act of secondary witnessing contributed to the public's positive reception of *Ya vuelvo*. Colombians felt a deep sorrow for the murdered politician and for María José. The curators intended, at least momentarily, to make the visitors reflect on the other's position, without taking their place. Being a secondary witness also implies that the mourning process is different.[69] Therefore, we could say that the museum's narrative mediates second witnesses' memories. Secondary witnessing encourages citizens to unite against elements that might threaten their identity. *Ya vuelvo* condemned corruption and violence in the country and manifested that the Palace of Justice's Siege, for instance, cannot be forgotten but enmity can be superseded in the name of peace.

Along with empathy, the curators of *Ya vuelvo* used nostalgia to make an impression on the audience. Although the institution's professionals could not control the visitors' reception of the images at the exhibition, they aimed to promote sentiments and to influence memory production. Since Pizarro was associated with reconciliation, peace, hope, and underrepresented marginal groups, the curators were able to use these concepts in the exhibit's favor. Over 50,000 people attended the exhibition.[70] However, the impact that *Ya vuelvo* caused on them varied according to their age range. In an interview, María José stated that people over 40 and 50 years understood the significance and influence of Pizarro in Colombia's recent political life but that citizens 30 or below had no idea who he was. Therefore, claimed María José, "We certainly are a country without memory." Since only those over 40 felt nostalgic and remembered the history of the M-19 and its demobilization, the curators of the Bogotá version, likewise, used that nostalgia to move the public. As noted by Arnold de Simine, museums present intimate narratives to achieve the public's empathy. María José Pizarro aimed to tell a family account to reconcile with the absence of her father, but the museum display broadened the scope of the story to give a larger account of the country's history.

Finally, and directly associated with the nostalgia raised by *Ya vuelvo*, Colombians approved the curator's audacity to question the Colombian government for its actions during the Palace of Justice Siege and to criticize the state's failed attempts to promote peace processes. This was possible by turning an intimate family and personal narrative into a national account. This idea, however, is not new to museum displays. Max Lejeune, President of the Conseil Général and former Defense Minister of France at the time of the Suez Canal crisis (1956), for example, created a national narrative exhibition for children based on his own experience as a kid. He put together an intimate recollection of his infancy along with the stories of many children of the 1920s and 1930s who were also affected by the war.[71] This effort of converting personal stories into national narratives that marked the Colombian version of *Ya vuelvo,* may have paved the way for a critique of state policy. The emphasis on memory during the late twentieth century in Colombia gained significance due to the acknowledgment that people across the nation are still overwhelmed by traumatic recollections of the violence from the 1980s to the early 2000s. The curators of the National Museum intended *Ya vuelvo* to act as a reminder of a sense of shattered hope. They emphasized the continuity between past and present oppression, marginalization, persecution, and suffering. With the inclusion of the two failed peace processes in which Pizarro partook, *Ya vuelvo* prompted Colombians to recall the failed historical efforts to reach an agreement between the government and rebel armed groups. This exhibition, in addition, presented two different and radical perspectives of the Palace of Justice Siege: the military and the guerrillas' viewpoints. In this sense, *Ya vuelvo* was a milestone in Colombian museums' representations of historical memories. This is one of the reasons why the curators decided to present a burned typewriter during the Siege, as well as an audio recording of a victim's voice begging to stop the fire. The National Museum of Colombia not only collects, preserves, and imbues artifacts with meaning; its curators and professionals also create new sensory experiences and environments, which are the fruit of a decision-making process.[72]

## Conclusions

Only ten years passed between the failed attempt to acquire and exhibit Tirofijo's towel at the National Museum of Colombia, the popular *Ya vuelvo,* and *Galán vive* all the same institution. Over this decade, the team of professionals of the museum aimed to give prominence to representations of the recent violence in the country and to discuss the conventional nature of the venue's role in Colombia's political life. The political context of the beginning of Santos's first mandate was more propitious for these experiments. Even though Colombians expected his administration to continue Álvaro Uribe's policies, Santos soon distanced himself from the former government. From the very beginning, he endeavored to achieve peace, which he did in 2016 when the Colombian state and the FARC-EP signed a ceasefire treaty after four years of conversations in Cuba. As he stated in 2010: "The time has come for national unity, the time has come for harmony, the time has come for us to work together for the prosperity of Colombia."[73] In this context, *Ya vuelvo* had official support, which guaranteed a forum at the National Museum. The ten years between Tirofijo's failed towel initiative and the launching of *Ya vuelvo* also demonstrate the ongoing and dynamic nature of historical memory production.

In addition, Pizarro's reinvention as a peacemaker contrasted with Tirofijo's notoriety. While Colombians recoiled that the leader of the FARC-EP denied a dying boy the right to see his father for the last time, Pizarro traveled the country preaching a narrative of reconciliation and forgiveness. María José and the curators of *Ya vuelvo* emphasized this facet because they knew of the debates surrounding Pizarro's figure and wanted him to make history as a peace advocate. This intention pervades the Colombian version of *Ya vuelvo* and illuminates the changing understandings of the role of museums and the kinds of memories that storied institutions in Colombia consider worthy of showcasing.

Museum professionals in Colombia and throughout Latin America have realized since the 1990s that these venues need to tackle polemical matters. They had also come to acknowledge that difficult pasts and heritages also comprise part of a country's identity. Grappling with different perspectives on political violence, such as the guerrilla and military versions of the Palace of Justice Siege, museums can tell tough stories without the need to exalt perpetrators or offend viewers. In this sense, the narratives of *Ya vuelvo*, for example, encourage diversity and signify the museum as a site for reflection and critique in revisiting past violent events.

Another pivotal contribution of *Ya vuelvo* was the opportunity the curators saw to bridge the gap between high and popular culture and its hierarchies in the Colombian context. *Ya vuelvo* attracted visitors to the museum who had not felt represented in the venue before. It appealed to the poor and working class, the ones Pizarro fought for. Through *Ya vuelvo*, curators and museum professionals indicated that a venue such as the National Museum of Colombia is a space that must include all Colombians without distinction of class, education, gender, or political affiliation.

However, battles over historical memory not only take place in the hallowed halls of the National Museum. In Colombian peripheral towns, victims of political violence also represent in memory venues the brutalities they endured. The next two chapters address the cases of rural communities where the inhabitants of small municipalities constructed alternative spaces for the survivors of violence to mourn and grieve the absence of their loved ones.

## Notes

1 Casa América Catalunya, "Juan Manuel Santos, presidente electo de Colombia, se 'lleva' nuestra exposición "Ya vuelvo" al Museo Nacional de su país," May 22, 2010, http://americat.barcelona/es/juan- manuel-santos-presidente-electo-de-colombia-se-lleva-nuestra-exposicion-ya-vuelvo-al-museo-nacional- de-su-pais-
2 "Inauguración 'YA VUELVO. Carlos Pizarro, una vida por la paz'," by America Catalunya, a video in carlospizarro.org, 2009.
3 María José Pizarro and Catalina Ruíz (Curators), *Hacer la paz en Colombia, "Ya vuelvo", Carlos Pizarro. Documentación Exposición* (Bogotá-Catalunya: Museo Nacional de Colombia, Casa América Catalunya, Fundación Carlos Pizarro, Ministerio de Cultura de Colombia, 200 Culturaes Independencia Bicentenario de las Independencias 1810–2010, 2011).
4 María Victoria de Angulo de Robayo, director of the National Museum of Colombia (2005–2014), Interview by Jimena Perry, Bogotá, February 12, 2017.

5 Sharon MacDonald, *Difficult Heritage. Negotiating the Nazi Past in Nuremberg and Beyond* (New York: Routledge, 2009), 2.
6 Bourdieu, *Distinction*, 7.
7 "Hacer la paz en Colombia: *Ya vuelvo,* Carlos Pizarro," Museo Nacional de Colombia, http://www.museonacional.gov.co/exposiciones/pasadas/Paginas/HacerlapazenColombia13.aspx.
8 "El Museo Nacional se prepara para renovación de sus guiones," http://www.museonacional.gov.co/el-museo/Paginas/planes2.aspx. Daniel Castro, director of the National Museum of Colombia, Interview by Jimena Perry, Bogotá, August 8, 2017.
9 Olga Lucía Martínez Ante, "El Museo Nacional abre tres nuevas salas de exposición," *El Tiempo*, April 14, 2019, https://www.eltiempo.com/cultura/arte-y-teatro/museo-nacional-de-colombia-abre-nuevas-salas-de-exposicion-349272
10 Francisco Romano, Chief Archaeology Curator, National Museum of Colombia, interview by Jimena Perry, Bogotá—Colombia, June 4, 2020.
11 "Renovación, historia y virtualidad en la agenda del Museo Nacional," *El Nuevo Siglo*, April 4, 2022, https://www.elnuevosiglo.com.co/articulos/02-26-2021-renovacion-historia-y-virtualidad-en-la-agenda-del-museo-nacional
12 "La pandemia cambió la forma cómo nos relacionamos con el arte: Directora del Museo Nacional". Interview. *Semana*, July 18, 2021, https://www.semana.com/mejor-colombia/articulo/cuando-veo-entrar-a-un-nino-al-museo-nacional-pienso-que-no-va-a-ser-el-mismo-al-salir-juliana-restrepo/202100/
13 Elvira Cuervo de Jaramillo, "¿Qué mostramos, ¿qué escondemos?," *El Espectador*, March 1, 2001, National Museum of Colombia Archive.
14 Casa América Catalunya, "María José Pizarro abre en el Museo Nacional de Colombia la exposición sobre su padre muerto," December 22, 2010, http://americat.barcelona/es/septiembre-21-maria-jose-pizarro-abre-en-el-museo-nacional-de-colombia- la-exposicion-sobre-su-padre-muerto.
15 Pilar Lozano, "El exguerrillero Carlos Pizarro ametrallado en un avión en vuelo," *El País*, April 27, 1990, http://elpais.com/diario/1990/04/27/internacional/641167201_850215.html.
16 Juan Antonio Pizarro, *Carlos Pizarro* (Bogotá: Círculo de Lectores, 1992), 11.
17 Rosemberg Pabón, *Así nos tomamos la embajada* (Bogotá: Editorial Planeta, 1984), 16.
18 Andrés Grillo, "November 6 de 1985. La herida abierta," *Semana*, May 30, 2004, National Museum of Colombia Archive.
19 Jorge Aníbal Gómez Gallego, José Roberto Herrera Vergara, and Nilson Pinilla Pinilla, *Informe final: Comisión de la verdad sobre los hechos del Palacio de Justicia* (Bogotá: Universidad del Rosario, Fundación Hanns Seidel, Comisión de la verdad Palacio de Justicia, 2010), 20.
20 Enrique. Parejo González, *La Tragedia del Palacio de Justicia. Cúmulo de errores y abusos* (Bogotá: Editorial Oveja Negra, 2010), 14.
21 Diana Carolina Durán Núñez, "Los muertos equivocados del Palacio de Justicia," *El Espectador*, July 25, 2015, https://www.elespectador.com/noticias/investigacion/los-muertos-equivocados-del-palacio-de- justicia-articulo-574961.
22 Anna Nicolás Marín, "Desaparecidos del Palacio de Justicia: una búsqueda de varias generaciones," *El Espectador*, November 5, 2017, https://www.elespectador.com/colombia2020/justicia/verdad/desaparecidos-del-palacio-de-justicia-una- busqueda-de-varias-generaciones-articulo-855986.
23 Anna Carrigan, *El Palacio de Justicia. Una tragedia colombiana* (Bogotá: Editorial Ícono, 2009).
24 "'El peor error de la historia del M-19': Antonio Navarro, exdirigente de esa guerrilla, da su mirada sobre los hechos del Palacio de Justicia," *El Tiempo*, October 31, 2015, http://www.eltiempo.com/archivo/documento/CMS-16417823.

25 Laura Gallo Tapias, *Recuerdos de un sobreviviente del Palacio* (Crónica Política y Sociedad. Bogotá: Uniandes, 2012), https://cerosetenta.uniandes.edu.co/recuerdos-de-un-sobreviviente-del-palacio/.

26 "El legado de Carlos Pizarro Leongómez," *El Tiempo*, September 14, 2010, http://www.eltiempo.com/archivo/documento/MAM-4141014.

27 Roberto Romero Ospina, *Unión Patriótica. Expedientes contra el olvido* (Bogotá: Centro de Memoria, Paz y Reconciliación, Agència Catalana de Cooperació al Desenvolupament, Alcaldía Mayor de Bogotá, Bogotá Humana, 2012), 140.

28 Darío Villamizar Herrera, *Las guerrillas en Colombia: Una historia desde los orígenes hasta los confines* (Bogotá: Penguin Random House Grupo Editorial Colombia, Kindle Edition Locations): 9340–9341.

29 "La exposición 'Ya vuelvo' recompone la figura del asesinado líder del M-19," *El Mundo,* September 14, 2010, http://www.elmundo.es/america/2010/09/10/colombia/1284138292.html.

30 Casa América Catalunya, "Más de 50.000 personas visitan en el Museo Nacional de Bogotá la muestra 'Hacer la paz en Colombia. Ya vuelvo. Carlos Pizarro,'" April 8, 2010, http://americat.barcelona/es/mas-de-50-000-personas-visitan-en-el-museo-nacional-de-bogota-la-muestra-hacer-la-paz-en-colombia-ya-vuelvo-carlos-pizarro.

31 El Heraldo, "Más De 40 Casos Emblemáticos, Elevados a Crimen De Lesa Humanidad," EL HERALDO, accessed July 26, 2022, https://www.elheraldo.co/colombia/mas-de-40-casos-emblematicos-elevados-crimen-de-lesa-humanidad-617164.

32 María José Pizarro, curator of the exhibition "Ya vuelvo." Interview *La Silla Vacía*, September 16, 2010.

33 https://www.eltiempo.com/cultura/arte-y-teatro/museo-nacional-de-colombia-abre-nuevas-salas-de-exposicion-349272

34 El Tiempo. "El Museo Nacional expone objetos de Luis C. Galán." August 13, 2009. Museo Nacional Archive.

35 El Espectador. "Exposición Galán vive." August 10, 2009. Museo Nacional Archive.

36 Robinson, Eugene, "Colombia Buries Slain Candidate," *The Washington Post*, August 21, 1989; Robinson, Eugene, "Colombian Candidate Murdered," *The Washington Post*, August 20, 1989; Los Angeles Times, "Colombia Presidential Candidate Assassinated: Extradition Treaty with U.S. Reinstituted in Effort to Combat Drug-Related Killings," August 19, 1989; The New York Times, "Colombian Presidential Candidate is Slain at Rally," 1989.

37 Semana, "El Nuevo Liberalismo," March 20, 2005. Accessed, June 13, 2018, https://www.semana.com/enfoque/articulo/el-nuevo-liberalismo/71546-3

38 Surgimiento del Nuevo Liberalismo, Accessed June 14, 2018, http://luiscarlosgalan2.blogspot.com/p/surgimeintos-del-nuevo.html

39 Alonso Salazar, *Profeta en el desierto. Vida y muerte de Luis Carlos Galán* (Bogotá: Editorial Planeta, 2003), 71.

40 Corbett, Craig, "Profiles. Luis Carlos Galán." Colombia Reports. April 1, 2017, Accessed June 14, 2018, https://colombiareports.com/luis-carlos-galan/

41 El Tiempo, "En el Tolima se planeó crimen de Galán: Testigo," August 15, 1991, Accessed, June 14, 2018, http://www.eltiempo.com/archivo/documento/MAM-137342

42 *El Tiempo*, "Galán en 10 frases," August 16, 2014, Accessed June 14, 2018.

43 Booke, James, "Drug Traffickers in Colombia Start a Counterattack," *The New York Times*, Archives, 1989, Accessed, June 14, 2018, https://www.nytimes.com/1989/08/25/world/drug-traffickers-in-colombia-start-a-counterattack.html

44 Corbett, Craig, "Profiles. Luis Carlos Galán," Colombia Reports, April 1, 2017, Accessed June 14, 2018, https://colombiareports.com/luis-carlos-galan/

45 El Tiempo, "Las pruebas contra los dos nuevos capturados del caso Galán," March, 11, 2013, Accessed, June 14, 2018, http://www.eltiempo.com/archivo/documento/CMS-12674660
46 Kienyke, "Luis Carlos Galán y su lucha contra Escobar," August 18, 2017, Accessed June 14, 2018, https://www.kienyke.com/kien-fue/galan-el-martir-de-pablo-escobar
47 Alonso, *Profeta en el desierto. Vida y muerte de Luis Carlos Galán* (Bogotá: Editorial Planeta, 2003).
48 Lozano, Pilar, "Atentado político en Colombia. Muerto a tiros el líder de la izquierda Bernardo Jaramillo. La esposa de Jaramillo le protegió con su cuerpo," *El País*, March 23, 1990, Accessed June 15, 2018, https://elpais.com/diario/1990/03/23/internacional/638146801_850215.html.
49 https://www.elespectador.com/judicial/la-memoria-intacta-de-un-lider-de-paz-y-justicia-article-194153/
50 http://centromemoria.gov.co/bernardo-jaramillo-ossa/
51 "Juez que condenó a Plazas Vega presentará una tutela para pedir protección," *El Universal*, December 16, 2015, http://www.eluniversal.com.co/colombia/juez-que-condeno-plazas-vega-presentara-una-tutela-para-pedir-
52 The Center for Justice and Accountability, *Colombia: The Justice and Peace Law*, https://cja.org/where-we-work/colombia/related-resources/colombia-the-justice-and- peace-law/.
53 Human Rights Watch, *World Report 2011: Colombia. Events of 2010*, https://www.hrw.org/world- report/2011/country-chapters/colombia.
54 Catalina Ruiz, Interview by Jimena Perry.
55 Silke Arnold de Simine, "Memory Museum and Museum Text: Intermediality in Daniel Libeskind's Jewish Museum and W.G. Sebald's *Austerlitz*," *Theory, Culture & Society*, (SAGE: Los Angeles, London, New Delhi, and Singapore, 29, no. 1, (2012).
56 Michael Brennan, "Why Materiality on Mourning Matters," (*The Materiality of Mourning. Cross- Disciplinary Perspectives*, eds. Zahra Newsby and Ruth E. Touson (Routledge: Abingdon and New York, 2019), 222–243.
57 "El sombrero pieza de museo," *El Tiempo*, April 25, 2010, National Museum of Colombia Archive.
58 Mateo Malahora, "Del sombrero caribeño al sombrero de la paz," *El Nuevo Liberal*, April 22, 2016, http://elnuevoliberal.com/del-sombrero-caribeno-al-sombrero-de-la-paz/.
59 Humberto Diez, "Asaltan Quinta de Bolívar y el Concejo," *El Tiempo*, January 18, 1974, https://news.google.com/newspapers?nid=N2osnxbUuuUC&dat=19740118&printsec=frontpage&hl=en.
60 "Después de 16 años el M-19 deja hoy las armas," *El Tiempo*, March 8, 1990, https://news.google.com/newspapers?nid=N2osnxbUuuUC&dat=19900308&printsec=-frontpage&hl=en.
61 Pizarro, *Carlos Pizarro. De su puño y letra*.
62 Entrevista: "Cuando la guerra pasa por la vida de uno arrasa con todo," *Siete Digital. Periodismo regional*, August 27, 2015, https://sietedigital.wordpress.com/2015/08/27/entrevista-cuando-la-guerra-pasa-por-la-vida-de-uno- arrasa-con-todo/
63 Adriana Patricia Giraldo Duarte, "'Las víctimas son la reserva moral y ética de la sociedad': María José Pizarro," *El Espectador*, November 10, 2016, https://www.elespectador.com/noticias/cultura/victimas-son-reserva-moral-y-etica-de-sociedad-articulo- 664808.
64 Pizarro, *Carlos Pizarro. De su puño y letra*, 66–71.
65 Casa América Catalunya, "María José Pizarro abre en el Museo Nacional de Colombia la exposición sobre su padre muerto."
66 Silke Arnold de Simine, *Mediating Memory in the Museum. Trauma, Empathy, Nostalgia* (London: Palgrave MacMillan, 2013), 44.

67 Virginia Garrard-Burnett, *Terror in the Land of the Holy Spirit: Guatemala under General Efraín Ríos Montt 1982–1983* (New York: Oxford University Press, 2010).
68 Arnold de Simine, *Mediating Memory,* 40–41.
69 Dominick LaCapra, *Representing the Holocaust* (Ithaca, NY and London: Cornell University Press, 1994), 194–195.
70 Casa América Catalunya, "Más de 50.000 personas visitan en el Museo Nacional de Bogotá la muestra 'Hacer la paz en Colombia. Ya vuelvo. Carlos Pizarro,'" April 8, 2010, http://americat.barcelona/es/mas-de-50-000-personas-visitan-en-el-museo-nacional-de-bogota-la-muestra-hacer-la-paz-en-colombia-ya-vuelvo-carlos-pizarro.
71 Jay Winter, "The Memory Boom in Contemporary Historical Studies," *Raritan* 21 (2001): 52–66.
72 Arnold de Simine, *Mediating Memory.*
73 "Juan Manuel Santos wins Colombia presidential election," *The Guardian*, June 21, 2010, https://www.theguardian.com/world/2010/jun/21/juan-manuel-santos-colombia-president.

# 3
# MEMORY, HEALING, AND JUSTICE
## The Hall of Never Again, Granada, Antioquia

In 2005, when the Colombian Congress issued the Justice and Law 975, under the second mandate of Álvaro Uribe Vélez, many Colombians believed they might have a respite from violence. In this context, the inhabitants of Granada, Antioquia Department, in Colombia's central northwestern region, created the Asociación de Víctimas de Granada, Asovida (Association of Victims of Granada), heartened by the mentioned law. The Association aimed to encourage survivors of the armed conflict, which started in 1980, to remember the atrocities they endured, help them heal, and aspire to a future free of violence. It also strove to help the survivors of violence to return to their territory, following forced displacement by insurgent armed groups; to aid in the community's rehabilitation; and to encourage individual grieving processes and memory sites.

Four years later, in 2009, the members of Asovida founded the Salón del Nunca Más (Hall of Never Again). Its purpose is to raise awareness about the brutalities endured by the inhabitants of Granada, compile histories of the municipality, and record historical memories of the conflict. Its founders included Gloria Elcy Ramírez, President of Asovida and victim of forced displacement; Gloria Elcy Quintero, Vice President of Asovida, who suffered her brother's disappearance by paramilitaries in 2001; and Jaime Montoya, Treasurer of Asovida and a survivor of forced displacement as well.

In the Hall, visitors find heart-rending stories, like this one found in Bitácora No. 3 at the Archive of the Hall of Never Again, dated August 28, 2010:

> Dear brother, you cannot imagine how sad we feel to not know anything about you. We do not know if you are alive or not. I refuse to believe that you are not alive, you are always in my heart and my soul, and in my thoughts too. I have not forgotten about you for a minute, I always

DOI: 10.4324/9781003283997-4

dream you are alive. When I heard the news of your disappearance, I did not want to believe it, something inside me tells me you are still in this world, if this is so, we only need a signal. Your sons have looked for you constantly without success. Each one of them has their own family: Harvey has two beautiful girls of which you met one. Daniel has a daughter called Daniela. Isaías has a boy called Santiago. I pray to God that you are alive and come back, if not I wish your soul rests in peace. I love you very much. Your sister.

This testimony is only one of the hundreds put in writing at the Hall of Never Again. It is in a *bitácora,* an intimate and personal journal where relatives and friends of the victims of the country's war express their sadness due to the absence of their loved ones. The *bitácoras* are notebooks that complement the permanent exhibition of the venue and have become memory records, devices which help in the community healing process. Through them, the people of Granada have found some solace and a way to communicate with their departed relatives and friends. On the other hand, the Hall's main exhibition is a wall covered with approximately 200 photographs of some of the 3,000 or more people murdered by armed groups in Granada since the 1980s.[1] The wall is a public register of those who lost their lives due to violence.

The Hall of Never Again is one of the 33 Colombian memory sites registered in the Red Colombiana de Lugares de Memoria (Colombian Network of Memory Sites) created in 2015. The participants of the IX Encuentro Regional de la Red de Sitios de Memoria y Reconciliación Latinoamericanos, RESLAC (IX Regional Meeting of the Latin American Network for Memory and Reconciliation Sites), which took place in Bogotá, created this network during the same year. The Colombian Network's main goal is to articulate and protect memory initiatives to strengthen the country's democracy and promote cultural diversity and human rights. The members of the Network also work to achieve a recognition of memory in Colombia's public policies. They strive to help grassroots projects, such as the Hall of Never Again, to consolidate their work over the previous ten years or more and to guarantee participation, autonomy, sustainability, and security for memory production.[2]

This chapter, the third case study of four, has a two-fold objective. First, I examine the nature of the Hall since its creators and Granada inhabitants do not consider it a museum. Second, I explore how the exhibitions found at this memory site shed light on the relationship between memory and transitional justice in Colombia. Due to the outspokenness of the members of Granada's community in memorializing, representing, and displaying the atrocities they endured, I argue that the foundation of a conventional museum would not have served as well their purpose of grieving and healing. Granada's memory site allowed this social group to make their voices count politically, besides validating their collective and personal histories.[3] In addition, I claim that state agents must consider the contents of the Hall in their policies of transitional justice. By the latter term, I mean the "set of processes and mechanisms, including accountability, justice, and reparations, operationalized by those seeking to come to terms with the multiple legacies of large-scale past abuses and to ensure nonrecurrence."[4]

To discuss why the Granada inhabitants do not wish to consider the Hall a museum, I delve into its character, exhibitions, history, description, objectives, and cultural context. For this, I follow the discussion by philosopher Hilde Hein in her book *The Museum in Transition: A Philosophical Perspective*. Hein analyzes how museums have changed in the last two decades, adapting to new ideas, technologies, epistemologies, generational changes, and newly warranted museum objects.[5] Another important work is *The New Museology* (1989), edited by art historian Peter Vergo, in which the new museology field questioned the "old" methods of assigning meaning to artifacts and stories, which generally overlooked why exhibitions were produced and in what context. Other publications worth mentioning are two essay collections of the Smithsonian Institution: *Exhibiting Cultures: The Poetics and Politics of Museum Display*, 1991, and *Museums and Communities: The Politics of Public Culture*, 1992, which analyze in detail how the relationships between museum professionals and communities need to work, ethics of display, and how the participation and collaboration of the people cannot be ignored. Other contributions are *Different Voices: A Social, Cultural, and Historical Framework for Change in the American Art Museum*, 1992; the United Kingdom Entitled *New Research in Museum Studies*, Vol. 1, (1990); and *The Epistemic Museum* by David Chapin and Stephen Klein in the summer of 1992. Besides, seminal pieces in the new museology field are James Clifford's *Routes: Travel and Translation in the Late Twentieth Century*, 1997, in which he discusses museums as contact zones; and the already mentioned *The Museum in Transition*, 2000, by Hilde S. Hein, where the author talks about how contemporary museum professionals are not centered anymore in displaying objects but narratives, sometimes marginal, which is one of the objectives of the new museology.

Inspired by Klein and Vergo, I extend this discussion to the Hall. Through this grassroots example—which is an exhibition space, has a script that tells a story, has glass cases, and other features of conventional museums—I explore why the Granada community does not perceive the Hall as a museum. In fact, their exhibitions are non-artifact, but story centered, following the principles of Hein and the new museology. The decision of the Hall's creators to focus more on histories than material pieces illuminates how conventional museums often fall short in their diversity and inclusivity endeavors.

In this chapter, I also argue that the people of Granada, through the Hall of Never Again, made the cultural choice to recall brutalities in two ways: one that relieves them in their individual and intimate grieving processes, found in the *bitácoras*; and another, collective and public, which aids in Granada's social fabric restoration, seen in the permanent exhibit of the Hall.[6] For this, I build on sociologist Maurice Halbwachs' characterization of autobiographical and historical memory, which are interrelated. The first one accounts for individual remembrances that refer to people's personal lives and that make them feel unique despite being part of a group. The second denotes collective matters in which each society member's memories serve the community's interests. In addition, I concur with Professor Andrew Rajca and the attention he devotes to the overuse of "Never More" (Nunca Más). He questions the romanticized narratives of the slogan due to the disconnection perceived between words and the continued use of violence against local and marginalized populations "who do not count as subjects of human rights."[7] Rajca analyzes the convergences between memory and human rights in three sites: the Memorial da Resistência (Resistance Memorial, MDR) in São Paulo, Brazil; the Centro Cultural y Museo de la Memoria (Cultural Center and Museum of Memory, MUME) in Montevideo, Uruguay; and the Espacio para la Memoria y la Promoción y Defensa de los Derechos Humanos (Space for Memory and the Promotion and Defense of Human Rights, EMPD DHH or Espacio Memoria) in Buenos Aires, Argentina. Resorting to art and its relationship to politics, the author discusses how the artistic interventions in these memorials overturn what is visible and who should be the legitimate subjects of memory and rights in post-dictatorship contexts. Building on philosopher Jacques Rancière's concept of dissensus, which "is not a conflict of interests, opinions, or values; but a division inserted in 'common sense': a dispute over what is given and about the frame within which we see something as given,"[8]:Rajca goes beyond established and official narratives about human rights and memories to examine how problematic it is to take them for granted. Employing the slogan "Never Again" frequently utilized by associations of victims and survivors of atrocities to state that violent pasts should not repeat themselves, the author of *Dissensual Subjects* illustrates how these words are not necessarily what cause disagreements but their different meanings, which are generally subjective and politically charged. I believe this applies to the Colombian Hall. For this community initiative, "Never More" has a special meaning. For the Granada inhabitants, the slogan significance goes beyond the purpose of non-repetition. It additionally implies building empathy with those who did not directly endure violence, teaching new generations their traumatic past, and forging cultural traditions which would allow them to envision a better future. Although I agree with Rajca's assertion that the indiscriminate use of "Never More" has caused it to lose some of its strength in contexts such as the post-dictatorial ones he studies, for the social groups which the Colombian Hall serves, the slogan has inspired their work.

Drawing on the content of the approximately 200 *bitácoras* found at the Hall, interviews and oral histories, exhibitions, documents of the National Center for Historical Memory Archive, photographs, newspapers, and magazines,

I suggest that the two interrelated levels of memories promoted at the Hall—autobiographical and collective—are examples of the kind of local knowledge and input that Colombian transitional justice needs in order to guarantee a fuller reconciliation, recourse for justice, and prevention of future atrocities. After periods of extreme violence in other Latin American countries, such as Argentina, Guatemala, Chile, Bolivia, Uruguay, El Salvador, and Peru, projects of transitional justice helped to reestablish democracy. Regular legal procedures or ordinary judicial mechanisms seem not to be enough to process what happened after an extended time of traumatic events.[9] Thus, it is necessary to go through a provisional stage to provide societies with answers, create strategies to prevent violence from recurring, make perpetrators accountable, and find ways to compensate the survivors. So, Transitional Justice is much more than a truth quest. It is a legal and state endeavor to recognize and acknowledge the survivor's voice and suffering. In Colombia, the first attempt to create a project of transitional justice in 2005 did not thrive, as explored later in the chapter.

In the words of Gloria Ramírez, President of Asovida and founder of the Hall, "[this is a] place set up for our reparation, not the state one, but our own."[10] I explore her statement by paying attention to what scholar Francesca Lessa has called memory narratives, which are stories that change, evolve, and represent the different ways in which people remember contested pasts.[11] In Granada's case, the Hall encouraged the survivors of violence to activate certain histories with the political purpose of using them to justify the adoption of transitional justice policies. The main exhibition of the Hall, the wall covered in pictures, is meant to help in this process and to prevent Granada's inhabitants from forgetting. The members of Asovida, as the founders of the Hall, believe that to omit or disregard their traumatic past will not lead to healing.

On the other hand, the content of the *bitácoras* provides useful information about the individual grieving processes of the Granada population. Like Halbwachs and Jelin, Lessa insists that individual memories are not isolated; they come into existence through "the shared narrative act" of recounting and listening.[12] Thus, elements and mechanisms of transitional justice are memory conduits and political projects directly related to the production of historical memories.

## "Museums are for the dead": The Hall of Never Again's Challenge

Since the twentieth century, the attempts to provide a definition of what is a museum have not ceased. During the 1950s, international debates centered on assigning meanings to the institution and it became the focus of normative museology in organizations such as the International Council of Museums (ICOM). Since the post-war period, when UNESCO and ICOM were created, the role of museums for the development of societies and their reconnection with nation-states was stressed and reiterated in international recommendations and rules that secured the long-term existence of these modern institutions. In Latin America, we can trace these debates to 1972 when the Roundtable of Santiago de Chile took place.[13] Concurring with museologist and anthropologist Bruno Brulon, during this event, now considered a landmark in redefining and re-evaluating museums in the region, museum professionals discussed the term decolonizing for the first time, for example, and stated how problematic it is to attempt limited definitions. In Chile's meeting, Latin American researchers promoted thinking about community-driven museums and self-determined with some level of state mediation with experts' support. This statement triggered conversations about immaterial heritage, object-centered museums, and the romanticization of the community, which paved the way for the 1970s and 1980s' ongoing approaches to museums.[14] This trend is very popular in Brazil, Mexico, and Cuba, and recently in countries such as Colombia, which did not participate in Chile's Roundtable. Drawing from premises from the new museology[15] and its pledge to break the European universal narrative of progress and civilization, social museum narratives went beyond the old/new binary and questioned methods of assigning meaning to objects and stories, which generally overlooked why exhibitions were produced and in what context. As posed by Brulon, nowadays, it is impossible to overlook the museum's political role and its long history of promoting inequalities and tensions created between objects and people.[16]

Until 2019, the ICOM defined a museum as: "A non-profit, permanent institution in the service of society and its development, open to the public, which acquires, conserves, researches, communicates, and exhibits the tangible and intangible heritage of humanity and its environment for education, study, and enjoyment."[17] However, in September of the same year, the ICOM held a meeting in Tokyo in which the Executive Board revised the above definition and realized that museums must keep up with current times. Therefore, they came up with the following alternative characterization:

> Museums are democratizing, inclusive and polyphonic spaces for critical dialogue about the pasts and the futures. Acknowledging and addressing the conflicts and challenges of the present, they hold artifacts and specimens in trust for society, safeguard diverse memories for future generations and guarantee equal rights and equal access to heritage for all people. Museums are not for profit. They are participatory and transparent, and work in active partnership with and for diverse communities to collect, preserve, research, interpret, exhibit, and enhance understandings of the world, aiming to contribute to human dignity and social justice, global equality, and planetary wellbeing.

This alternative approach to museums reflects ICOM's interest to update and discuss preconceived notions of these institutions, as well as the significant role they play in societies that use them as devices to aid in reconciliation and reparation processes. This definition also jibes with the concerns expressed by the creators of the Hall, who identify with the principles of the new museology. However, it is still begging for approval since in some ICOM branches, its members thought that the omission of the words education and collection, for instance, still needed to be part of the definition.[18] From August 20 to 28, the ICOM held its 26th General Conference in Prague and apparently reached an agreement on the question of what a museum is. The new approach states:

> A museum is a not-for-profit, permanent institution in the service of society that researches, collects, conserves, interprets and exhibits tangible and intangible heritage. Open to the public, accessible and inclusive, museums foster diversity and sustainability. They operate and communicate ethically, professionally and with the participation of communities, offering varied experiences for education, enjoyment, reflection and knowledge sharing.[19]

However, during the first decades of the twenty-first century, museums have taken many turns and are being highly influenced by social movements, decolonization statements, and participation of historically underrepresented groups such as indigenous populations, racial minorities, LGBTQI+ associations, and other people in the periphery of nation-states and neoliberal markets, as stated by museologist Bruno Brulon.

During the 1970s and 1980s, the demand for local museums encouraged the French movement of new museology, partially based on the ideas of the "ecomuseum," a community-based initiative devoted to promoting development in regional cultures.[20] Nevertheless, the new museology's ideas go back to the 1930s, when theorists such as T.R. Adams stated that museums have, or need to have, a relationship with social justice. Adams also argued that these institutions must play a significant role in the struggle to maintain and encourage social freedom.[21] This advanced the discussion about the social and political roles of museums, encouraging new communication and new styles of expression in contrast to classic, collections-centered museum models.[22] Librarian and curator Deirdre Stam, however, claims that despite the possible continuities in the narrative of the 1930s and 1990s, few new museologists are aware of the history of the discipline and assume that it started during the 1980s and 1990s. She also states that historical theory is the foundation for the new museology's principles.[23] Stam shows how the Annales school of historians in 1950 and beyond devoted their attention to material culture, everyday life, and political and economic interpretations of objects. During the 1970s and 1980s, the approach of historians such as Thomas J. Schlereth, in *Artifacts and the American Past*, provided insights on how to use objects as historical sources.[24] Many other historians have influenced the development of the new museology, such as Fernand Braudel, Philippe Ariès, Emmanuel Le Roy Ladurie, E. A. Wrigley, Keith V. Thomas, and Peter Gay.

The new museology addresses issues such as value, meaning, control, interpretation, authority, and authenticity in museums; this field's focus also includes redistribution of curatorial power and challenges the relationship between venues and the represented communities. The nature of this change calls for more interaction between diverse marginal groups and museum professionals; therefore, it includes more visibility of "regular" people and the venue's audiences. This shift has also incorporated terms like "cultural empowerment," "social re-definition," "dialogue," and "emotion" into the museum narratives to make the institution more participatory and appreciative of people's lives, which in turn comes with an awareness of social accountability and responsibility in the museum.[25] But only in 1989, with the publication of The New Museology, edited by Peter Vergo, was an academic field consolidated. In this compilation, the author addressed the discipline's methodological and theoretical challenges. Vergo asserts that conventional museum studies focused too much on the methods and too little on the venues' purposes.[26] By claiming this, he implied that one limitation of the "old" museology is to assign preconceived questions about how people produce exhibitions and in what context. Vergo's concerns sparked an extensive discussion and critique of the knowledge and authority conveyed by conventional museums. Along these lines, museum scholar Edwina Taborski views the meanings of artifacts displayed as arbitrarily assigned, therefore, part of a social narrative that allows for interpretation.[27] In this context, new museologists focus on how museum professionals present stories that represent members of the public—narratives with which the public can identify. The new museology informs the novel approach used by ICOM in 2019, which emphasizes access and interpretation for all kinds of museum audiences.

Even though it is possible to trace some of new museology's principles at the Hall of Never Again, its creators assert that their space should not be thought of as a museum. This insistence reflects their conviction that museums are static places for antiquities and dead animals, institutions that have nothing to do with life, while the Hall is devoted to life.[28] The founders of the Hall also believe that the stationary character of conventional museums imposes limitations on what people want to represent. For instance, on account of the community's ingrained Catholicism, a non-museum-like site was more appropriate to display their personal religious narratives, such as the following found in the following *bitácoras*:

*Bitácora 5.*
[...] Your disappearance caught us by surprise. We still do not believe that you had left without a trace, like the wind. Who wanted to forbid you from being among your loved ones? But in God we trust that soon

we will hear from you. Please, God, help us find out what happened so we can end this suffering.
*Bitácora 7.*
Dear son, we miss you so much. Your mom and brothers always remember you. I must tell you that your father died because of your absence. I pray to God to have you in his glory if you are dead [...].
*Bitácora 9.*
[...] Thanks, father, for helping me achieve my dreams from where you are. I hope you are enjoying Heaven besides God and the Virgin [...].

In the *bitácoras*, survivors also ask for divine protection from the dead:

*Bitácora 17.*
Hello mom, I know that from Heaven you are watching over me and that is why I want to ask you to shield me against bad friendships. Since you are gone my heart is broken [...].
*Bitácora 155.*
[...] I am sure you are in God's company. Today I pray to the same God to protect your home and children.
*Bitácora 146.*
[...] Blessings. You are an angel from Heaven protecting your family in earth. God sent us sadness but also resignation.

The almost ever-present references to God and religion found in the *bitácoras* and other artifacts of the Hall would not have had the same presence and significance in a secular institution like the National Museum of Colombia, for example. The Granada inhabitants feel that the Hall they have provides enough freedom to display what they need and want (Figure 3.1).

In addition, the liberty felt by the Hall creators allows them to include in the main exhibitions' images and objects that, as mentioned in former chapters, would belong to the realm of "kitsch" or popular culture. Artifacts that high culture considers tasteless, following Pierre Bourdieu, do not carry enough cultural capital to belong in a museum but belong at the Hall, like the Virgin of the image.[29] Therefore, the founders of the Granada Hall do not want the restrictions imposed by a high-culture institution that does not serve them well. In concurrence with Stuart Hall, "[...] popular work helps the serious artist to focus the actual world, to draw upon common types, to sharpen his observation and to detect the large but hidden movements of society."[30] This means that the Granada inhabitants' popular expressions find a place at the Hall without any objection. In this context, the founders of the Hall challenge conventional museum exhibitions and find answers and solace in their own representations of their violent past.

**114** Memory, Healing, and Justice

**FIGURE 3.1** This image is a view of the wall that displays the approximate 200 victims of the recent armed conflict in Granada, Antioquia. Picture by Jimena Perry, 2017.

In addition, distancing the Hall from conservative conceptions of museums as static or embalmed, Gloria Quintero, Vice President of Asovida, one of the founders and guides of the Hall, notes:

> The community made the difference. The Natural Science site, for example, is a museum, the Hall is not. The Granada inhabitants do not want to call the Hall a museum. For them, a museum is where things go to die, and the Hall celebrates life. The Hall is about life.[31]

The apparent contradiction of talking about life while displaying death clears away when we understand what the people of Granada mean. They think of the Hall as the place in which they can revisit their past to let it go and transform it into hope for the future. In this sense, it is a space devoted to life. Museums are not for this community; these institutions do not allow any interpretation of the past. Thus, the organizers faced the challenges to define the venue, its functions, actions, and name. The creators of Granada's memory site need and want the validation that a museum provides, but not the actual label of "museum."

Granada's only museum, in this context, is the one devoted to Natural History, which opened to the public on November 10, 2016. Managed and directed by Carlos Abel Aristizábal, the permanent exhibition of the institution contains dissected animals, species of the region, and others from the coast. This place is designed for school children's field trips, for recreation, and to learn more about Granada's natural history.[32] It is a place for preserved specimens, and that is why the creators of the Hall and many members of the community believe that "museums are for the dead."[33]

Although both the Hall and the Museum of Natural History represent Granada's history, the former is thought of as a place in which there is no room to interpret the past because its items (dissected animals) are viewed more as objects than artifacts, following Johannes Fabian distinction mentioned in Chapter 1. Artifacts belong to culture; therefore, they are part of a narrative that privileges the history of their production. In the case of Granada's Natural History Museum, its objects belong to nature.[34] Besides, the Hall of Never Again is a space to grieve. The goal of the founders of the Hall is to exhibit Granada's violent past and to avoid rigid and fixed understandings of the brutalities inflicted upon the region's inhabitants.

Sometimes, though, for funding and financial reasons, the creators of the Hall of Never Again make it pose as a museum. The main characteristics of the space also can encourage an outside visitor to think of it as a museum: It is nonprofit; its creators wish to establish it as a permanent institution at the service of society and its development; it is open to the public; and its members acquire, conserve, research, communicate, and exhibit the tangible and intangible heritage of the region for education and study. However, in concordance with the new museology's ideas, the Hall is more socially oriented, "instilling confidence in a society's potential for development."[35] The challenge at Granada's site is to give the visitors the sense of a living past, one that is present and needs to be known to prevent its recurrence. Nevertheless, the Hall's creators and the members of the community want to differentiate the venue from a museum, continuously making the efforts to turn this site into a critical historical space for mourning, criticism, and reflection.

The Hall of Never Again is a community's response to the legal impunity and state silence that has surrounded the atrocities that the inhabitants of Granada endured. Its funding does not come from the Colombian government, and due to its scarce resources, it only opens on the weekends or when someone calls Gloria Quintero or Gloria Ramírez, President and Vice President of Asovida, respectively, and asks for a guided tour. The Hall has received financial assistance from international agencies such as the Agencia Española de Cooperación Internacional para el Desarrollo (Spanish International Cooperation Agency for Development), and it has won national peace prizes such as the

Special Category Award of the Orlando López Prize in 2010. The fact that the Colombian government does not fund this Hall, despite several requests from its creators, shows the state's indifference toward small towns and municipalities that are far from the center of power and do not carry significant economic or political weight in the country.

## Memory and the Hall of Never Again

During the mid-1980s, concurrent with the proliferation of memory studies outside and inside Latin America, the academic memory field gained strength and facilitated reflections about how societies that have endured brutalities come to terms with their violent pasts.[36] In Europe and North America, for example, contemporary memory studies began with the works of historians Yosef Yerushalmi, *Zakhor: Jewish History and Jewish Memory* (1982), and Pierre Nora's anthology, *Lieux de Mémoire* (1984). In these texts, the authors approach memory as a collective endeavor when remembering major significant traumatic events such as the Holocaust and the industrialization that replaced peasant culture in France.[37]

During the 1980s, the influence of these seminal books helped Latin American scholars such as cultural critics Idelber Avelar, Nelly Richard, Alberto Moreiras, and Beatriz Sarlo comprehend the dictatorships of the Southern Cone.[38] In Colombia, for instance, the proliferation of grassroots, academic, and artistic memory endeavors was particularly extensive. The publication of historian Gonzalo Sánchez's book, *Guerras, memoria e historia,* in 2003, was one of the first academic reflections about memory studies in Colombia. In this work, Sánchez argues that the effect of repeated attempts to reach peace in the country has been felt by Colombians as an imposition to forget, which is precisely what the creators of the Hall do not want to do.

Another milestone for the Colombian memory field was the mentioned above Justice and Peace Law of July 2005. President Álvaro Uribe's efforts to exonerate the paramilitaries for responsibility in human rights violations and mass forced displacement in the country, and blame the guerrillas for the armed conflict, paved the way for an official, but biased acknowledgment of the internal war and led to the creation of the Comisión Nacional de Reparación y Reconciliación (National Commission for Reparation and Reconciliation) and the Grupo de Memoria Histórica (Historical Memory Group). The main goals of these institutions were to reconstruct historical accounts of the country's internal violence.[39] However, during Uribe's mandate, memory production was biased and mainly focused on negating the country's armed conflict. One of the president's most renowned consultants, José Obdulio Gaviria, stated on several occasions that in Colombia there was not a war but a terrorist threat, not forced displacement but voluntary migration, and no unemployment but informal jobs.[40] These arguments bedeviled the work of the Historical Memory Group professionals because their findings clashed with state policies. Nevertheless, other publications such as the general report of the Historical Memory Group *Basta ya! Colombia: Memories of War and Dignity* became part of the wave of the country's memory studies, with an emphasis on reconciliation and peace communication channels. Colombia's context marks the difference between memory studies in Argentina and Chile. While in the latter two countries, academics agree that conflicts and differences are part of healthy democracies, the ongoing nature of Colombia's political context challenges the memory studies field. Another obstacle for memory policies in Colombia is still the negation of the conflict by some parts of society, such as the Army and the right-wing president Iván Duque (2018–2022), Uribe's protégé. However, as mentioned in several parts of the book, the June 19th presidential elections results are bringing a new sense of hope for Colombians. For example, the victims' associations, who have supported Gustavo Petro's policies since 2018, feel relieved and optimistic to be heard again.

The emergence and consolidation of the memory field in Latin America and Colombia encouraged new research about ways to remember and to organize museums, exhibitions, and representations of violence. The slogan Nunca Más (Never Again), for example, utilized by human rights activists and scholars of the Southern Cone, inspired the founders of Granada's memory site.[41] By naming it the Hall of Never Again, they hope that its exhibitions and narratives will raise awareness of the impact of violence on Granada's community and prevent its recrudescence. The creators of the Hall exhibit brutalities straightforwardly to impact members of the community as well as outsiders. They believe that this method will place people, at least for a moment, in the victim's shoes and therefore personalize the need to put a stop to the violence.

## Paths to Transitional Justice in Colombia

For the members of the International Center for Transitional Justice, the concept "refers to the ways countries emerging from periods of conflict and repression address large-scale or systematic human rights violations so numerous and so serious that the normal justice system will not be able to provide an adequate response."[42] With this idea in mind, the founders of the Hall view their site as a space in which reparation and restoration are possible since the state would not pay attention to their needs.

Political scientist John H. Herz used the term "transitional justice" for the first time in 1982[43] in an edited volume in which several academics discussed the transition of authoritarian and totalitarian regimes to democracy; in 1986, Philippe C. Schmitter, Guillermo O'Donnell, and Laurence Whitehead also discussed this concept in their book *Transitions from Authoritarian Rule: Comparative Perspectives*.[44] Since then, the idea of transitional justice has gone through two more developments, as stated by the Deputy Director of Research at the

International Center for Transnational Justice, Paige Arthur.[45] After the Cold War, in 1989, the term became associated with democratic processes and modernization, and used in conflict resolution within a context of justice, law, and society during the late twentieth century. Legal scholars such as Ruti Teitel applied the concept of transitional justice to broader political contexts, not only post-conflict situations.[46] This makes the concept a flexible and ongoing field that interfaces directly with memory production.

Political scientist Alexandra Barahona de Brito insists on the advantages of studying the connections between transitional justice and memory. She analyzes the politics of memory, defined as the shifts in how societies view their past. These changes also represent a kind of memory-making in which elites or marginal communities create boundaries, patterns of social and political inclusion and exclusion, and new social and political continuities and discontinuities. Through this process, victims can acquire a voice, societies condemn repression, and repressors become outsiders.[47] Following Lessa, Barahona de Brito, and other human rights scholars such as Juan E. Méndez, I emphasize the pivotal significance of the survivor's voice for the connection between transitional justice and memory. When policymakers and state agents talk about reparations in truth commissions, trials, and amnesties, the victims' narratives need acknowledgment, not only for healing purposes but also for legal arguments that could aid in advancing social processes.[48] Furthermore, during the third phase of transitional justice as described by Ruti Teitel,[49] the victims' active participation is crucial to construct and preserve memory settings and to determine what, whom, why, and how people remember.[50] Communities such as the inhabitants of Granada make these decisions about memory preservation in a way that determines their future—or at least that is their hope. In this sense, Barahona de Brito claims that transitional justice is a component of the politics of memory, a form of memory-making in the aftermath of atrocities. This gives transitional justice a broader historical context, as Teitel explains in her article "Transitional Justice Genealogy."[51]

In addition, Barahona de Brito introduces two notions that advance our understanding of the memories represented by the Granada inhabitants. These are mnemonic communities and institutions and memory. The first idea refers to the coexistence of several memories within a social group and to the fact that people adopt and put into practice those that make sense to them as members of that society. This is seen in the representations of violence in the Hall of Never Again, analyzed further in the chapter. The second notion refers to the way memory institutions, including courts, schools, universities, museums, and the media, transmit narratives about historical atrocities. Studies of memory sites and museums enrich the relationship between transitional justice and memory and deepen the analysis of circumstances that lead to the inclusion and participation of survivors, perpetrators, and authoritarian elites in memory sites and venues. Memory scholarship, thus, helps to reframe transitional justice.[52]

Lawyer Carlos Felipe Rúa asserts that the first time we could find elements of transitional justice in Colombia was in 2005[53] due to the Law of Justice and Peace 975 issued by Congress, which in turn led to the creation of the National Center for Historical Memory.[54] Through this law, President Álvaro Uribe Vélez aimed to encourage the standards for assessing atrocities (such as kidnappings, genocide, forced disappearances, and torture) committed by guerrilla fighters and paramilitaries who wished to lay down their weapons and reincorporate into civilian life. The law also aimed to guarantee the victims of the armed conflict their rights to know the truth, to claim justice, and to seek state reparations.[55] However, the Justice and Peace Law did not specify who the victims were or how they should obtain redress, and according to Colombian scholars María Victoria Uribe and Pilar Riaño, this law did not give victims any kind of participation in legal proceedings.[56] In addition, the victims had to deal first with the fact that their testimonies were not credible due to the government's refusal to acknowledge the armed conflict. Only in 2011, when the Congress issued Law 1448, was the term "victim" legally defined. Article 3 of the law reads:

> For the purposes of this law, victims are those persons who individually or collectively have suffered damage due to events that occurred as of January 1, 1985, as a consequence of violations of International Humanitarian Law or of serious and manifest violations of the norms of International Human Rights, which occurred on the occasion of the internal armed conflict.[57]

Although this characterization establishes and acknowledges, for the first time, the Colombian victims of the armed conflict entitled to reparations, it leaves open the concept of suffering damage. For instance, the psychological repercussions and the conflict's effects on second- and third-generation victims still require clarification. In August 2017, the Comisión de Implementación y Monitoreo de la Ley Víctimas (CIMLV), which represents the Mesa Nacional de Víctimas, reiterated what their members denounced since 2016: the scarcity of public funds and programs devoted to assist victims. Even though Asovida arose in 2005, the victims and survivors of Granada's violence did not feel represented in the public policies related to recognition and reparation. The members of Asovida think that the government ignores the cultural particularities of each Colombian region affected by the armed conflict, so their programs do not respond to real needs. Thus, the Hall is part of their continuous struggle to make their voices heard.

In 2016, the Granada inhabitants and many other communities of the country hoped that the creation of the Jurisdicción Especial para la Paz, JEP (Special Peace Jurisdiction), would aid in their efforts to become visible to the government and attain truth, reparation, and compensation. On December

11, 2016, the Colombian state created the JEP as part of the Sistema Integral de Verdad, Justicia, Reparación y no Repetición (Integral System of Truth, Justice, Reparation, and no Repetition) to manage transitional justice in the country and acknowledge the crimes committed within the armed conflict. It cannot last more than 20 years. The JEP's main goal is to identify the truth of the violent acts committed during the armed conflict and let the victims know it. Other objectives are to fight against impunity, held perpetrators accountable, and adopt decisions to achieve juridic security for the demobilized, exerting the state obligation to research, judge, and sanction crimes that are not subject of an amnesty. The JEP is autonomous and independent from the country's judicial branch, and its recipients are the ex-combatants who signed the peace treaty of 2016, state agents, and those who participated indirectly in the armed conflict. The JEP however has suffered several attacks, especially by right-wing politicians and the army, who do not agree in having members of the FARC-EP in politics and public positions. This has led to more violence against the demobilized guerrillas and constant sabotage of the entity.

The JEP was a result of the peace treaty signed between the Colombian government and the FARC-EP after four years of dialogue in Cuba (2012–2016). However, this ceasefire is controversial because many Colombians have a problem forgiving the crimes committed by this guerrilla and their assimilation into civilian life. Thus, many citizens voted against the agreement in a plebiscite held also in 2016. On this occasion, voters stated their opposition to support the Cuban dialogues and open pathways to reach peace in Colombia. Finally, President Juan Manuel Santos (2010–2018) signed the accord by decree in an attempt to salvage the efforts to reach peace in a country historically racked by violence.

Many Colombian lawyers and politicians have expressed their concerns about the JEP's situation and are especially surprised with the results of the plebiscite. Although this is still a matter of study, I believe it is safe to say that Colombians have very deep wounds that do not let them see beyond the FARC-EP crimes, which is understandable, but it also reveals the political polarization in the country. Those against the JEP worry that this organism might become an impunity pact because its final version removed the initiative to not benefit those who do not fulfill their duties toward the victims. This is an ongoing, heated debate. In addition, some activists and politicians state that one of the biggest issues of the JEP is Iván Duque's government (2018–2022) efforts to not recognize the organism. It is known that these transitional justice processes must be negotiated to reach consensus, which has not happened yet in Colombia.[58]

Sociologist Milciades Vizcaíno affirms that transitional justice was the core of the negotiation between the state and the FARC-EP because it defined what should be justice, truth, reparation, and no repetition. However, he continues, this would only be credible if it is applicable and applied, which is a challenge for three reasons. First, transitional justice agreements are always controversial; second, past trends inform future uncertainties; and third, the current situation weakens the no repetition goal. Since 2018, Colombians are witnessing an increase in violence, which makes it very difficult to keep a strict differentiation between victims and perpetrators. Therefore, according to Vizcaíno, transitional justice is an attempt to repair the victims of the armed conflict and by the same token it is recovering the responsibilities of the perpetrators for past crimes and no repetition. This implies that the state must lead these processes and exert its control in the territories, which has not happened since 2018 and even before.[59]

Another issue that has impeded a smooth pathway toward peace in Colombia, as mentioned before, is the deep division of political positions. Historically, as addressed by lawyer Nicole Summers, the most successful transitional justice processes have been those who investigate the past to inform and establish a fair and peaceful future.[60] This has been a problem in Colombia due to the right-wing attempts to rewrite history from the point of view of the perpetrators of violence, dismissing the victims' versions. This policy became a visible problem when Iván Duque took office, and even before, because it was reflected in the choices he made, like appointing historian Darío Acevedo, known for his immovable position that there is no armed conflict in Colombia, as director of the National Center for Historical Memory. This, however, is changing. Following Vizcaíno, this shows that no consensus has been reached in the country because the victims and survivors are claiming to have their testimonies and stories considered, to know the truth, and be repaired.[61] The following case study is an example of a grassroots memory site devoted to achieving truth, justice, and reparation despite the government oblivion.

## The Hall of Never Again: Location, Violence, and Its Representations

In the town of Granada, a critical zone of the Department of Antioquia lies the Hall of Never Again. It is the gateway to eastern Antioquia and home to an area of water reservoirs that generates 35% of the electricity of the country. Antioquia, one of the 32 Colombian departments, is in the central northwestern part of the territory, with a narrow section that borders the Caribbean Sea. Most of its area is mountainous, with some valleys, and is part of the Andes Mountain range. Besides being one of the richest municipalities of the department, harvesting coffee, beans, sugar cane, and berries, Granada is near the José María Córdoba airport free zone, and it is close to the highway that connects this part of Colombia with Bogotá, the capital city. Due to its location and topographic conditions, Granada is a strategic corridor for the different armed groups (Army, paramilitaries, drug lords, and guerrillas) and is the path used to commercialize the drugs that come from the lands near the water reservoirs.[62]

The Hall of Never Again is situated in one of Granada's two squares. The venue is strategically located not in the town's main plaza but in a more convenient and visible place, where the buses from other municipalities and Medellín arrive, thus an area with many stores and restaurants. The newcomers' first sight when they get off the bus is one of Granada's two churches, the Community Center, and the Hall. Like many Colombians, the Granada inhabitants are mostly Catholic, and this church is essential for them. In this place, most of the religiously significant events such as baptisms, weddings, first communions, and funerals take place and has become a symbol of endurance for the Granada people because it is a place where they feel protected (Figure 3.2).

The stairs seen in the image above and the space in front of the church are gathering places for communal activities such as protests or just a meeting space. It is one of Granada's most significant reference points. Granada's main church is in the town's primary square, not visible for newcomers; it is necessary to hike to get there, making it more difficult to access.

Besides the church seen in the picture, there is the community center of Granada, composed of a library, the Natural History Museum, and a sports field. The Hall of Never Again is a two-story building adjacent to the center that the mayor lent to Asovida in 2009. Initially, the loan consisted of the first floor only because the second one housed a children's daycare. However, in

**FIGURE 3.2** View of Granada's church from the bus station. Photograph by Jimena Perry, August 2017.

## Memory, Healing, and Justice 123

2015, Asovida expanded the Hall to include the second floor, where they host workshops and leadership training events.

The leaders of Asovida and the founders of the Hall decided to mourn by purposely remembering what happened to their community. Therefore, they built the Hall with the explicit intention to inform outsiders of the violence endured in Granada since 1980. On this site, the survivors evoke crimes such as more than 630 disappearances, 83 victims of land mines, 80 instances of "false positives," and the massive displacement of 97% of the rural inhabitants and 73% of the urban population. Colombia's so-called "false positives" process refers to the extrajudicial killings in which the military killed thousands of civilians, then dressed their victims as guerrillas to present them as combat kills to the media.[63] Gloria Ramírez, President of Asovida and one of the creators of the Hall, remembers when the venue opened:

> When we started the process of the Hall, many people of Granada did not believe us, some thought this was just a waste of time, but we just kept going. We understand that these processes may not serve everybody, we respect that. However, we are convinced that the Hall, as a memory exercise and to help us heal, is worth it. When we opened the Hall in 2009, an old lady approached me and thanked me. She told me that one of the pictures of the permanent display belonged to her son and that because he disappeared, she did not have a place to visit him. She did not have a place to grieve. The woman felt relieved that now she could go somewhere to see and even talk to her son. She could finally heal. This is the kind of reparation we look for. If there is just one person who feels the Hall aids in her or his process, we have succeeded.[64]

Gloria Ramírez believes, as do the members of Asovida, that if the inhabitants of Granada do not heal their violent past, then resentment, anger, and sadness will remain present in their lives and in the memories they pass on to new generations. Thus, she and other community leaders insist on revisiting the past to let it go.

The members of Asovida found inspiration for the Hall in two similar Latin American venues. The methodology of collecting testimonies follows the example of the Recuperación de Memoria Histórica (Recovery of Historical Memory—Remhi) in Guatemala.[65] Project Remhi was launched in 1995 to document a non-official version of the violence that occurred in Guatemala during the twentieth century and to account for the victims' pain. The Remhi Project achieved these objectives through workshops, and the Granada community emulated this process. The purpose was to acknowledge another's pain and to understand and sympathize with his or her experiences.

Another influence on the Hall of Never Again was the Peruvian exhibition *Para recordar, relato visual del conflicto armado interno en el Perú, 1980–2000, Yuyanapaq* (For Remembering, Visual Narrative of the Armed Conflict in

**124** Memory, Healing, and Justice

Peru, 1980–2000, Yuyanapaq), founded by the Centro de Información para la Memoria Colectiva y los Derechos Humanos (Center of Information for the Collective Memory and Human Rights), established by Peru's National Truth Commission. The organizers used testimonies and photographs in the display to bring together the observer with the survivor and his or her family.

In this context, the primary intention of the Hall's 200-photograph display is to impress upon visitors that the victims of violence were people just like them: people whose lives affected a community and who therefore deserve remembrance. On another wall, beside the photographs, there are children's paintings and products of workshops organized by Asovida to help families talk about their traumatic memories. The other two significant artifacts displayed at the Hall are the fragment of a gas cylinder the FARC-EP used to attack Granada in 2003, addressed later in the chapter, and an art installation called *Río abajo* (Downriver), which emulates a mass grave. Artist Erika Diettes crafted the piece to raise the viewer's awareness of victims with No Name ("N.N."), and to invite observers to reflect on what they might feel if trapped underground. That is why the person observing Downriver can see her or his reflection in the glass that contains the grave's representation (Figure 3.3).

**FIGURE 3.3** Entrance to the Hall of Never Again. Photograph by Jimena Perry, 2017.

Andrew Rajca, besides debating the Never Again slogan, as mentioned before, also uses the interaction between art and politics as a dissensus manifestation to explore how the sites he studies do not constitute final and fixed monuments to honor those who endured brutalities but places that provide moments of subjectivation for certain groups. Due to the nature of the Hall of Never Again, a local, peripheral, and politically committed memory site, visitors can clearly sense the tension between notions of human rights and memory which in turn, following Rajca, produces contradictions challenging state remembrances of violence and even perpetuating the exclusion of the victims' voices. As an example of this situation, Rajca highlights the Memorial da Resistência (Resistance Memorial, MDR) in São Paulo, Brazil, and the challenges this site faces when the state attempts to engage with the remembrances of activists, students, workers, armed militants, and cultural figures. Rajca points out how problematic state intervention can be because in the attempt to create an all-encompassing narrative it leaves out what it considers are "non-political" citizens, perpetuating exclusion. This happened with the Hall of Never Again and many other Colombian sites, which have suffered setbacks when the state intervenes. Not to say that governmental support and acknowledgement is not needed, but it must be done in the terms of the victims and survivors. The "moments of political subjectivation" noted by Rajca get lost when the social groups' cultural nuances get lost. However, Rajca also notes what happens when the opposite is done. Using the Centro Cultural y Museo de la Memoria in Montevideo, Uruguay, the author of *Dissensual Subjects* points out the attempts made by the MUME's curators to create dissensual interventions in the victim-perpetrator binary. He demonstrates how this memory site devotes more attention to those "non subjects" to encourage other meanings of memory and human rights in post-dictatorship settings. The MUME in Uruguay uses temporary exhibitions and installations to explore how art disrupts prevailing concepts of politics, remembrance, and representation, which, following Rajca, promotes new spaces of inclusion and subjectivity.[66] On a small scale and stemming from community-based initiatives, the founders of Granada's Hall of Never Again are proud of the Downriver installation because it refers to the mass graves found not only in this part of Colombia but all over the country.

Continuing the Hall's tour, to the left of the picture display, visitors can see images of 15 mass graves found in Granada, displayed intentionally so the spectator "assumes and puts him or herself in the victim's place."[67] In another room, the public can see a large photograph of a march that took place on December 9, 2000, three days after the FARC-EP destroyed the town. The photograph below illustrates the 200-picture wall (Figure 3.4).

Since one of the main aims of the Hall is to make visible the pain of Granada residents, Gloria Quintero, Vice President of Asovida, also a guide of the venue, researched the massacres in the region. She identified more than 22 massacres from 1988 until 2004, but she insists there are more. The results of her research

**126** Memory, Healing, and Justice

**FIGURE 3.4** View of the main display of the Hall: The 200 photographs of Granada's victims. Photograph by Jimena Perry, 2017.

now adorn four panels as part of the permanent exhibition in the Hall, in which there is a list of the massacres documented by Quintero. The following chart summarizes them (Table 3.1):

The massacre of El Vergel deserves special attention, according to the Granada community, because of the cruelty inflicted upon the victims' bodies, which paramilitaries stabbed and dismembered. For this reason, it has a detailed description.[69] On April 20, 2001, the latter armed group killed nine people in three *veredas* from the municipality of Granada, El Vergel being one of them. Among the victims were four brothers. The next account of the event was not in a bitácora but in the transcription of a workshop conducted by professionals of the National Center for Historical Memory. The following text is displayed in a panel of the Hall of Never Again, and it includes the description of the massacre that took place on April 20, 2001. It is my translation:

> April 20, 2001: Seven people in the Vergel Vereda. This day, while working in their plots, armed men of the AUC interrupted a group of peasants. The paramilitaries went through the Vergel Vereda stabbing seven innocent men. Among them was José Joaquín Ramírez, his wife, and other people from the municipality of Santuario. The AUC members

**TABLE 3.1** Massacres Committed in Granada, Antioquia, 1998–2004

| Date | Number of Victims | Place | Perpetrator |
|---|---|---|---|
| June 11, 1988 | 4 guerrilla fighters | Town Granada | Coordinadora Guerrillera Simón Bolívar, CGSB (Simón Bolívar Guerrilla Coordinating Board, composed by the FARC-EP, the M-19 Movement, the ELN, the Popular Liberation Army, EPL, the Workers Revolutionary Party, and the Movimiento Armado Quintin Lame composed the Simón Bolívar Coordinating Board, from 1987 to the early 1990s.)[68] |
| September 30, 1999 | 4 policemen | Granada, coliseum | Not established |
| October 29, 1999 | 3 policemen | Not established | Ejército de Liberación Nacional, ELN (National Liberation Army) |
| March 5, 2000 | 3 soldiers | Not established | Ejército de Liberación Nacional, ELN (National Liberation Army) |
| July 4, 2000 | 4 civilians | Alto del Palmar (El Palmar Height) | Autodefensas Unidas de Colombia, AUC (United Self-Defenders of Colombia, paramilitaries) |
| November 3, 2000 | 19 civilians | Not established | Autodefensas Bloque Metro (paramilitaries) and Colombian National Army |
| November 3, 2000 | 2 civilians | Paraje Cristalina-Cebadero | Ejército de Liberación Nacional, ELN (National Liberation Army) |
| November 4, 2000 | 1 policeman, 1 civilian | Not established | Ejército de Liberación Nacional, ELN (National Liberation Army) |
| December 6, 2000 | 15 civilians, 5 policemen | Not established | Fuerzas Armadas Revolucionarias de Colombia-Ejército del Pueblo, FARC (Revolutionary Armed Forces of Colombia-People's Army) |
| April 5, 2001 | 4 civilians | Not established | Autodefensas Bloque Metro (paramilitaries) |

*(Continued)*

| Date | Number of Victims | Place | Perpetrator |
|---|---|---|---|
| April 20, 2001 | 7 civilians | Vereda El Vergel. Vereda is a unit smaller than a town or municipality. It is a term specific to Colombia. | Autodefensas Unidas de Colombia, AUC (United Self-Defenders of Colombia, paramilitaries) |
| July 14, 2001 | 4 civilians | Not established | Fuerzas Armadas Revolucionarias de Colombia-Ejército del Pueblo, FARC (Revolutionary Armed Forces of Colombia-People's Army) |
| July 17, 2001 | 5 civilians | Not established | Colombian National Army |
| November 17, 2001 | 4 civilians (3 women and 1 man) | Not established | Ejército de Liberación Nacional, ELN (National Liberation Army) |
| April 21, 2002 | 3 civilians | Not established | Not established |
| June 4, 2002 | 5 civilians | Vereda El Edén | Autodefensas Unidas de Colombia, AUC (United Self-Defenders of Colombia, paramilitaries) |
| June 6, 2002 | 5 civilians | Vereda El Edén | Not established |
| July 2002 | 3 civilians | Not established | Not established |
| October 14, 2002 | 3 civilians | Not established | Autodefensas Bloque Metro (paramilitaries) |
| November 12, 2002 | 6 civilians | San Luis | Colombian National Army |
| January 13, 2003 | 5 civilians | Corregimiento Santa Ana. Term used in Colombia to define subdivision of municipalities. | Colombian National Army |
| April 15, 2003 | 3 civilians | Vereda Las Faldas | Not established |
| September 28, 2003 | 3 civilians | Not established | Not established |

approached them asking for their IDs, and when they saw that José was from Granada, gave the order to the other people there, including his wife, to stay inside a house where they took them. The peasants stayed there from 10:00 am to 2:00 pm. The AUC also killed Humberto Ramírez. He was a community leader, a Christian, known for his generosity. They also killed Darío Aristizábal, Javier and Humberto Duque Arias (two brothers), and their brother-in-law. Darío had two girls and a pregnant wife. The other two victims were young men. The paramilitaries also murdered an elderly man, José Vicente, and his son.

Gloria Quintero investigated painstakingly this massacre, an initiative which in turn encouraged more enquiry about the atrocity. Currently, this event is part of the National Center for Historical Memory database, and its information is available online. In 2004, one survivor of El Vergel's butchery remembered it like this:

> I am from El Vergel. On April 20, 2001, there was a massacre there. Paramilitaries killed seven good people, they were good people and my *vereda* was beautiful. The paramilitaries arrived, I lived further away, but neither my brothers nor my father were victims because it is a big vereda (...) It was an Easter Friday at 10:00 am. They arrived from that side. They told the women who were working with their husbands and to those from Santuario (another vereda) to hide. The women left; their husbands were all from Granada. They killed them all (...) In an indescribable way. They only untouched part of their bodies were their faces, all the rest of the bodies was severely damaged, with knives, they destroyed them. We had to tie them up so they would not disintegrate (...) and they put salt on them.[70]
>
> The stabbed bodies, the dismembered and disfigured corpses, add to the humiliation and shame of being murdered like animals. "You would find bodies, lift their shirts and see they were stabbed. It was overwhelming with a young man because they opened his stomach like a pig. It is very traumatizing to see people killed like that."[71] The Autodefensas Unidas de Colombia, AUC (United Self-Defenders of Colombia) performed this massacre.[72]

The seven people assassinated in this massacre left families behind them. Their pictures hang on the Hall's wall, and each one of them has a *bitácora*. In their notebooks, there is nothing but narratives of sadness. The collective imprint this event left in the community relates to a private and intimate memory that highlights processes of mourning. Here is another remembrance of the massacre found in a *bitácora* at the Hall:

*Ramiro's Bitácora No. 54*
  Nine years ago, you departed because they took your life. I did not know you because when they killed you, my mother was pregnant with

me. I hope you are in heaven and know that you will always have a place in my heart.

Hi uncle, when they tell me how they killed you, I hurt. Those who killed you must be very bad. I want you to light my way. I know you are watching me and loving me from heaven. Your niece.[84]

The Vergel massacre exemplifies the two levels of remembrance the Hall's creators encourage and promote. Also, some of the narratives found so far in the *bitácoras* confirm that memory is diverse, follows cultural models, and is multifaceted, and that mourning does not have a handbook. These *bitácoras* and the language used in them strengthen the previous point about how a Hall serves better this community.

Since the first massacre and guerrilla attack in 1988, the inhabitants of Granada have endured bombings, kidnappings, forced displacements, disappearances, and targeted killings. The second intrusion, in 1990, damaged the local Caja Agraria, the national Colombian institution that promotes rural development, shuttered in 1999. Besides, during the 1980s the FARC-EP and Ejército de Liberación Nacional (ELN) fought one another to control the territory. In 1997 and 1998, the guerrillas kidnapped the mayors of Granada, and in 1998, there were massive displacements from the rural areas. During 1999, the ELN killed three police officers. From 1998 to 2000, the town of Granada's population dropped from 18,000 inhabitants to 5,500 as the displacement of its inhabitants approached 70%.[73] Some of the people who fled their lands went to other parts of the Department of Antioquia, such as Medellín, the capital, or other municipalities such as Nare and Puerto Berrío.

In the last decade, when the community attempted reconstruction, violence returned. In April 2001, the paramilitary group Autodefensas Unidas de Colombia (AUC), Bloque Metro, killed seven peasants. In July, the FARC-EP executed the mayor. In 2002, another 3,500 people suffered displacement by paramilitaries, and the AUC ordered the local administration to shut down. In October of the same year, the FARC-EP tried to take over the municipality, but the Colombian Army repelled the assault.

It was also during these years that Granada suffered one of the most severe guerrilla attacks in its history. In 2003, a truck loaded with 400 kilograms of dynamite exploded in the town's main square. It left 21 people dead and 14 wounded. The material damage was incalculable. This incident is one of the most vividly recalled by the population because it destroyed almost all of the urban area. That same year, there was another attempt to blow up the Police Command of Granada, but it failed because a gas cylinder thrown by the guerrillas did not detonate.

From 2005 until 2007, due to the National Army's operations in the region, FARC-EP, the ELN guerrillas, and the paramilitary group Cacique Nutibara retreated. These actions made the inhabitants of Granada feel that the armed conflict was over, but the violence persisted. In 2007, the National Army committed three extrajudicial executions, and the FARC-EP attacked a bus and killed a community leader and her daughter and wounded three people. In the same year, Granada suffered another two explosions in the urban area: one in a nightclub and the other in a storage facility. Violence finally abated by the end of 2007, but the emotional, psychological, and economic damage remained.[74]

From 2008 onwards, the reconstruction of Granada began. That year coincided with the opening of the highway between Medellín and Bogotá, the trials of some members of the Army who committed massacres, and projects that encouraged the return of displaced populations, instilling hope in the future for Granada residents. Also, in 2008, Colombian authorities captured soldiers and guerrillas involved in several massacres, confiscated war material, and started to clear land mines planted by the guerrillas. The reconstruction of Granada continued, and reparations for the victims of the armed conflict began. Nevertheless, that same year, the FARC-EP detonated two bombs in Granada, fortunately with no casualties. In this context, in 2009, community leaders founded the Salón del Nunca Más.

From 2009 to 2013, the National Army kept finding weapons of the FARC-EP and the ELN, and the displaced population continued to return. Finally, in 2011, with the passage of Law 1448, the victims strengthened their organizations, some protests took place, and the state implemented programs related to land restitution. The report *Granada: Memorias de guerra y reconstrucción* (Granada: Memories of War and Reconstruction), published in 2016 by the National Center for Historical Memory, states that of 11,045 inhabitants of Granada (3,155 families), 7,484 people (2,138 families) returned to the town between 2012 and 2015.[75]

In 2013, the population of Granada commemorated the tenth anniversary of the bomb that destroyed the main square of their town. In the words of Gloria Quintero, this commemoration signals "the value of remembering. Our loved ones die when we forget them. We want children to learn that forgetting is not the way to mourn."

According to the researchers who wrote the report about Granada's convulsive past, until 2022, the region is currently violence-free. Paramilitaries, guerrilla, and Army are gone, and the reconstruction of the town's infrastructure has encouraged people to recover their life and recuperate from the horrors of war. However, a comprehensive reparation, one that includes economic, physical, psychological, and social components, is still pending. The Granada inhabitants must deal with the deep and unsettling damage inflicted by the country's armed conflict.

In addition to the struggle to restore their social fabric and infrastructure, Granada residents continue to fight against stigmatization and shame, as stated by historian Gonzalo Sánchez. Like most of the survivors of brutalities in Colombia, the inhabitants of Granada found themselves in the middle of a polarizing label conflict. For the guerrillas, the Granada people supported paramilitaries, and for the paramilitaries, they allied with guerrillas. Sánchez claims that when rural communities fall into one of these categorizations, it is generally due to unfounded assumptions. A common and erroneous belief of those unaffected by the horrors of war is that residents of combat zones must belong to an armed group or at least identify with one of them. Sánchez insists that to deal with stigma and shame means to explore the relations between the armed actors, the inhabitants of a region, and the territory—and to understand the history behind their actions.[76] The relevance of these local voices and histories influenced the creators of the Hall to create the venue. Jaime Montoya, a writer and community leader who has been involved with Asovida and the Hall from its start, states,

> One of the main purposes of the Hall of Never Again, which we started in Granada, is to encourage other towns of Colombia to do the same. The Hall is meant to be a mirror in which we can look at ourselves, reconcile with life, as an act of collective grief. A collective memory exercise that acknowledges the faces displayed in the wall. We want to tell everybody that they were humans too, that violence truncated their dreams, and that they deserve remembrance. Our immediate task is to find allies to help us disseminate, fund, and keep constructing memories. This must be a project that speaks to everyone, a project that inspires solidarity with the past and that encourages constructing a tolerant and more democratic society.[77]

Montoya's words have a twofold meaning: To emphasize the solidarity and impact the Hall must have beyond Granada and to encourage people to think how venues such as the Hall can help to eliminate the stigma and shame that Colombian violence has brought to the survivors of brutalities.

The process to bring the Hall of Never Again to fruition took the members of Asovida six years. After the last massacre, in 2003, the community gathered in their grief and carried out activities, such as Stations of the Cross, a *chocolatada* (one of the traditional drinks of their region, hot chocolate), a *sancocho* (a stew of Latin America and the Caribbean made from various meats, tubers such as yams or cassavas, and other ingredients), and a fundraiser called *Granadatón*. These efforts gave the people a sense of solidarity and a new hope that they could overcome their violent past. Currently, in the Hall, community leader Gloria Quintero sells coffee from Tejipaz and *alfajores* (a kind of cookie) to help fund the venue. The members of Asovida also created in 2016 the non-profit entity Association Weaving Territory for Peace (Asociación tejiendo territorio para la paz), Tejipaz, which is an organization for the commercialization of products, such as coffee, produced by the peasants of the region. Tejipaz's purpose is to contribute to the sustainability of peace through economic development, strengthening the community's relationship with their territory, and deepening the resilience of the armed conflict victims, minorities, and general population. By promoting fair trade and training peasants in planning and management, Tejipaz seeks to solidify the local economy. The aim is to improve competitiveness and economic sustainability for rural and urban Granada inhabitants.[78] According to Gloria Ramírez, the collaboration between the Hall of Never Again and Tejipaz strengthens constantly. The leaders of both organizations, Ramírez and Giraldo, develop joint projects devoted to draw attention to the region's peasants products and ways of life, such as organic fertilizer workshops and crop transformation. In addition, since 2018 they have created innovative ways to attract tourism to Granada. The project Rutas de memoria y paz (Paths of Memory and Peace) is one of them. These routes are guided tours of emblematic places of Granada's municipality in the urban and rural areas with the purpose of creating awareness, reflecting, and getting to know better Granada's history, culture, traditions, landscape, current situation, and future. Also, this endeavor attempts to promote peasant economies to help achieving a long-lasting and sustainable peace by creating alliances with cultural tourist companies and encouraging knowledge exchanges between urban and rural areas. The routes include visits to productive farms, to the Hall of Never Again, and coffee tastings in the Tejipaz Coffee Shop, created in 2019, for visitors and locals´ gatherings and listening to live music, poetry readings, storytelling, and where specialists train those who want to become baristas. "All these initiatives have the goal to show people and the whole country that in Granada there are also good things to show, not everything is about violence and its horrors."[79] Ramírez words show how the Granada community understand memory processes and are aware that they shift, evolve, and adapt. Her reflections demonstrate too that the inhabitants of the region have pondered about the ways in which they narrate their violent past and are coming to realize their need to go beyond graphic descriptions and depictions of the war aftermaths. Although the main exhibition of the Hall of Never Again remains as it has since 2009, the projects it has prompted are taking memories one step further.

The Granada community also gathers on the first Saturday of every month to discuss local concerns. During these assemblies, the municipality's inhabitants discuss and learn about conflict resolution, forgiveness, human rights, and law. They also address issues related to the economic compensation some of the community members received as beneficiaries of Law 1448. Many peasants obtained some financial aid to return to the lands from which paramilitaries drove them out, but often the reparation is insufficient to cultivate their land again. In addition, some people are unwilling to return to their former plots because of the emotional toll. So far, in the words of some Granada inhabitants, only a few compensation cases have succeeded. Gloria Quintero underscores the necessity of the state agents to consider the current economic realities and expectations of the people. She referred, for example, to one Granada woman trained as a hair stylist with the indemnification fund from the government. "This was good use of the money," believes Quintero.

All the processes undertaken by the Granada leaders and the community were considerably affected by the Covid-19 pandemic. The Hall of Never Again had to close more than usual, only being opened when someone called one of the guides or creators for a guided visit, and the community assemblies were postponed being reactivated in March 2022. The memory paths also stopped, and the peasants were not able to commercialize their products, such as coffee and fruits. The coffee shop had to close too, and the barista training stopped. This caused a disruption of the cultural tourism efforts, which are being slowly reactivated.

## The Bitácoras and Ways to Remember

The first time I visited the Hall was in the summer of 2014, where I found some of the *bitácoras* and stories. Gloria Quintero read this *bitácora* during a guided visit she did for me, but it is still not classified; therefore, it does not have a number as the others do.

> I have many things to tell you, my dear father, I am older now, much older, time goes by so fast. My love, my life has changed dramatically since you are not here. God gave me many things, but there are some many questions I need to ask you because you are the best teacher. Due to all the things, you taught me I have been able to succeed. My dream is to see you again. I have suffered and I know that you did too. [...] Father, no time is enough to thank you for what you did for me. [...] Now I understand so many things of life, however, I do not understand what happened to you, I do not understand, father. I do not understand, I never will. Why did they destroy my family? [...] They sent you to a place you did not deserve to be. From where you are, they broke my life and soul in a thousand pieces. I owe you what I am now. I love you, father, I love you.

The permanent exhibition of the Hall includes more than 200 *bitácoras*, which are public records for visitors to read, and anyone can even write in them. Most of their content is full of emotion, like the former one, and reflect the private lives of those who survived violence. Every victim of the brutalities committed in Granada not only has an intimate and personal story to tell but also shares a group narrative with which the community members identify as a group. The personal accounts of the *bitácoras* complement the permanent exhibition, which refers to the events in a broader way. Therefore, the notebooks become a device to aid in both levels of the survivors' journey to recovery. In his book *The Collective Memory*, Halbwachs calls attention to the fact that group membership definitively influences individual remembrances. This is the case with the Granada inhabitants, who have also found in the Hall a collective reinforcement for their cultural identity. Despite having diverse recollections of the violent events past, the people of Granada come together in their pain to claim reparation and find their own voice.[80] They participate in two kinds of memory, as the creators of the Hall are aware.

The founders of the Hall designed the *bitácoras* for the survivors of violence, for the families and friends of the departed to relieve their pain and communicate with their dead loved ones. But there are also records to keep track of when and how people disappeared, died, or were displaced. They are a way for people to continue their relationships with loved ones taken away, to let the public know what happened to the victims and their families, and perhaps to press for accountability for the perpetrators in the future. In this sense, they are testimonies that strengthen projects of transitional justice.[81]

The texts found in the *bitácoras* are mainly intimate and personal and usually highlight the good qualities of the person, why they are gone, and the pain of their absence. Of the 200 *bitácoras*, 91 belong to victims of homicide, 28 to the disappeared, six to victims of massacres, and the 75 remaining do not specify a cause of death. In their pages, it is possible to find mothers talking to their children. I changed the names of the bitácoras to respect the victims' and survivors' privacy:

> *Pedro's Bitácora No. 30.*
> I will never forget the good things that happened when you were here with us. I will also never forget the tough and cruel moment I found you lying on the floor lifeless and sad. May God forgive the people with such a bad heart, and I hope God has you in all his glory. Thanks for all the happy moments your short life gave us.

Sisters to brothers:

> *Luis's Bitácora No. 44.*
> Dear brother, I remember today when I heard the incessant shooting and ran to the phone to check on my family. It was unbelievable that when the shooting stopped someone came to tell me you were dead. I had just talked to you just moments ago and I asked you about our other sister, you told me she was out, I thanked you and said goodbye. You said my name and goodbye. For some reason, you are not in this world anymore, God has a purpose for everything, and I know that with you it is no different.
>
> *Carlos's Bitácora No. 88.*
> Dear brother, six long years ago we do not know anything about you. We do not know if you are dead or alive, but my biggest wish is

that you are still alive. You are always in my heart because you were such a good person. Dear brother, we have looked all over for you, but we have not been able to find you, neither dead nor alive. Your children and wife are very sad with your disappearance. Dear brother, me and our mother are very depressed due to your absence. Not to know anything about you is very hard. Bye dear brother, I wish to find you very soon.

Daughters to their fathers:

*Juan's Bitácora No. 62.*
Hello dear father, I want to tell you that I miss you very much, I know you know that. Please, promise me that you will take care of me, do not let anything bad happen to me, help me, and never leave my side. Please, also take care of my mom and all my family. I ask you for the strength to forgive those who hurt you and my brother. Please, help us overcome our difficulties at home and school. I love you very much and I will never forget the moments we had together. I love you father, take care of me and all of us.

Friends to friends:

*Abel's Bitácora No. 128.*
He was my friend. Helpful, kind, community leader. May you rest in peace. I know you were very spiritual and that you only wanted to help others. Unfortunately, the violence destroyed everything, and it is ending with humankind. That is why all these spaces are definitive to create awareness of what we have lost and of the need to find paths of peace, dialogue, and forgiveness. That is the only way to build a different world, with love, and if war is a human invention, the human mind can also invent peace.

Narratives of people who did not know the deceased:

*Mario's Bitácora No. 60.*
Although I did not know you, they tell me that you were a great leader and that you won the award for the best mayor. I did not have the chance to talk to you, but I would have loved to because I like social causes and learning something from you would have been very valuable. I know your story from Asovida and from their process, which I am part of. When I tell your story I feel proud, I want to be like you. In your memory and as a homage the institution receives your name. Bye.

And even texts about the Hall itself:

> *Alberto's Bitácora. No 102.*
> Today we celebrate a year of the Hall of Never Again ventures. A place to cry but at the same a place designed to not forget our victims and to mourn. We are also pleased to have a place to vent and to remember our loved ones.

But besides being a personal device to help individual grieving and healing processes, through the *bitácoras* the visitors to the Hall learn about local histories that link the people in the community to reconstruction processes.

The *bitácoras* also reveal the tension between surviving family members. Some of their contents evidence frictions among relatives even before the violence. Therefore, the creators of the venue are careful not to idealize the time before or since armed conflicts reached the region. In this sense, the *bitácoras* are accounts of everyday life that also bear witness and truth telling. The following narratives demonstrate these family relationships:

> *Ricardo's Bitácora. No. 22.*
> Dear father, I miss you very much because my grandmother hits me very hard, she does it with ropes and I want to tell my mother to put me in a boarding school. That way she would not have to suffer for me because she loves my sister more than me. I want to die; I cannot handle more sadness. I cannot live without you. I am only happy sometimes, I cry all the time, and cannot be with my grandmother anymore. My mother is trying to find a house for us because she also does not get along with my grandmother. She is asking a friend for help. I must go because my aunt is waiting for me. I miss you every day. […] I love you very much, father. When my grandmother hits my sister, I get very sad. I am also sad because you are not here. I want you to come back. I am only nine years old.

> *Francisco's Bitácora not classified yet.*
> The truth, I do not know where you are. I do not want to be harsh, but you deserve it for being so bad with me and abusing me without a motive. I do not know what to feel for you. I do not know if I should pray for you or hate you. All the beating, one day you almost choked me with no reason. To know that my son was born sick because of your beatings, your jealousy... It is your fault that my son is no longer with me. You paid the price for humiliating me. You paid even a higher price for insulting me. My son would have been four years old. I hate you; it is your fault that he is not with me.

The case of the *bitácoras* of the Hall of Never Again evinces the interaction between autobiographical and collective memories and how communities remember. These notebooks also reveal the significance of Granada's local cultural history, which is the input necessary for transitional justice to afford aid to social groups to heal and restore their social fabrics after violence. If state policy makers acknowledge and recognize the particularities of communities such as Granada, their compensation and reparation projects could serve people better because the state would be attentive to their needs.

## Conclusions

Despite the influence of the new museology in many traditional museums, a conventional institution would not have thrived in producing historical memories in Granada. The creators of the Hall of Never Again and the members of the community decided that an exhibition space could help them grieve and process their violent past in their own cultural terms. That is why the Hall has the configuration described in the chapter. In this memory site, the people of Granada decided to privilege life over death in the exhibitions and continuously state that this space is to celebrate life. They honor the casualties caused by the armed conflict left and insist that their site is not a museum. The rigidity of conventional institutions, for the community of Granada, are elements that they want to avoid in their narratives of the violence they endured.

The founders of the Hall created the venue with the main objective of helping people not forget. This objective counteracts María José Pizarro's statement about Colombians having no memory, mentioned in Chapter 2. Particularly for the Granada community, remembering has become a valuable tool to understand that in order to build a future without violence, they must know what happened and why. Therefore, they need the freedom that a conventional museum does not allow to display their intimate thoughts about life, death, and religion. The selection of artifacts found at the Hall reflects the personal nature of the displays and the aim to make visitors realize that each life taken is unique, special, and irreplaceable.

While we can agree on the universality of grief, how individuals and communities manifest this sentiment is quite diverse. For instance, in the case of the Hall of Never Again, its founders' decisions of portraying violence encouraged a close relationship between the Granada inhabitants and the material cultural displayed at the site. This means, following sociologist Michael Brennan, that artefacts such as the bomb fragment, the *bitácoras*, and the art installation, have the purpose to channel memories through them. The items selected by the creators of the Hall have a specific goal: to remind the viewers of a traumatic past that cannot be overlooked or forgotten. For the Granada inhabitants, the violent events of the past serve as a constant remembrance of the situations they hope to prevent from recurring. Therefore, the relationship developed by the Granada community with the artifacts displayed at the Hall acquires a double meaning. First, the pieces trigger memories of violence due to the emphasis on the destruction and pain violence caused. Second, the same items help the people of Granada to express repressed feelings that, perhaps, prevent them from complete grieving process. The agency of the material culture at the Hall and the interaction between survivors of atrocities and artifacts generate an interaction that allows people to heal, consonant with Brennan's insights.[82]

How the Granada inhabitants use the Hall of Never Again for producing historical memories informs this particular community's relationship with its past, which in turn reveals their expectations from the government: visibility, reparation, and justice. As Gloria Quintero noted, the state must acknowledge and recognize the concrete needs of the survivors of brutalities. Boilerplate approaches cannot help them because policymakers are unaware of the current realities of the community. Generic policies for displaced persons might not accomplish their goal simply because people's lives shift as does their willingness to return to their communities.

The Hall of Never Again in Granada is only one example of the multiple grassroots memory sites that Colombian rural communities create to process the pain caused by violence. The next chapter addresses another such local case of memory production, likewise devoid of Colombian state support.

## Notes

1 "Sepultadas 21 personas de la masacre en Granada, Antioquia," Caracol, 2000, http://www.caracol.com.co/noticias/judiciales/sepultadas-21-personas-de-la-masacre-en-granada- antioquia/20001105/nota/75878.aspx.
2 ¿Cómo definimos la Red Colombiana de Lugares de Memoria? http://redmemoriacolombia.org/site/quienes-somos.
3 "El Museo Nacional De La Memoria, Un Deber Moral," Dejusticia, https://www.dejusticia.org/column/el-museo-nacional-de-la-memoria-un-deber-moral/.
4 M. Brinton Lykes and Hugo van der Merwe, "Exploring/Expanding the Reach of Transitional Justice," *International Journal of Transitional Justice* 11, no. 3 (November 1, 2017): 371–377.
5 Hilde S. Hein, *The Museum in Transition. A Philosophical Perspective* (Washington, DC: Smithsonian Books, 2000).
6 Maurice Halbwachs, *On Collective Memory*. Translated by Lewis A. Coser (Chicago, IL and London: The University of Chicago Press, 1992), 52.
7 Andrew C. Rajca, *DISSENSUAL Subjects: Memory, Human Rights, and Postdictatorship in Argentina, Brazil, and Uruguay* (Evanston, IL: Northwestern University Press, 2018), 4–5.
8 Jacques Rancière (Steven Corcoran, Translator). *Dissensus: On Politics and Aesthetics.* (London-New York: Continuum International Publishing Group Ltd, 2010).
9 Roberta Villalón, ed., *Memory, Truth, and Justice in Contemporary Latin America* (London: Rowman and Littlefield, 2017).
10 Gloria Ramírez and Lorena Luengas, "Salón del Nunca Más, Granada. Un proceso comunitario. Oriente Antioqueño," in *Museos, comunidades y reconciliación. Experiencias y memorias en diálogo. XIV Cátedra de Historia Ernesto Restrepo Tirado* (Bogotá: Museo Nacional de Colombia, Universidad Externado de Colombia, 2009), 55.
11 Francesca Lessa, *Memory and Transitional Justice in Argentina and Uruguay. Against Impunity* (New York: Palgrave-McMillan, 2013), 19.

12 Elizabeth Jelin, *State Repression and the Labors of Memory*. Translated by Marcial Godoy-Anativia and Judy Rein. (Minneapolis: The University of Minnesota Press, 2003), 24.
13 Ibermuseos. *Roundtable of Santiago de Chile, 1972. Vol. 1*. http://www.ibermuseos.org/en/resources/publications/mesa-redonda-de-santiago-de-chile-1972-vol-1/. (23 May 2022).
14 Bruno Brulon, "Decolonising the Museum? Community Experiences in the Periphery of the ICOM Museum Definition," *Curator: The Museum Journal* 64, no. 3 (2021): 439–455.
15 Peter Vergo, *The New Museology* (London: Reaktion Books, 1989).
16 Brulon, "Dcolonosing the Museum?"
17 "Museum Definition." ICOM, http://icom.museum/the-vision/museum-definition/
18 https://www.theartnewspaper.com/2020/08/13/icom-in-turmoil-after-row-over-new-definition-of-museums
19 "ICOM Approves a New Museum Definition," International Council of Museums, Accessed September 14, 2022, https://icom.museum/en/news/icom-approves-a-new-museum-definition/#:~:text=NetworkICOM%20approves%20a%20new%20museum%20definition&text=The%20new%20text%20reads%3A,exhibits%20tangible%20and%20intangible%20heritage.
20 Brulon, "Decolonising the Museum?"
21 T. R. Adam, *The Museum and Popular Culture* (New York: American Association for Adult Education, 1939), 28.
22 Vikki MacCall and Clive Gray, "Museums and the 'New Museology': Theory, Practice, and Organizational Change," *Management and Curatorship* 29, no. 1 (2013): 1–17.
23 Deirdre, C., "The Informed Muse: The Implications of 'The New Museology' for Museum Practice," *Museum Management and Curatorship* 12, no. 3 (1993): 267–283.
24 Stam, "The Informed Muse."
25 MacCall and Gray, "Museums and the 'New Museology.'"
26 Peter Vergo, *The New Museology* (London: Reaktion Books, 1989), 3.
27 Edwina Taborsky, "The Discursive Object," in *Objects of Knowledge, New Research in Museum Studies 1*, ed. Susan Pearce (London and Atlantic Highlands: The Athlone Press, 1990), 52.
28 Gloria Ramírez and Lorena Luengas, "Salón del Nunca Más, Granada," 34.
29 Pierre Bourdieu, *Distinction*.
30 Stuart Hall and Paddy Whannel, *The Popular Arts* (Durham, NC and London: Duke University Press, 1964/ 2018).
31 Gloria Quintero, Interview by Jimena Perry, Granada, Antioquia, August 14, 2012.
32 Carlos Abel Aristizábal, Interview by Jimena Perry, Granada, Antioquia, May 9, 2017.
33 Gloria Ramírez, Interview by Jimena Perry, Granada, Antioquia, May 12, 2017.
34 Johannes Fabian, "On Recognizing Things. The 'Ethnic Artefact' and the 'Ethnographic Object,'" *L'Homme*, no. 170, ESPÈCES D'OBJETS (avril/juin 2004): 47–60.Published by EHESS, Stable URL: http://www.jstor.org/stable/40590211
35 Andrea Hauenschild, "Claims and Reality of New Museology: Case Studies in Canada, the United States, and Mexico," http://museumstudies.si.edu/claims2000.htm#2.
36 Silke Arnold-de Simine, *Mediating Memory in the Museum: Trauma, Empathy, Nostalgia* (London: Palgrave MacMillan, 2013); Marek Tamm, "Beyond History and Memory: New Perspectives in Memory Studies," *History Compass* 11, no. 6 (2013): 458–473; and Jay Winter, "The Generation of Memory: Reflections on the 'Memory Boom' in Contemporary Historical Studies," *Canadian Military History* 10, no. 3: 57–66.
37 Kerwin Lee Klein, "On the Emergence of Memory in Historical Discourse," *Representations*, no. 69, *Special Issue Grounds for Remembering* (Winter, 2000): 127–150.

38 Michael J. Lazzara, "The Memory Turn," in *New Approaches to Latin American Studies. Culture and Power*, ed. Juan Poblete (New York: Routledge, 2018), 14–32.
39 Michael J. Lazzara, "The Memory Turn," 18.
40 "El país según José Obdulio," *El Tiempo*, August 13, 2008, https://www.eltiempo.com/archivo/documento/CMS-4445405
41 Jelin, *State Repression*, 93.
42 International Center for Transitional Justice, "What is Transitional Justice?", https://www.ictj.org/about/transitional-justice.
43 John H. Herz, *From Dictatorship to Democracy: Coping with the Legacies of Authoritarianism and Totalitarianism* (Westport, CT: Greenwood Press, 1982).
44 Guillermo O'Donnell, Philippe C. Schmitter, and Laurence Whitehead, *Transitions from Authoritarian Rule: Comparative Perspectives* (Baltimore, MD: John Hopkins University Press, 1986).
45 Paige Arthur, "How 'Transitions' Reshaped Human Rights: A Conceptual History of Transitional Justice," *Human Rights Quarterly*, 31, no. 2 (May 2009): 321–367.
46 Ruti G. Teitel, "Transitional Justice Genealogy," *Harvard Human Rights Journal*, 16 (Spring 2003): 69–94.
47 Alexandra Barahona de Brito, "Transitional Justice and Memory: Exploring Perspectives," *South European Society and Politics* 15, no. 3 (September 2010): 359–376.
48 Juan E. Méndez, "Victims as Protagonists in Transitional Justice," *International Journal of Transitional Justice* 10, no. 1 (March 2016): 1–5.
49 Teitel, "Transitional Justice Genealogy," 8.
50 Méndez, "Victims as Protagonists," 4.
51 Teitel, "Transitional Justice Genealogy," 4.
52 Barahona de Brito, "Transitional Justice and Memory."
53 Carlos Felipe Rúa Delgado, "Los momentos de la justicia transicional en Colombia," *Revista de Derecho* 43 (2015): 71–109.
54 María Victoria Uribe and Pilar Riaño Alcalá, "Memory Amidst War: The Historical Memory Group of Colombia," *International Journal of Transitional Justice* 10 (2016): 6–24.
55 Andrea Peña, "La Ley de Justicia y Paz," *Semana*, February 5, 2006, https://www.semana.com/on- line/articulo/la-ley-justicia-paz/76931-3.
56 Uribe and Riaño Alcalá, "Memory Amidst War."
57 Ley 1448 de 2011, http://www.unidadvictimas.gov.co/sites/default/files/documentosbiblioteca/ley-1448-de-2011.pdf. My translation.
58 "Jurisdicción Especial Para La Paz: Fundamentos Teóricos y …—Scielo," accessed July 28, 2022, http://www.scielo.org.co/scielo.php?script=sci_arttext&pid=S0121-47052019000200003.
59 Vizcaíno, M., "La justicia transicional: ¿un paso hacia la paz?" *Revista Derecho Penal y Criminología* 36, no. 100 (2015): 75–88.
60 Summers, N., "Colombia's Victims' Law: Transitional Justice in a Time of Violent Conflict?" *Harvard Human Rights Journal* 25 (2012): 220–235.
61 "Jurisdicción Especial Para La Paz: Fundamentos Teóricos y …—Scielo," accessed July 28, 2022, http://www.scielo.org.co/scielo.php?script=sci_arttext&pid=S0121-47052019000200003.
62 Gloria Ramírez and Lorena Luengas, "Salón del Nunca Más, Granada," 26.
63 Néstor Alonso López, "Granada, Antioquia, el pueblo que dijo 'Nunca más' a la violencia," *El Tiempo*, November 21, 2010.
64 Gloria Ramírez, Interview by Jimena Perry.
65 Gloria Ramírez and Lorena Luengas, "Salón del Nunca Más, Granada," 35.
66 Andrew Rajca, *Dissensual Subjects: Memory, Human Rights, and Postdictatorship in Argentina, Brazil, and Uruguay* (Evanston, IL: Northwestern University Press, 2018).
67 Gloria Ramírez, Interview by Jimena Perry.

68 Virginia M. Bouvier and Santiago Restrepo, *Colombia la construcción de la paz en tiempos de guerra* (Bogotá: Editorial Universidad del Rosario, Escuela de Ciencias Humanas, 2014).
69 Martha Inés Villa Martínez, *Granada: Memorias de guerra, resistencia y reconstrucción* (Bogotá: Centro Nacional de Memoria Histórica, 2016), 185–186.
70 Centro Nacional de Memoria Histórica. *Masacre de Granada 2001*, http://rutasdelconflicto.com/interna.php?masacre=537.
71 Testimony from a woman collected during a workshop organized by the National Center for Historical Memory during June 27 and 28, 2004. Villa Martínez, *Granada: Memorias*, 185.
72 Testimony from a man collected during the same workshop. Villa Martínez, *Granada: Memorias*, 186.
73 "Restaurando a Granada," March 22, 2013, http://www.traslacoladelarata.com/2013/04/22/restaurando-a-granada/
74 Villa Martínez, *Granada: Memorias*, 128.
75 Villa Martínez, *Granada: Memorias*, 133.
76 Gonzalo Sánchez, *La Masacre de El Salado: esa guerra no era nuestra* (Bogotá: Centro Nacional de Memoria Histórica, 2009).
77 Jaime Montoya, Interview by Jimena Perry, Granada, Antioquia, May 12, 2017.
78 Claudia Milena Giraldo, Interview by Jimena Perry, Granada, Antioquia, May 10, 2017.
79 Gloria Elcy Ramíez, Interview by Jimena Perry, Granada, Antioquia, April 25, 2022.
80 Halbwachs, *The Collective Memory*, 48–50.
81 Gonzalo Sánchez, "Testimonio, Justicia y Memoria. Reflexiones preliminares sobre una trilogía actual," *Estudios Políticos* 53 (2018): 19–47.
82 Michael Brennan, "Why Materiality in Mourning Matters," in *The Materiality of Mourning: Cross-Cultural Perspectives*, eds. Zahra Newby and Ruth E. Toulson (London: Routledge, Taylor & Francis Group, 2019), 223–242.

# 4

# MEMORY AND INTANGIBLE HERITAGE

## The Traveling Museum of Memory and Identity of Montes de María, El Mochuelo

In 1994, a group of journalists, teachers, cultural advocates, and community leaders created the Corporación Colectivo de Comunicaciones Montes de María Línea 21 (Montes de María Line 21 Corporation Collective of Communications) in Carmen de Bolívar, one of the 15 peasant communities that compose the Montes de María region in the Colombian Caribbean. The other towns are María La Baja, San Juan Nepomuceno, San Jacinto, Córdoba, Zambrano, and El Guamo in Bolívar; Ovejas, Chalán, Colosó, Morroa, Toluviejo, Los Palmitos, San Onofre, and San Antonio de Palmitos in Sucre. The Collective's aim is to encourage the inhabitants of the area to exercise their rights to identify and participate in projects of citizenship building. Under the leadership of journalist Soraya Bayuelo—who survived the killing of one of her nieces by the FARC-EP—the Collective's purpose is to motivate children, teenagers, and adults to construct a future without violence through community television, radio, cinema, and printed media.[1] As a result, the Collective won the Colombian National Peace Prize in 2003. *El Tiempo*, *El Espectador*, and *El Colombiano* newspapers, *Semana* magazine, radio, and television network Caracol, and the German foundation Friedrich-Ebert-Stiftung en Colombia, Fescol, promote the award. The Collective won the fifth national prize for being a tool that favors peace initiatives, solidarity, socio-economic development, and understanding among Colombians.[2] In addition, in 2020, the Collective was awarded the Fundación Alejandro Ángel Escobar solidarity price for their persistent work. These two acknowledgements have called the attention of national and international NGOs, activists, and researchers, which makes visible the peace efforts of the Montes de María inhabitants.

The members of the Collective, inspired by Woody Allen's movie *The Purple Rose of Cairo*, also organize annually a community cinema festival with the

DOI: 10.4324/9781003283997-5

same name. This Montes de María event started in 2002 and in 2022 celebrates 20 years of existence, becoming a landmark for the communities of the region. One of the key features of this festivity is its itinerancy. The cinema moves around the 15 municipalities of Montes de María, so the film projections can reach as many people as possible. The Collective's creators devote much attention and resources to design traveling venues because they know that for some people of the area it is difficult to access these activities. Therefore, since 2008, the affiliates of the Collective started to think about an itinerant museum and inaugurated it after 11 years of planning.

Nicknamed El Mochuelo, traditional songbird of region, the Traveling Museum of Memory and Identity of Montes de María, opened its doors on March 15, 2019. El Mochuelo started its journey in Carmen de Bolívar and visits the 15 townships of the region prior to returning where the tour began. The creators of the venue emphasize its non-static nature because they believe in the cultural enrichment produced by the interaction between socially dynamic actors, such as the inhabitants of the region's municipalities. They also highlight its peripatetic character, which allows for the venue not to exhibit conventional glass cases and museological artifacts, such as pottery, paper documents, or material culture from the region. Instead, the designers of El Mochuelo envisioned it as a space for interactive displays, pictures, videos, paintings, and other structures easy to set up and move around. The founders of the museum wanted the site and its exhibits to promote reflections about the peasant life of Montes de María, recreate the region's oral traditions, and help survivors remember that they can rely on their cultural mores to heal and move on from the violence they endured.

The purpose of this memory site, like the Hall of Never Again (discussed in the previous chapter) and the nearly 30 other Colombian memory venues, is to remember and honor the victims of the decades-long armed conflict. However, at El Mochuelo, the inhabitants of Montes de María do so in a unique way: They carry out an inventory of their "immaterial or intangible heritage."[3] Although representations of brutalities exerted upon them still have a place at El Mochuelo, the aim of the community leaders is not to present graphic or shocking descriptions.

In this chapter, the final case study of four, I explore the relationship between memory and intangible heritage through El Mochuelo's exhibitions, narratives, images, setting, and cultural context. I examine how and which remembrances the Montes de María communities select to pass on to future generations. I also analyze why the creators of El Mochuelo decided to recover and preserve their cultural traditions to strengthen and restore their social fabrics affected by violence, for preventing atrocities to recur. In addition, I discuss why the creators of El Mochuelo thought an itinerant or peripatetic venue would serve better than a conventional static museum.

Drawing on oral histories, interviews, the archive of the National Center for Historical Memory of Colombia, newspapers, and magazines, I analyze the nature and reasoning behind the creation of El Mochuelo, its particular production process of historical memories, and the voids it attempts to fill. Lastly, I contrast this site with the Hall of Never Again's case to enhance our comprehension of the ways in which Colombian cultural diversity manifests and operates.

Scholars such as anthropologist Veysel Apaydin who examines the relationship between memory and heritage insist in the impossibility of approaching one concept without the other because individuals and groups are the ones who assign meaning to them. Despite Apaydin's focus on tangible or material heritage, he raises discerning thoughts about their interconnection due to his research, in which he poses the always present debate about what is material and immaterial heritage. Although the anthropologist works concentrate on monuments and materiality, he calls our attention to look at the deep cultural connotations that surround objects. Oral narratives, social knowledge, or to use Bourdieu's idea of social capital, are expressed in concrete items; thus, limits are blurry. Furthermore, Apaydin reiterated that the values culturally assigned to heritage and the memories they trigger are a significant symbol for collective identity because they bring communities together. This is the case seen at El Mochuelo, where the 15 social groups of Montes de María gathered to strengthen their social identity. Thus, intangible heritage is a war casualty too; not only statues, artifacts, or monuments are lost, but also the information and perceptions linked to them, which also indicates that memories are gone. Cultural heritage, as proven at El Mochuelo, helps groups and individuals overcome traumatic pasts and survive in adverse environments.[4]

Concurring with Apaydin, in *Museums, Exhibitions, and Memories of Violence in Colombia, 2000–2014*, I privilege the cultural decisions made by members of the communities examined. As El Mochuelo shows, the non-direct reference to violence in its displays does not entail forgetting, what it demonstrates is that for grassroots initiatives to thrive, they must be grounded in cultural and collective decisions. As stated by Apaydin, "It is strongly suggested here that cultural memory and heritage are processes that actively engage the social, economic, and political life of the present; they are living processes and a tool for the resilience of communities." Therefore, as mentioned throughout this book, there is no standard way to remember, represent, and grieve atrocities endured and, as the local case studies presented in this text show, Colombian cultural diversity is far from over.

## Immaterial or Intangible Heritage in Colombia

In his article *Time and Heritage*, historian Francois Hartog asserts: "Heritage is a recourse in times of crisis."[5] This provocative statement inspires this chapter's discussion because it is related to UNESCO's goal of preserving and protecting cultural diversity by creating awareness of those material and immaterial elements communities think of as heritage. Therefore, Hartog's assertion and UNESCO's mission trigger three interrelated concerns: What is worthy for communities to protect and preserve, why, and how. These are universal questions with several answers; however, they attempt to address a long-time worry related to what scholar Andreas Huyssen notes: "The contemporary public obsession with memory clashes with an intense public panic of oblivion."[6] It seems that most memory efforts are struggles against forgetting, perhaps because the events they remember and represent are too horrific for people to pretend they never happened. Thus, memory and heritage seem to have the common idea of remembering as salvaging.

By attempting to recover and salvage the immaterial heritage (songs, poems, and oral traditions) of the Montes de María region, the creators of El Mochuelo encourage a particular process of memory production to fill in the silences and voids of the region's violent history. These communities decided not to dwell in the past but to overcome it by looking into the present for building the future. Even though El Mochuelo is a museum, it is still in the making, and due to its peripatetic character, its displays are continuously changing.

The effort of collecting the oral traditions of the region started in the 1990s, as mentioned before, when community leaders such as Bayuelo began to fear their culture was in danger. As with most Colombian communities, the recent violence disrupted the Montes de María population's life, activating recovery efforts for its preservation. Conveniently, the Convention for the Safeguarding of the Intangible Cultural Heritage issued by UNESCO in 2003 framed these endeavors, which purpose is to salvage cultural traditions that are getting lost. Although this idea of preservation is based on good intentions, it is also problematic because it does not consider how diverse cultural processes work. Social groups decide what becomes part of their heritage and what they want to remember; so, if a tradition or costume falls into oblivion in the absence of cultural repression, it is most likely because certain cultural actors meant for this to happen.

In the Convention's context, many local Colombian communities found a space to acknowledge their traditions. However, not all cultural expressions become heritage, and as historian Jessica Moody claims, "...heritage is not [only] a physical thing left over from the past but an actively constructed understanding, a discourse about the past which is ever in fluctuation."[7] Her heritage approach resonates with contemporary uses of memory, such as Huyssen's, who claims that it is not enough to remember or represent the past but to envision alternatives for the future. Understanding heritage and memory as processes related to the past provides a better understanding of cases such as El Mochuelo because there is a representation of their history, but most of the venue's attention is devoted to the present and the future of the communities it serves. El Mochuelo's work team believe that when they move the museum from one town to another, they transport its displays and the knowledge that the community members have. These dialogues, products of cultural interactions, comprise the museum's cultural inventory of immaterial heritage.

Furthermore, the creators of El Mochuelo strive to pass mostly oral traditions from one generation to another, choosing what to preserve and deciding which knowledge to protect. In this sense, and following Paul Ricoeur's *History, Memory, Forgetting*, and Moody, not everything is remembered. Ricoeur highlights the cultural meaning of forgetting, which becomes part of significant historical memory processes, thus relevant when we think about heritage. Ricoeur also opens the discussion about when and how diverse cultures choose not to forget, omit specific remembrances, and freely select how they want new generations to perceive their past.[8] The El Mochuelo creators largely bypassed direct violent references, a decision which confirms Ricoeur's assertion that to ignore specific remembrances is also part of the dynamics of memory-making. To exclude historical memories at El Mochuelo reflects what the venue's organizers and the inhabitants of Montes de María wish to consider worth preserving as part of their immaterial cultural heritage and memory.

Colombian scholars began using the term "immaterial or intangible heritage" in 2006. In that year, the country ratified and adhered to the United Nations Educational, Scientific, and Cultural Organization (UNESCO) Convention for the Safeguarding of the Immaterial Cultural Heritage, issued in Paris during its 32nd meeting on October 17, 2003. The summit defined immaterial or intangible heritage as:

> [...] practices, representations, expressions, knowledge, skills—as well as the instruments, objects, artefacts, and cultural spaces associated therewith—that communities, groups and, in some cases, individuals recognize as part of their cultural heritage. Communities constantly transmit their cultural heritage from generation to generation, and recreated it in in response to their environment, their interaction with nature and their history, and provides them with a sense of identity and continuity, thus promoting respect for cultural diversity and human creativity. [...] it manifests in the following domains: (a) oral traditions and expressions, including language as a vehicle of the intangible cultural heritage; (b) performing arts; (c) social practices, rituals and festive events; (d) knowledge and practices concerning nature and the universe; (e) traditional craftsmanship.[9]

UNESCO's elucidation of intangible heritage encouraged Colombian academics and rural communities to think about ways to collect and safeguard cultural traditions lost to the armed conflict. In this context, the members of the Montes de María Collective of Communications made the most of the term to preserve and promote their own culture.

Before the mid-1990s, the term used for cultural expressions was folklore, but the UNESCO specialists realized it implied a separation from the material components of culture. The notion of cultural heritage, instead, was broad enough to avoid the binary distinction between intangible and tangible patrimony. The notion of intangible cultural heritage came to include cultural expressions and knowledge used in the production of material items, such as monuments, museums, and other infrastructures, which are directly linked with oral traditions, memorialization, commemoration, and historical events, El Mochuelo being one of them.[10]

The notion of immaterial cultural heritage implies passing mostly oral traditions from one generation to another, choosing what to preserve, and deciding which knowledge to protect. Since the 1930s, scholars such as social psychologist Frederic Bartlett, in his book *Remembering: A Study in Experimental and Social Psychology* began to hint toward constructing the concept of "cultural heritage"—without discerning between tangible-material culture and intangible. Bartlett addressed the function of remembering in specific contexts and emphasized the relevance for social groups to recall daily life events. He also stated that the place rumors, stories, and designs acquire in a culture is the result of decision-making processes transmitted from person to person through the years. "In this way," he continues, "cultural characters which have a common origin may come to have apparently the most diverse forms."[11] These statements illustrate how, despite enduring brutalities similar to the community of Granada, mentioned in Chapter 3, the Montes de María inhabitants decided to organize public memorials differently. While in El Mochuelo, violence is not as graphic because its creators opted to display oral traditions, the creators of the Hall decided to do the opposite: display graphic violence accounts. About El Mochuelo, Soraya Bayuelo states, "The dead ones were my friends and acquaintances, I knew them all, therefore, I was not able to show their pictures or describe how they died. That relives the trauma, and we need to heal." While Gloria Ramírez, from the Hall of Never Again, notes, "It is important for us that the outsiders that come to the Hall see with their own eyes the terrible violence we went through." These distinctive ways to remember and represent brutalities do not compete among each other and are not mutually exclusive. They are examples of how Colombian cultural diversity, communal dynamics, and local histories influence the public manifestation of historical memories.

Another pivotal book for understanding immaterial cultural heritage is Maurice Halbwachs's book On Collective Memory (1950). While the historian does not refer specifically to the notion of immaterial cultural heritage, his analysis of how memories get imprinted in people's minds after processes of transmission from one generation to another encouraged the concept's development. The historian argues that different generations acquire from their parents and grandparents their remembrances of the past and that, even though there is a bond between generations, the younger ones create their own memories to pass onto a newer age group. This means that each recollection and therefore allusion to Montes de María cultural traditions at El Mochuelo, for instance, is the result of selective community determinations. Halbwachs also underscores the interactions between collective and autobiographical memory, prompting reflections about what communities and individuals value and remember, mentioned also in Chapter 3.[12]

In Paul Ricoeur's *History, Memory, Forgetting*, the author also emphasizes on memory and heritage. He highlights the cultural significance of forgetting, which becomes part of significant historical memory processes, thus relevant when we think about heritage. In medical or biological terms, it is a popular belief that forgetting signals bad memory. However, and in accordance with Ricoeur, memory reflects cultural decisions. "Could forgetting then no longer be in every respect an enemy of memory, and could memory have to negotiate with forgetting, groping to find the right measure in its balance with forgetting?"[13] Ricoeur's question opened the discussion about when and how diverse cultures choose not to forget but to omit certain remembrances and to freely select how they want new generations to perceive their past. The El Mochuelo creators largely bypassed direct violent references, a decision which confirms Ricoeur's assertion that to ignore certain remembrances is also part of the dynamics of memory making. To exclude historical memories at El Mochuelo reflects what the venue's organizers and the inhabitants of Montes de María wish to consider worth preserving, therefore, as part of their immaterial cultural heritage.

In Montes de María, since 1994, when Soraya Bayuelo founded the Collective, a cultural inventory of the immaterial heritage of the region started. The Collective's efforts and El Mochuelo concentrate on taking stock of the old and new oral traditions that the traveling venues promote. As Soraya emphasizes, "We strongly believe in the cultural exchanges that take place when people travel. When going somewhere, people bring with them oral knowledge. When leaving, it is the same since they take what they have learned with them." Soraya and El Mochuelo's work team believe that when they move the museum from one town to another, they transport not only its inventory but also its immaterial heritage. The oral traditions displayed at the venue are poems, songs, and stories of Montes de María.

As mentioned, the UNESCO's 2003 Convention promoted an explicit awareness of the need to conserve, maintain, and pass onto new generations the cultural expressions that are at risk of disappearing. Although this idea of preservation is based on good intentions, it is also problematic because it does not consider how diverse cultural processes work. Generally, social groups decide what becomes part of their heritage and what they want to remember; so, if a tradition or costume falls into oblivion in the absence of cultural repression, it is most likely because certain cultural actors meant for this to happen. Both El Mochuelo and the Hall of Never Again are clear examples of these selections.

## The Violence in Montes de María

The 15 towns that compose the Montes d María region are between the Colombian Caribbean Departments of Sucre and Bolívar in the country's coast. Due to its location and wealth of natural resources, the zone has been highly coveted during the twentieth century, especially since the 1980s. Guerrillas, drug lords, the army, and paramilitaries disputed the control of the area because it permits access to the Caribbean Sea at the Gulf of Morrosquillo,[18] which is a corridor for the commercialization of cocaine in the Department of Bolívar. This part of the country also has great diversity of flora and fauna and is propitious for agricultural production, including corn, rice, cassava, yams, plantains, tobacco, coffee, and avocado, earning the name of the "Caribbean pantry" for the abundance of its production. Montes de María is also the home of the Zenú Indigenous community. The region is not only diverse in biological and natural terms. It is also home to 15 social groups, which devote a lot of their time to create and re-create oral expressions such as songs, poems, and stories. The citizens of the area value these cultural activities. Therefore, when the violence of the 1980s started, all their social structures were deeply disturbed, and fear gripped increasingly isolated households.

In the decade of the 1980s, the appearance of three of the main guerrillas of the country, Ejército Revolucionario del Pueblo, ERP (People's Revolutionary Army), FARC-EP, and the ELN, engulfed Montes de María in violence. These insurgents stole cattle and kidnapped owners of small-, medium-, and large-scale pieces of land to finance their operations.[14] They also sabotaged, harassed, and attacked civilians such as farmers, whom they tried to recruit or brainwash. To counteract the guerrillas' presence, locals turned to the Asociación Nacional de Usuarios Campesinos de Colombia, ANUC (National Association of Peasant Users of Colombia), created in 1967 to promote and defend the sharecropper cultures of Colombia.[15] Drug lords exacerbated violence in the area with their arrival in the 1990s. From 1996 to 2005, there were approximately 234,098 victims of atrocities in this region, according to official figures of the Comisión Nacional de Reparación y Conciliación (National Commission of Reparations and Reconciliation).[16]

Paramilitaries and guerrillas perpetrated most of the massacres in the 15 Montes de María towns. The victims of these atrocities were community leaders, peasants, students, unionists, human rights activists, members of the LGBTQ communities, and Indigenous peoples. The following chart lists the most notorious massacres in Montes de María, perhaps because of their coverage in the media (Table 4.1).

Table 4.1 lists 31 massacres; however, the inhabitants of Montes de María, with Soraya Bayuelo's help, have documented 117. An interview with anthropologist Bexielena Hernández, founder of Estudio Mapping, company that designs and produces exhibitions, complemented the information presented in

**TABLE 4.1** Some Massacres Perpetrated in the Montes de María Region between 1991 and 2007[17]

| Rural Area | Municipality | Year |
| --- | --- | --- |
| El Palmar | Ovejas | 1991 |
| La Haya | San Juan Nepomuceno | 1991 |
| El Cielo | Chalán | 1992 |
| Pichilín | Colosó | 1996 |
| La Pelona | San Onofre | 1997 |
| La Libertad | San Onofre | 1997, 2000 |
| San Isidro | El Carmen de Bolívar | 1999 |
| Caracolí | El Carmen de Bolívar | 1999 |
| Capaca y Campoalegre | Zambrano | 1999 |
| Las Palmas | San Jacinto | 1999 |
| El Salado | Carmen de Bolívar | 2000 |
| Las Brisas, San Cayetano, Mampuján | María la Baja y San Juan Nepomuceno | 2000, 2001, 2002 |
| Mata de Perro | El Carmen de Bolívar | 2000 |
| Flor del Monte, Canutal y Canutalito | Ovejas | 2000 |
| Chinulito y el Cerro | Colosó | 2000 |
| Chengue | Ovejas | 2001 |
| Retiro Nuevo | María la Baja | 2001 |
| Macayepo | El Carmen de Bolívar | 2000 |
| La Aventura | Córdoba | 2002 |
| Los Guámaros y el Tapón | San Juan Nepomuceno | 2002 |
| Arenas | San Jacinto | 2003 |
| La Sierra | Carmen de Bolívar | 2004 |
| Don Gabriel | Ovejas | 2005 |
| Bajo Grande | Carmen de Bolívar | 2007 |

the chart. This firm oversaw the design of El Mochuelo during 2015; thus, its team of professionals outlined a timeline of the violence in Montes de María.

The exact number of massacres and instances of victimization is still a matter of debate. The researchers of the Centro Nacional de Memoria Histórica, CNMH (National Center for Historical Memory), have reported sixty extermination acts, but based on the information gathered by members of the Montes de María communities, it is highly probable that there are more; therefore, investigations continue. In the Truth Commission Report submitted to the country in June 2022, there are accounts of violence survivors in Montes de María, like the following, in which paramilitaries committed acts of sexual violence against afro descendant women:

> [...] they had total control of the population, which allowed them to impose rules, patterns of behavior, and sanctions to those who did not

> follow their parameters. Mostly they punished women. Those punishments consisted in sexual aggressions which implied that these were generalized conducts within the armed organization [paramilitaries].[18]

The Colombian Truth Commissioners gathered testimonies like this one to show how the country's internal war left a myriad of victims, not only casualties but survivors with deep emotional, cultural, social, and mental scars. Thus, to provide a number or definitive quantity of victims is still a matter of time and research.

One of the best-known massacres in Montes de María, which received the greatest media coverage, occurred in the El Salado township in 2000. Four hundred and fifty paramilitary fighters left more than one hundred dead peasants over five days in February. This atrocity was one of the bloodiest of the region. It attracted special attention because, although local authorities alerted the state to the presence of paramilitary groups in their towns, government officials failed to act, allowing for one of the worst bloodbaths in the history of Colombian violence during the 2000s. The victims ranged in age from six to 65 years old. The researchers of the CNMH identified 60 fatality victims: 52 men and eight women; three 18-year-old individuals; 12 between the ages of 18 and 25; ten young adults between ages 26 and 35, 23 adults between ages 23 and 36, and ten older adults. The atrocities included torture and decapitations.

Three paramilitary groups, with the help of powerful families of the region, perpetrated the El Salado massacre. Historian Gonzalo Sánchez led the team of researchers of the CNMH who reconstructed the brutality. They presented their findings in their 2009 report, *La Masacre de El Salado: esa guerra no era nuestra* (The Massacre of El Salado: That Was Not Our War).[19] In this text, the investigators describe and carefully analyze the context, the violent acts, and their aftermath. It includes testimonials of the survivors, such as the following:

> In the court they told us, "men to one side, women to the other," and they threw us upside down there, immediately they took a young man, they told him, "You stay here with us because you escaped in Zambrano, but you will not get away this time." He was the first one killed in the court. They put a bag over his head, he screamed for his life, not to kill him, they beat him on the belly, kicked him, punched him in the face, they destroyed all his face first, they said to us, "Look and learn, this will happen to you, so you better start talking." We responded, "What would we say if we know nothing." After they threw the young man in the court, they killed him, they shot him [...]. They cut off one of his ears; he cried and screamed; he was the first one killed there. [...]. It took a while for him to die. That agony is horrible, to see how someone suffers.

Although the massacre of El Salado and those mentioned in the table are the best-known atrocities that occurred in Montes de María, there were other mass killings that did not receive the same attention. According to scholar José Francisco Restrepo, the first registered massacre in the region took place in September 1992 in a small town called Cielo, in Chalán, Department of Sucre. A group of armed men—whose identities remain unknown until today—entered the house of a family and killed eight people. Afterward, several paramilitary and guerrilla groups took over the region, and the police force left.

After this brutality, on June 27, 1995, the FARC-EP killed the former governor of Sucre, as confirmed by the 2009 report. This was a breaking point that unleashed a very bloody and violent time. Kidnappings started to rise, farmers reported millions in losses, and bombings became a common occurrence. In addition, the confrontations between paramilitaries and guerrillas increased, leaving civil society in despair. The armed groups killed, kidnapped, bombed, set farms on fire, and kept enlarging their forces. The state's military forces did not intervene much, instead mistreating the region's inhabitants and accusing them of being paramilitaries or guerrilla fighters, which escalated the conflict. Three different forces attacked peasants and Indigenous communities of Montes de María, putting them in the crossfire.

In March 1996, paramilitaries shot a civic leader couple while holding their baby in front of their house and killed 15 councilors of the Civic Movement of Sucre. Simultaneously, the FARC-EP intensified their attacks against the farmers of the region; in response to the state's inaction, these farmers created the Cooperativas de Seguridad Rural, Convivir (Cooperatives for Rural Security), in Sucre and Bolívar. Around the same time, another group of farmers reached out to the nearby Urabá region paramilitaries, searching for some more help to defend themselves against the guerrillas. Their appeal succeeded, and many other paramilitary groups started to enter Montes de María. The infamous Castaño Brothers came into the scene, making the inhabitants of the region very wary of their surroundings.

Fidel, Carlos, and Vicente Castaño Gil founded the Peasant Self-Defenders of Córdoba and Urabá (ACCU), a far-right paramilitary organization in Colombia. They were known for their cruelty and associations with drug traffickers. Their victims exceed 140,000 people. They were sworn enemies of the guerrillas since their father got kidnapped and killed by the FARC-EP in 1980; from then on, the brothers devoted their lives to fight these rebel groups. They are also ill-reputed because they killed each other due to rivalries and jealousies. The researchers of the CNMH have proved the involvement of Carlos in the El Salado massacre and in the death of Carlos Pizarro Leongómez, discussed in Chapter 2. The presence of paramilitaries determined to decimate the guerrillas intensified the war. The inhabitants of Montes de María stopped going out at night and lived in constant fear.

This extreme paramilitary advance did not eliminate the guerrillas. Its real achievement was the destruction of entire families. The armed groups took away people's land and left thousands of women and children in absolute poverty. The assault also opened corridors for drug trafficking. In response to the paramilitary attacks, the guerrillas strengthened and increased their offensives. Between 1994 and 1999, homicides, massacres, and kidnappings were part of everyday life for the people of Montes de María. When the paramilitary demobilization started in 2005, the guerrillas were still bombing state infrastructure in this zone. However, without the paramilitary menace, the army entered Montes de María and reduced the guerrillas. This brought some tranquility to the population of the region, which came together and created victims' associations to confront the atrocities endured.[20] Let us remember that during 2005, the Justice and Law Peace, mentioned in Chapter 3, provided a legal framework approved by the Congress to facilitate the demobilization of paramilitaries in Colombia. Supposedly, it would also encourage guerrilla groups to lay down their weapons.

After some years of calm, the government identified the presence of newly armed actors in the region and other parts of the country. These groups receive the name of Bandas criminales, or bacrim (Criminal Bands) and include former paramilitary fighters involved in drug trafficking and extortion. In 2010, the Instituto de Estudios para el Desarrollo y la Paz, INDEPAZ (Institute of Studies for Development and Peace), said that the bacrim were now responsible for more violence than the guerrillas. "With names like the Águilas Negras (Black Eagles), Erpac, and Rastrojos, these bacrim combine control of cocaine production and smuggling with extreme violence, but do not have any apparent political agenda."[21]

In 2018, when President Iván Duque took office, as mentioned before, the violence increased, not only in Montes de María but all over the country. During that year, the Colombian Ombudsman's Office warned the government about the presence of armed illegal groups again. On this occasion, the paramilitary organization Autodefensas Gaitanistas de Colombia, AGC (Gaitanist Self-Defense Forces of Colombia), attempted to control the territory for trafficking drugs, weapons, and people. They killed two peasants and forcibly displaced 27 families. However, the authorities refused to take any action arguing that there was no such presence despite being enough proof that the AGC were regrouping and gaining momentum in the area. As a result, once again the inhabitants of Montes de Maria felt coerced and afraid to collaborate with the illegal organization. In addition, when the Covid-19 pandemic started, many people could not leave due to the quarantine. When the Ombudsman's Office issued the alert, it was established that young unemployed men were targeted by the AGC, luring them with money and making evident the need for state intervention, but this did not happen.[22] Since then, the 15 communities have been living in a tense calm, hoping that brutalities do not recur.

Recently, the communities of Montes de María are experiencing a violence upsurge. In January 2022, the region's inhabitants denounced the killing of six individuals and denounced the presence of armed individuals on motorcycles with face coverings. They are threatening people so they do not leave their houses and painting graffities related to the Autodefensas Gaitanistas de Colombia, AGC (Gaitanist Self-Defense Forces of Colombia), also known as the Gulf Clan, on walls of several municipalities. Social leaders of the region, who want to keep a low profile, are fearing for their lives while the AGC coerces them to vote for candidates they do not believe in. In addition, high-end cars, traditionally used for drug smuggling, are becoming frequent again.[23] In April and May 2021, Montes de María suffered an escalation of violence. Social leaders such as Bayuelo had to lay low and take extra security measures for a while. The paramilitary group, The Gulf Clan, terrorized the townships of Colosó and San Jacinto, not allowing the peasants to commercialize their products amid a national strike. People of these municipalities denounced publicly the presence of the armed actors, but nobody listened. This situation made worse the social leaders' stigmatization, and in another of the 15 municipalities forced displacement, and dead policemen and civilians still occur. Let us remember that the massacre of El Salado could have been prevented if somebody had paid attention to the population's cries for help.[24] Community associations have issued several warnings to the public opinion accusing the national government of its inaction. Forced recruitment of minors, extortion of the inhabitants of the region, and the existence of a paramilitary informant network have a significant presence in Montes de María once more. In May 2022, peasants made a far cry to the national government to demand protection without any success, as usual.[25] After the results of the presidential election on June 19th, marginalized and local social groups felt a ray of hope and awaited their turn to achieve justice.

According to the report submitted by the Truth Commission on June 28, 2022, the violence endured by the Montes de María inhabitants was worse than the one described here. Survivors' accounts included in the text attest to the cruelty paramilitaries, guerrillas, the army, and drug lords subjected them to. The report also did not uncover but confirmed the alliances between traffickers and paramilitaries and the army, as one high commander stated: "Politicians and military men colluded to control cocaine production and commercialization to get rich as happened in Montes de María."[26] In addition to the corruption that comes with drug dealing and violence, the truth commissioners made sure that Colombians were aware of subtle but embedded ways of exerting power and committing atrocities against civilians. Within the armed conflict, armed groups used extreme acts of violence to terrorize populations, such as the black ones. The report presents the transcription of a survivor's account, a woman marked with incandescent iron by the commander of the AUC. She recalled:

> I have never been able to forget that. I have that here; I have not forgotten. I believe they did that to me because I am black. I think he marked me because the color of my skin as if I was a slave. During slavery, they marked Black women like the paramilitaries marked me.[27]

This testimony speaks to the structural racism present in Colombia despite slavery being abolished in 1851. Armed actors thought that having dark skin was reason enough to brutalize Black communities and individuals. The members of the Truth Commission also found that the violence exerted on Colombians depended on their ethnic background, which explains why it was viciously inhumane against Black and Indigenous people, who have been historically discriminated and considered less valuable. Therefore, there were several violences. White and mestizo populations did not suffer the same kind of barbarity.[28] The inhabitants of Montes de María are mostly Black, mestizos, and Indigenous people who have found ways to coexist. However, when the recent violence took over the region, the perpetrators unsettled this, and targeted individuals based on their ethnicity. Another minority that suffered a great amount was the LGBTQAI one, as will be addressed further in the chapter.

According to historian Gonzalo Sánchez, besides the legacy of violence, the survivors also must fight against stigma. He states: "Many peasants ended up being the target of judgmental glances that implicated them with one armed group or another."[29] It is to counteract this humiliation that the people of Montes de María decided to create another image of their communities and the attacks they suffered through the Collective and now El Mochuelo. Thus, revisiting the massacres through a peripatetic venue, one which does not privilege shocking images of brutalities, becomes a methodological tool to create and tell a new history. In this sense, memory is also a way to eliminate stigma and "essential in restoring dignity."[30] As historian Giovanny Castro, curator of El Mochuelo, originally from the Nariño Department, notes, one of the museum's main purposes is to distance its displays from violence. The aim of the venue, according to Castro, is not to "shock or overwhelm the public with gory images of dismembered, tortured, and dead people. The purpose is to present community selected narratives of culture and resilience, songs, and stories." The violence displayed is minimal. One of the purposes of the creators of El Mochuelo is to attract children and young people who did not experience the violence directly. By collaborating closely with them, it is possible to convey the message that peace and hope are achievable even after violent events.

El Mochuelo, in addition, "is a response not only to the bloodbath of El Salado, the most documented of the massacres, but to other ones like Chengue, Macayepo, Las Palmas, and many others that did not have the same public exposure," states Castro. Regarding his work, he says,

> I am a mediator between the museum and the community. I listen to them and suggest ways to put their memories on display. I am the one that helps to make their pain visible. This always makes me wonder if we really can provide something valuable to the communities in exchange for them telling and retelling the stories of what they lived.

Giovanni Castro joined the El Mochuelo project in 2013. Soraya Bayuelo contacted and offered him the curatorship of the project, but due to the region's violent situation and living conditions he hesitated. In Carmen de Bolívar, there is no aqueduct and it suffers a harsh drought for most part of the year. These contingencies affected the design of El Mochuelo and played a significant role in its 11 years of planning.

Nevertheless, Castro accepted the appointment and began collaborating with the peasants of the region. He built on the work of the Collective and its communication strategies—radio, television, cinema, and community workshops—to reach the members of the 15 municipalities and start creating historical memory initiatives. In 2013, Castro and the members of the Collective organized regional meetings for young people, which became a breeding ground for narrating memories. In these spaces, elders share their stories about their return to the region after enduring forced displacement and their processes of land recovery. From 2013 until today, Castro has been a fundamental actor in El Mochuelo's development. His work and support made the project viable, and he is deeply involved with the inhabitants of the region.

## Representations of Violence at El Mochuelo

The conceptualization of El Mochuelo started three years after President Álvaro Uribe Vélez issued the Justice and Peace Law of 2005, at the end of his first term (2002–2006). As previously mentioned, this law's intention was supposed to help armed groups, such as paramilitaries and guerrillas, demobilize and reintegrate into civil society. The actual number of demobilized members still needs more research. This regulation gave a sense of calm, or at least of some respite from violence, and encouraged many survivors of atrocities to return to their territories and ponder what had happened. In this context, Colombian memory sites began to proliferate. Communities felt safe to move around their regions again, which encouraged them to rebuild their social fabrics. They created several victims' associations, such as the Collective, which provided the basis for El Mochuelo and the Association of Victims of Granada.

While the experience of the violence endured by the 15 communities of Montes de María is not unique, what sets these social groups apart is how they choose to remember and represent what happened to them. As has been emphasized, they celebrate their cultural identity reflected in oral traditions such as poems, stories, and games. Even though they do not delve into graphic or detailed descriptions of the atrocities endured, there are still references to atrocities. For instance, at El Mochuelo, museum goers can find a panel that represents sexual violence against women. The images displayed are not graphic, but the idea conveyed in the exhibition reflects the necessity to acknowledge and tend to women who endured this kind of brutality and create awareness of the need of no repetition. They follow the logic with which Soraya Bayuelo and other community leaders created El Mochuelo: "This is a place for words."

Memory, identity, and territory are the three main thematic axes of the museum. The curators and producers of the venue believe that these topics are inclusive enough to enable El Mochuelo to become a space in which the residents of the region can recreate their traditional culture. At the Traveling Museum, territory is conceptualized as a foundation that allows people to think about themselves as lead characters of their history. Territory also addresses the body and spirit of the people of the region, represented with music and other ancestral and historic traditions. The identity element refers to the Montes de María inhabitants' social organization, ways of thinking, imaginaries, and distinct cultural expressions. Memory, in turn, is meant to be a collective exercise, transcending the private sphere. The communities' part in this process uses memory as a political tool to redefine themselves and their territories. The 15 social groups of Montes de María continuously reinvent the museum spaces.

The museum's script has five modules which illustrate its three axes. The first section welcomes the visitor. It has two rocking chairs, which represent the regional custom to sit in the doorways of houses to talk with friends. It also welcomes the visitors with a text written in *décimas*, ten-line stanza of poetry in Spanish and translated into some native languages, such as the one spoken by the Zenú Indians. Beatriz Ochoa, community leader and cofounder of El Mochuelo, authored this poem, which plays on a daily recording when the venue opens its doors:

> [...] To highlight our identity Words and the truth
> Now we created a museum
> Just as we dreamt about it As a bird of our territory That heals with its flight Our life project.
> We welcome
> This Mochuelo and its flight.
> Beatriz Ochoa (Philosopher and Cofounder of the Corporation Collective of Communications Line 21)[31]

This poem illustrates what the creators of the Traveling Museum expect from El Mochuelo. The text explicitly refers to the power of words, as highlighted by Soraya before, to their orality, therefore, their immaterial heritage. Both the inhabitants of Granada and Montes de María followed their commonsense when they decided to represent the brutalities endured. Per anthropologist Clifford Geertz, social groups resort to what is natural and obvious for them—culture—when narrating stories.[32] Therefore, when addressing violent and traumatic pasts, as these communities do in their memory sites, culture directly informs their depictions, which in turn confirms the heterogeneity of historical memories.

El Mochuelo's second section represents Montes de María with pictures and interactive maps. It also includes postcards with images of the region's cartography, territory, women, and children (Figure 4.1).

The third and fourth parts represent empowerment through music and gastronomy. The aim of El Mochuelo's creators is for the inhabitants of Montes de María to feel proud of who they are and their history and enrich their cultural immaterial heritage inventory.

The Mochuelo exhibits also represent the process of food sovereignty in the region.[33] For this there are some calabash tree bowls displayed near to a panel with pictures of traditional dances and musical instruments from Montes de María.

Since 2012, the concept of food sovereignty has been discussed by NGOs and Latin American state agents. The definition is under construction, and even though it suffers constant modifications, the basic premise is:

Food sovereignty is the ability of the states and people to exercise their right to freely define and implement their alimentary and nutritional policies and strategies. This should be done in a sovereign way with the aim to achieve alimentary and nutritional security and to organize production, access, and food consumption according to the populations' necessities. The priority of these

FIGURE 4.1 A man in San Jacinto municipality observing the timeline of the known massacres of Montes de María. Pictures taken by the members of the Corporation Collective of Communications Line 21.

**160** Memory and Intangible Heritage

policies and strategies is small family and community-based producers and local food consumption.

These sections also refer to the ways in which the inhabitants of Montes de María endured violence and how they remember it. In a panel called Memories of the Resistances, the visitors of El Mochuelo can read about the different strategies used to defend their territory and culture. Other artifact that keeps the flame of resistance alive is the so-called "memory sheet," a large cloth on which members of the communities have imprinted phrases of hope and their memories.

The fifth and last section is a space devoted to the communities' children, called "playground." Here, it is common to see children playing the traditional *golosa* game and women singing children's tunes. *Golosa*, or hopscotch, is a children's game played with several participants or alone. It is a popular playground game in which players toss a small object into numbered triangles or a pattern of rectangles outlined on the ground and then hop or jump through the spaces to retrieve the object. This section includes games and activities related to the knowledge of the territory and the cultural identity of the municipalities of Montes de María.[34]

An innovative aspect of El Mochuelo is also the inventive use the community, curators, and production team make of their intangible heritage. They not only conceive it as a resource activated in times of crisis, as mentioned at the beginning of the chapter, but also as a tool that can help them look into the future, as they want to be remembered by Colombians and the world. This implies that they do not think of their immaterial patrimony as something to preserve but as knowledge to help them build a peaceful present and future. For them, heritage is alive. Another purpose of the project is to "forgive, move on, and preserve the memory of more than 3,000 people killed by illegal groups."[35] In this sense, to understand El Mochuelo as an inventory of intangible heritage takes on significant aspects. One example of the creation and use of their immaterial heritage is represented in how a clothes iron renders loss. This artifact speaks to the tradition in Montes de María related to the cultural assignation of gender roles. Men go outside the house to work, and women do the domestic chores, such as ironing. "For a mother, a wife, not having to iron the shirts of their murdered relatives" is sad; it, therefore, becomes a cultural representation of a feeling of loss that is now part of their intangible heritage. El Mochuelo displays immaterial and abstract concepts, like loss and death, in material forms such as the iron, the hopscotch game, and the clothesline, as mentioned further in the chapter. The use of these pieces triggers memories related to the violence displayed in the museum, which become part of the cultural inventory of the region.

Another feature worth mentioning about El Mochuelo is the space the curators devoted exclusively to the LGBTQIA community. Since the museum is an inclusive venue in which "everybody is welcome, everyone fits, not a single inhabitant of Montes de María should be excluded," Soraya emphasized in a

2017 interview. She and her team were aware of the brutalities committed against this group during the armed conflict. So far, El Mochuelo is the only Colombian venue that raises awareness about how the war affected LGBTQIA groups. In Montes de María, for instance, paramilitaries mocked and tortured homosexual, bisexual, and transgender people in many ways. The most common one was to dress gender-non-conforming men as women, put them in a public ring, and make them fight to entertain the paramilitary leaders.[36]

Aware of the havoc violence causes and the significance of orality for the Montes de María inhabitants, in 2002, Soraya, along with teachers, cultural promoters, and other community leaders, came together to create the Traveling Cinema. As she stated during the same interview: "The peripatetic idea is fundamental because in the travels around the region people interact, share ideas and experiences, and this leads to innovative ideas, to innovative ways of participation. We have found out that traveling venues activate memories because people feel they are heard, and they count. We try to include as many communities as possible in our projects. When things come and go, the outcomes are richer." Related to immaterial heritage, the Cinema Club plays a key role because it recovers some of the oral spaces for social interaction, conversation, and storytelling that violence took away from the region. In the Colombian Caribbean, nights are a time for socializing. Families, neighbors, and friends gather outside their houses to talk, play board games, drink, and eat. These get-togethers are part of the Caribbean culture and play a fundamental role in bonding together families and friends; this is when people share their lives, strengthening their cultural identity. The Purple Rose of Cairo, therefore, intended to help the inhabitants of the region to regain confidence in going out at night and reclaiming their meeting spaces because the film screenings take place in the town squares. The efforts of this venue's creators aimed to overcome fear. Thus, the idea of creating a traveling museum in 2008 came as no surprise. That is also why El Mochuelo, launched in 2019, opens its doors at 4:00 pm and closes between 10:00 and 11:00 pm.

Among the first Colombian professionals who got involved with the project of El Mochuelo were anthropologist Italia Isadora Samudio Reyes, concerned with the study of gender, armed conflict, and peace research, and Giovanni Castro. They did considerable fieldwork, along with Soraya and other community members. Based on the information and data they gathered, they suggested effective ways to convey the inhabitants of Montes de María memories of the war, their cultural resistance, history, and diversity via the museum. As part of the work group, some graphic designers from the Pontificia Universidad Javeriana, located in Bogotá, were responsible for its mobile structure.[37] In this sense, the museum is the result of the work that journalists, anthropologists, historians, teachers, community leaders, and cultural promoters have conducted in relation to memory, territory, and communication, in conjunction with the victims of the armed conflict.

**162** Memory and Intangible Heritage

Like most Colombian memory sites, El Mochuelo does not receive funding from the Colombian state. Its resources come from international entities, such as the French Embassy in Bogotá, administered by the CNMH.[38] The Agencia Catalana de Cooperación al Desarrollo, AECID (Catalan Agency for International Development Cooperation), also funded the final part of the research for the museum. This organization combats poverty and works for sustainable human development. Its charter states that the agency fosters full development, conceived as a fundamental human right, with the fight against poverty as part of the process for building this right. To this end, the Agency follows the guidelines of the 4th Master Plan, in accordance with the international agenda of the Millennium Development Goals and with a focus on three cross-cutting axes: gender perspective, environmental quality, and respect for cultural diversity. The lack of Colombian state funding demonstrates once again the limitations of the national government in memorializing the suffering of victims and communities.

During the 11 years that passed between the conception and actual opening of the Traveling Museum of Memory and Identity of Montes de María, the venue went through some transformations. The most significant related to its

**FIGURE 4.2** The members of the Collective took these pictures a few days before launching of the site. The original 2008 idea changed significantly when the museum opened in 2019. Pictures taken by the members of the Corporation Collective Line 21.

structure; from a circular, bird-shaped tent, it became a traditional house with gabled roof. When El Mochuelo opened its doors, the structure was the one shown in Figure 4.2.

These changes in El Mochuelo's appearance were due to three main factors. First, as striking as the bird-shaped tent design was, to assemble and disassemble the infrastructure and all its components demanded enormous amounts of money, time, and training. In 2015, the Colombian design firm Estudio Mapping won the public bidding of the CNMH to produce the bird-shaped tent. However, according to Bexielena Hernández, anthropologist and founder of Estudio Mapping, "The bird-shaped structure was not realistic because all the technicalities it implied, such as refrigeration systems, due to the weather of the zone, electricity, and functionality." Another major concern for the Estudio Mapping team regarded the timeline suggested by the community. This museographic piece, commonly used in many venues, presented significant challenges for Estudio Mapping, such as the number of massacres. Due to technicalities, all the atrocities the communities wanted to include in the timeline did not fit, and as Hernández states, "Having the task to choose which massacre was more significant than others distressed us very much, we could not do that. It is extremely hard to think about victims, people, as objects of design." The other issue was the physical material used to display the timeline. The inhabitants of Montes de María wanted this piece made of their traditional hammock fabric, but it did not work because the information would not physically adhere to it. Lastly, the members of Estudio Mapping found it incredibly challenging to produce a piece called the "Tree of Life." This artifact meant to honor the victims of violence in a structure about ten-feet tall with branches where cards that display the names of the dead would hang. The idea was meaningful but proved inviable because it was too tall, and the height of the residents of the region made it impossible for them to reach the branches and see the names of the victims on the hanging cards. The members of Estudio Mapping worked with the Collective during 2015 but then withdrew from the project.

The other problems that the creators of El Mochuelo faced were questions of practicality and a lack of economic resources. Due to the physical conditions of Montes de María, the bird-shaped tent was an illusion. Therefore, the design team that came after Estudio Mapping exchanged the tent for an 18 by 12-meter wooden pavilion (five meters tall), which simplified its assembly and disassembly. Both the structure of the venue and the "Tree of Life" form changed; the architects suggested a clothesline-like piece on which 700 cards with the names, place of birth, and date would hang with clips (Figure 4.3).

Nevertheless, one of the constants of the traveling museum has been its logo, which has always been a mochuelo bird (Figure 4.4).

The curators of El Mochuelo only chose five pieces that directly represent the armed conflict starting in the 1980s. First, there is the structure called the

**164** Memory and Intangible Heritage

**FIGURE 4.3** The "Tree of Life," where 700 cards with victims' names hang. Giovanni Castro, curator of the venue, is sitting below. Pictures taken by the members of the Corporation Collective of Communications Line 21.

**FIGURE 4.4** Soraya Bayuelo at the entrance of El Mochuelo. Picture taken by the members of the Corporation Collective Line 21.

"Tree of Life," which deserves special attention due to the names of the 700 victims that are displayed in its "branches." The idea of the curators is to make visible tags or cards with the victims' basic information—name, place of birth, and age at death—and to encourage more inhabitants of the region to make public the names of killed relatives and friends.

Second are the tapestries of Mampuján, of the María La Baja municipality. These handicrafts tell the story of the forced displacements that local people suffered. They also represent women's efforts to ease their pain through sewing. The Mampuján weavers call one of these artifacts *Mampuján, día del llanto* (*Mampuján, day of mourning*). It depicts the massacre and forced displacement that took place on March 10 and 11, 2000. Right-wing paramilitaries entered Mampuján and gathered all its inhabitants in the town's main square. They accused 12 peasants of being guerrilla informants and killed them. These tragic days remain vivid in the survivors' memory. The paramilitaries arrived with machetes, threatened the population, and looted their properties. They ordered the inhabitants of the town to line up for their execution, but suddenly, after killing several people, the captain of the paramilitaries stopped the massacre, claiming he realized that the peasants were innocent. The survivors suffered displacement. Two significant Mampuján tapestries are currently displayed at the Memory and Nation Hall at the National Museum of Colombia, which speaks not only to the renovation plan of the institution addressed in Chapter 1 but also to the visibility the victims and survivors of Montes de María are gaining in the national scene.

Third, local artist Rafael Posso, and survivor of the 2001 massacre of Las Brisas, made some charcoal drawings depicting the brutalities inhabitants of the region endured. These art pieces were displayed near a burned rocking chair recovered after 15 years of the Massacre in Las Brisas. It is a symbol of how the war destroyed this community's way of living. Fourth, the previously mentioned panel in which the Montes de María women represent the sexual violence they suffered. Fifth, a burnt rocking chair which represents where the people use to sit during the night gatherings violence banned.

## Nature of El Mochuelo

Some of the features that make El Mochuelo unique are its lack of conventional museological objects and glass cases and the fact that the whole venue is peripatetic and not just one of its exhibits. Conventional museologists consider collections, logs, and archival records as markers of a museum, and El Mochuelo does not have them in the same manner. Instead, the pieces exhibited at the traveling museum are panels with oral traditions, videos, some drawings, pictures, and just a few artifacts, which makes more sense for traveling purposes.

As stated before, El Mochuelo's design is movable; therefore, traditional artifacts and display cases would be a major obstacle. These innovations have led historians such as Clara Isabel Botero to argue that this site is not a proper museum. For Botero, an appropriate institution must have another type of setting. The scholar compared El Mochuelo with another venue in Montes de María. She referred to an archaeological community museum in San Jacinto, founded in 1984, which has "700 archaeological objects registered at the Instituto Colombiano de Antropología e Historia, ICANH (Colombian Institute of Anthropology and History), which makes it a solid institution, a real one." The creators of the Community Museum of San Jacinto praise the venue for being a "true" museum that has an important object collection, registered at the ICANH, in a proper building, which displays its pieces in appropriate cabinets.[39] However, philosopher Hilde S. Hein notes that currently, museums face several challenges since they acquire different configurations. For instance, as in the case of El Mochuelo, many venues privilege the experience of the visitors and audience rather than artifacts, as seen in the poem mentioned previously.[40]

Despite the differences between these memory sites, the curators and creators of both El Mochuelo and the Community Museum of San Jacinto work together. They collaborate because both venues are part of the efforts of social leaders in Montes de María to remember, recover, and represent their traditional culture. The two work teams see each other's sites as spaces that share a common purpose. In fact, the director of the San Jacinto Museum functioned as a consultant during the 11 years of planning the peripatetic venue. Furthermore, during three weeks in October 2014, the Community Museum of San Jacinto housed a display called "Memoria e identidad en los Montes de María. Un preludio a El Mochuelo" (Memory and Identity in Montes de María: A Prelude to El Mochuelo). This exhibit had photographs, audio files, and videos the communities of Montes de María made to commemorate the victims of the violence in the area. In addition, there were supplementary activities such as workshops and lectures related to peasants' memory of their territories and the claims of victims of violence.[41] After this first opening in Cartagena, the exhibition traveled to the Community Museum of San Jacinto, where it will be hosted until the organizers of El Mochuelo decide otherwise.

El Mochuelo also found inspiration in The Caribbean Museum, a state institution founded in 2009 in Barranquilla, which relied on everyday scenes and landscapes to impart a sense of immediacy to the spectator. The Caribbean Museum does not have many artifacts either but instead displays interactive devices, videos, multimedia, and other technological equipment to enliven the visitor's experience. This museum's few displays of material pieces are only ancillary.[42]

The difference between the Caribbean Museum and El Mochuelo is that the grassroots venue did not receive any kind of funding from the Colombian government nor any significant publicity. This is due to the differences in the topics these museums present. El Mochuelo remembers the violent past from the peasants' perspective, emphasizes their oral and cultural traditions, and the stories and collective imaginary related to violence and survival. Implicitly, the Traveling Museum shames the Colombian government because it highlights its failure to protect citizens and to exercise the state's monopoly on the use of violence. The Caribbean Museum, on the other hand, exalts the geographic particularism and diversity of this Colombian territory.

In March 2020, when the Covid-19 pandemic started, museums in Colombia and around the world closed, but most institutions found ways to keep their displays available for the public, resorting to virtual options such as digital exhibitions, workshops, presentations, and meetings. However, this was not feasible for Colombian grassroots memory venues such as the Hall of Never Again and El Mochuelo. Due to the geographical location of these sites, Wi-Fi options are not always possible, and when they are, their connection does not have the best quality, interfering with the communication attempts. In El Mochuelo's case, its itinerancies flights, as the people of the region call them, stopped. The restrictions imposed by Covid-19 made it impossible for the museum to keep traveling around the 15 municipalities, and it was stored in Carmen de Bolivar's community center because its flights began there. The last itinerancy of the museum, before the pandemic, took place in Chalán, Department of Sucre, after that it came where it is resting now. If someone wants to visit El Mochuelo nowadays will find nine halls of the mentioned center with displays about the region's peasant culture, references to sexual violence against women, the tree of life, and some of the interactive devices. The reflections brought by stopping the venue's flights have also triggered other thoughts related to "other pandemics," such as violence, poverty, inequality, and racism, just to name a few. One of the silver linings for these groups has been the time to look within and regroup to keep fighting for a peaceful present and future.

Another significant innovation that the script of El Mochuelo is undergoing is emphasis the curators are doing to highlight a gender perspective. More than focusing on women who had already died, they want to celebrate those who are still alive. The Collective identified 15 women social leaders of the region and began working with them through workshops, dialogues, unstructured interviews, and just listening to their life stories. This exercise allowed the members of the Collective and El Mochuelo to find five cultural advocates, five planters, and five devoted to the promotion of human rights and memory. The activities done with these women started to multiply, and now there are several associations that have come forward or are being created, such as teachers, cultural promoters, and community mothers, among others. When El Mochuelo starts traveling again, the idea is to have a stronger and more developed gender research and perspective. This initiative is related too with the purpose of keep the LGBTQAI+ space El Mochuelo has. These groups have worked tightly with the members of the Collective to make their voices heard using audiovisual aids and promote workshops and conversations about the atrocities they endured due to their non-binary identity. Now that the conflict is hopefully coming to an end, the LGBTQAI+ community wants to keep collaborating with the curators of El Mochuelo to have more representation in the traveling displays.

As clearly expressed by Bayuelo in an interview she gave on July 12, 2022, "El Mochuelo and the processes it inspires, and triggers never end. The Museum is resting currently but that does not imply is finished. On the contrary, is more alive than ever and its influence is palpable." Since El Mochuelo's launch in 2019, it has become a landmark in the region and a pretext for motivating people to participate in local community building projects. However, at the mentioned center, the curators of the venue only had space to display some of the features of the entire site. The tree of life, emblematic piece, stands there, along with artifacts related to their peasant culture such as tools for working the land, references to sexual violence against women, and some tapestries and paintings. The gabled roof traditional house is kept in storage as are many of the technological devices that comprise the museum. In the same interview mentioned above, Bayuelo talked about El Mochuelo's future. She with the other members of the Collective are working on its script and physical structure so when time comes for the next flight it is renewed and stronger. Currently, the creators of El Mochuelo are working with a firm or architects on a way to make the play area's roof a structure to be opened and closed depending mainly on the weather conditions. Since the region is extremely hot, sometimes people cannot stand the intense sun since that part of El Mochuelo always has been open. The same happens with the activities and games that take place there. Another significant innovation that is taking place at the venue is a redesign of the tree of life, which is a great challenge since there are 3,800 names, so far, displayed at its branches, but Bayuelo insists that there are many more. The original material for creating this piece was meant to be wood, but for museographic reasons it did not go through. However, nowadays, taking advantage of the rest the pandemic imposed, the members of the Collective and the museum are considering going back to their first choice. This also is related to the number of victims the tree must display, which unfortunately is growing. Thus, the people involved with the traveling museum decided to take their time for relaunching a site that fulfills most of their objectives. They insist that whatever time it takes for them to start moving the venue again is worth it if it turns out as they wish. Cartagena, capital of Bolivar's Department in the Colombian Caribbean, is meant to be the first flight of El Mochuelo after its repose.

The curators of the museums decided that the El Mochuelo's first flight after the pandemic should be in Cartagena, capital of Bolivar's Department in the Colombian Caribbean. Not only because this city is a major Colombian port and a well-known touristic destination, but also because the members of the Collective and El Mochuelo have found there several allies that are helping them develop their projects. Teachers, politicians, activists, and journalists want to showcase El Mochuelo in Cartagena to give more visibility to the endeavor and try to find funds. The Colombian government has never provided any economic sources for the museum, and as a political posture during the last four years, the creators of the traveling museum distanced themselves with anything related to Iván Duque's government. They also stated vehemently their deep disagreement with the former director of the CNMH, Darío Acevedo, position of denying the country's internal conflict. Since all the community processes began in Montes de María, 35 years ago, the people of the region have found support and resources through international agencies, NGOs, and scholarships, but never have received funding from the Colombian state.

As stated above, currently the members of the Collective and El Mochuelo are implementing several processes to encourage and improve the participation of the community. They want to put into practice what public historians and other scholars are calling shared authority, although several social groups, such as the 15 towns in Montes de María, have advocated for it for a long time. Since the 1990s, scholars such as Michael Frisch, in his book *A Shared Authority: Essays on the Craft and Meaning of Oral and Public History,* discusses how oral history, as a secondary method, can help to build a much more productive relationship between researchers and communities by refuting the conventional conception that history should be institutional. Statement constantly challenged by public historians.[43] El Mochuelo creators and curators have the feeling that they do not need intermediaries to make their voices heard, and I believe this is a product of the memory exercise they do with their cultural immaterial inventory. They have come a long way, and now they are more empowered. The inhabitants of the region are willing to step up and make their own decisions; however, they are aware that they still need some intermediation. Therefore, Bayuelo spends most of her time looking for allies: "My goal is to find people that can help us, not only with money but helping us to promote the work we do." Currently, when they work with researchers, they are able to tell them how they want to be portrayed, what kinds of answers the investigation should address, and instead of being passive subjects, the inhabitants of the region are gaining clarity about how historical memories should help them build a peaceful future. It has been a lengthy process, but it is paying off. The process of the Hall of Never Again is different. They have less allies because its leaders have many other obligations, and a great part of the community is not as involved in memory endeavors. They have also experienced much resistance and people who think spaces such as the Hall are useless as mentioned in Chapter 3.

Finally, El Mochuelo has forged partnerships with academics and universities. In April 2022, they held their first international seminar devoted to reflecting about the relationship between memories, conflicts, and no repetition of violence. On the first day of the event, there were four panels, and on the second day, there were dance and community presentations. The seminar was a success, and a publication will follow. What this means is that El Mochuelo is getting plenty of exposure and attention, which its curators hope and believe will help them continue their work and development of the site. In addition, and related to the new government, Bayuelo and other members of the Collective have been summoned by the new leaders of the country to be part of workshops and discussions about how to have a more inclusive state. Their voices are being considered, but they are aware that this does not mean all of the recommendations they make will be implemented. What it indicates is the willingness of the president and vice president to have a multivocal government. Only time will tell if this was achieved.

## Conclusions

All the grassroots sites devoted to historical memories in Colombia emerged as an attempt to acknowledge and make visible marginal communities' pain and grief. Although their healing processes are different, as seen with the cases of the Hall de Never Again, discussed in Chapter 3, and the Traveling Museum of the Memory and Identity of Montes de María, both venues aim to preclude violence from commandeering their lives. The creators of El Mochuelo decided to remember by celebrating their traditional culture while the founders of the Hall preferred to be very explicit in their collective remembrances and to respect individual grievances through the *bitácoras*.

The differences in their recollections demonstrate that in a country like Colombia, memory is not only a recollection of facts but also the cultural decisions that intervene in the making of remembrances. This brings us back to historian Michael Rothberg's notion of multidirectional memory. The author notes that frequently when memories of the same event abound, a competitive feature appears and manifests in the need to assert one remembrance as the real or true over others. State narratives prevail over peripheral stories, thereby promoting and perpetuating exclusions. In his book *Multidirectional Memory: Remembering the Holocaust in the Age of Colonization*, Rothberg challenges the idea of state or official remembrances as the exclusive ones, underscoring those varied memories of the same event do not necessarily have to compete for attention because they are all valid and significant.[44]

Rothberg's claim about multidirectional memory applies to the Colombian case. Each of the 33 sites known so far, which display the remembrances of the brutalities endured in several forms, aspires for their inclusion in the country's project of nation building. One does not deserve more laurels than another, and one is not more accurate or appropriate than another. All must become part of Colombia's recent history and historical memory to honor the pluriethnic and multicultural character of the nation, stated in the Constitution of 1991.

## Notes

1 "Quiénes somos," https://montemariaaudiovisual.wordpress.com/quienes-somos/.
2 "Montes de María, Premio Nacional de Paz 2003," N.D. https://www.eltiempo.com/archivo/documento/MAM-1045178.
3 UN Educational, Scientific and Cultural Organization, UNESCO, *Convention for the Safeguarding of the Intangible Cultural Heritage*, October 17, 2003. https://ich.unesco.org/en/convention.

4 Apaydin Veysel, *Critical Perspectives on Cultural Memory and Heritage: Construction, Transformation and Destruction* (London: UCL Press, 2020). Kindle Edition.
5 François Hartog, "Time and Heritage," *Museum International* 57, no. 3 (2005): 7–18, https://doi.org/10.1111/j.1468-0033.2005.00525.x.
6 Andreas Huyssen, *Present Pasts: Urban Palimpsests and the Politics of Memory* (Stanford, CA: Stanford University Press, 2009).
7 Jessica Moody, "History and Heritage," in *Palgrave Handbook to Contemporary Heritage Research*, eds. Emma Waterton and Steve Watson (Basingstoke: Palgrave MacMillan, 2015), 113–129.
8 Paul Ricoeur, *History, Memory, Forgetting*, trans. Kathleen Blamey and David Pellauer (Chicago, IL and London: The University of Chicago Press, 2004).
9 UN Educational, Scientific and Cultural Organization, UNESCO, *Convention for the Safeguarding of the Intangible Cultural Heritage*, https://ich.unesco.org/en/convention
10 Manuel Salge, *El principio arcóntico del patrimonio. Origen, transformaciones y desafíos de los procesos de patrimonialización en Colombia* (Bogotá: Ediciones UniAndes, 2019), 42.
11 Frederic Bartlett, *Remembering. A Study in Experimental and Social Psychology* (Cambridge: Cambridge University Press, 1932), 118.
12 Darcia Viejo-Rose, "Cultural Heritage and Memory: Untangling the Ties That Bind," *Culture & History Digital Journal* 4, no. 2 (2015), 4.
13 Paul Ricoeur, *History, Memory, Forgetting*, 413.
14 Programa de las Naciones Unidas para el Desarrollo, "Los Montes de María: análisis de la conflictividad," June 10, 2010, http://www.undp.org/content/dam/undp/documents/projects/COL/00058220_Analisis%20conflcitividad% 20Montes%20 de%20Maria%20PDF.pdf.
15 Asociación de Usuarios Campesinos de Colombia, ANUC, http://anuc.co/dynamicdata/historia.php.
16 Giovanni Castro, Soraya Bayuelo Castellar, and Italia Isadora Samudio Reyes, "Museo itinerante de la memoria y la identidad de los Montes de María: tejiendo memorias y relatos para la reparación simbólica, la vida y la convivencia," in *Estudios para la paz: representaciones, imaginarios y estrategias en el conflicto armado*, ed. Mauricio Hernández Pérez (Bogotá: 2013), 162.
17 Edwin De los Ríos, Carmen Andrea Becerra Becerra, and Fabián Enrique Oyaga Martínez, *Montes de María: entre la consolidación del territorio y el acaparamiento de tierras. Aproximación a la situación de Derechos Humanos y el Derecho Internacional Humanitario en la región (2006–2012)* (Bogotá: Publicaciones ILSA, 2012), 11.
18 "Hay Futuro Si Hay Verdad: Informe Final Comisión De La Verdad," Hay futuro si hay verdad | Informe Final Comisión de la Verdad, accessed August 31, 2022, https://www.comisiondelaverdad.co/hay-futuro-si-hay-verdad, 576.
19 Gonzalo Sánchez, *La masacre de El Salado: esa guerra no era nuestra*, 24–27.
20 "¿Cómo se fraguó la tragedia de los Montes de María?"
21 "Profiles: Colombia's armed groups," *BBC News Latin America & Caribbean*, August 20, 2013, http://www.bbc.com/news/world-latin-america-11400950.
22 Beatriz Valdés Correa, "¿Por Qué Se Recrudece La Violencia En Los Montes De María?," ELESPECTADOR.COM, August 15, 2020, https://www.elespectador.com/colombia-20/conflicto/por-que-se-recrudece-la-violencia-en-los-montes-de-maria-article/
23 Radio Nacional de Colombia, "Comunidades En Los Montes De María Denuncian Intimidaciones De Grupos Armados," Denuncian intimidaciones de grupos armados en los Montes de María, accessed July 21, 2022, https://www.radionacional.co/noticias-colombia/denuncian-intimidaciones-de-grupos-armados-en-los-montes-de-maria.
24 Colprensa, "¿Regresa El Terror a Los Montes De María? Consejos Territoriales Lanzan SOS," www.eluniversal.com.co, May 5, 2022, https://www.eluniversal.

com.co/regional/regresa-el-terror-a-los-montes-de-maria-consejos-territoriales-lanzan-sos-CE6512400.ro
25 Colprensa, "Ataques Del Clan Del Golfo: Campesinos De Los Montes De María Piden Seguridad," Paro armado: campesinos de los Montes de María piden seguridad por ataques del Clan del Golfo, accessed July 21, 2022, https://www.radionacional.co/noticias-colombia/paro-armado-campesinos-de-los-montes-de-maria-piden-seguridad-por-ataques-del.
26 "Hay Futuro Si Hay Verdad: Informe Final Comisión De La Verdad," Hay futuro si hay verdad | Informe Final Comisión de la Verdad, accessed July 21, 2022, https://www.comisiondelaverdad.co/hay-futuro-si-hay-verdad.
27 "Hay Futuro Si Hay Verdad: Informe Final Comisión De La Verdad," Hay futuro si hay verdad | Informe Final Comisión de la Verdad.
28 "Hay Futuro Si Hay Verdad: Informe Final Comisión De La Verdad," Hay futuro si hay verdad | Informe Final Comisión de la Verdad.
29 "¿Cómo se fraguó la tragedia de los Montes de María?"
30 Sánchez, *La masacre de El Salado,* 13.
31 Beatriz Ochoa (Philosopher, Cofounder of the Corporation Collective of Communications Line 21). My translation.
32 Clifford Geertz, *Conocimiento local,* 107.
33 "Qué significa soberanía alimentaria"? La Vía Campesina. Movimiento Campesino Internacional, https://viacampesina.org/es/quignifica-soberanalimentaria/
34 Adriana Correa, *El primer vuelo del Mochuelo,* Centro Nacional de Memoria Histórica Archive, http://www.centrodememoriahistorica.gov.co/de/noticias/noticias-cmh/el-primer-vuelo-del-mochuelo.
35 Adriana De la Cruz, "Los nuevos vientos del Mochuelo," *El Universal,* August 3, 2013, http://www.eluniversal.com.co/bolivar/los-nuevos-vientos-del-mochuelo-130001.
36 Bello, *Basta Ya!,* 322.
37 "Apoyo de Francia al Centro de Memoria Histórica," French Embassy in Bogotá, http://www.ambafrance-co.org/Apoyo-de-Francia-al-Centro-de.
38 "El Mochuelo: un museo itinerante de la memoria en los Montes de María," French Embassy in Bogotá, http://www.ambafrance-co.org/UN-MOCHUELO-PARA-LA-PAZ.
39 Clara Isabel Botero, "La construcción del museo comunitario de San Jacinto, Montes dee María, Bolívar," *Boletín de historia y antigüedades* 101, no. 859 (2014): 493–515.
40 Hilde S. Hein, *The Museum in Transition. A Philosophical Perspective* (Washington, DC: The Smithsonian Institution, 2010).
41 Giovanny Castro, "Inicia en Cartagena el primer vuelo del 'Mochuelo,'" October 17, 2014, http://mimemoria.org.
42 Andrés Forero, "Sí, el Caribe también tiene sabor: producción de identidades regionales en el Museo del Caribe," in *Baukara, bitácoras de antropología e historia de la antropología en América Latina,* eds. Clara Isabel Botero and Jimena Perry (Bogotá: Universidad Nacional de Colombia, 2013), 45.
43 Michael H. Frisch, *A Shared Authority: Essays on the Craft and Meaning of Oral and Public History* (Albany: State University of New York Press, 2011).
44 Michael Rothberg, *Multidirectional Memory.*

# FINAL THOUGHTS

Many things have happened since I started this research, and many others are unfolding as I write this conclusion. Since 2002, Colombia has undergone deep changes and especially since 2022 citizens of the country are hopeful that the long-awaited peace can finally become a reality. There are also high expectations from the victims and survivors of the internal war related to the current government compared with the way in which Iván Duque's government, 2018–2022, approached historical memory policies. As stated throughout the text, the new Colombian President and Vice President, who took office on August 7, 2022, are promoting a social, participative, and inclusive government. On June 19, 2022, Colombians democratically elected as President Gustavo Petro, demobilized member of the M-19 guerrilla and seasoned politician; and Francia Márquez, social leader and lawyer with a long history of fighting for inclusion, participation, and community projects. Francia is the first black woman elected democratically by Colombians to hold this position. She has escaped two failed attempts to end her life by hired assassins and receives constant threats; however, this only makes her want to fight harder against racism and inequality.[1] In addition, Márquez has endured all kinds of discriminatory slurs from people who deeply disagree with a black woman holding a high governmental role. It is common to hear some Colombians saying: "Is not enough being black to be in that job." However, they are forgetting that Márquez is lawyer and graduated from a university, as most Colombian public officials do. Both she and Petro have a long history of dealing with exclusion, therefore, they have clearly stated their intention to listen to the people, make citizens safe, and strongly advocate for peace.

Their stances were proclaimed, once again, on the day of their possession. In a powerful and symbolic ceremony, the national event started with a speech

DOI: 10.4324/9781003283997-6

from Roy Barreras, President of the Congress, in which he referred to violence, memory, and peace:

> We are here today to try stopping dead and make Colombia a world a life world power. We want to heal our wounds, that is our purpose. To heal them we need to know them, remember them. We are product of a history full of brave voices that claim rights and justice for everyone but only until today they have found a path for vindication.[2]

His discourse signaled the goal of the new country's leaders: to resume peace conversations, give victims and survivors of the armed conflict the opportunity to remember their past without any fear, and be included in national policies. Barrera's words were well received by an audience composed of several minorities, a phenomenon that had not occurred in Colombia during the last mandates.

Being the first Colombian left government, the mentioned speech was very significant because it alluded as well to Gustavo Petro's past as a guerrilla leader. In this context, Barreras summoned María José Pizarro to the stage: "Now I call a daughter of the left, of history, a history interrupted by bullets but thanks to you [Gustavo Petro] as a representative of that, we are back on track. I leave you Senator María José Pizarro." In a moving act, she imposed the presidential sash on the incoming head of state. As the daughter of Carlos Pizarro as stated in Chapter 2 of this book, this action brought the audience to tears, as she was crying too. Besides, she had sewn on the back of her jacked a picture of her father. She said:

> My father was murdered being a presidential candidate, 45 days after laying down his weapons, after signing a peace agreement. At the time, surveys showed he was leading in the elections. After his assassination, one of his dreams came true: a national conversation that ended with the 1991 Constitution and that now is coming true again with the national agreement Petro is calling for.[3]

Journalists, academics, and politicians saw this as a gesture to keep alive the memory of those silenced by violence, not only Pizarro but also Luis Carlos Galán and especially Bernardo Jaramillo, leader of the UP. A small group of survivors of the UP genocide were also part of the event and cheered when Petro delivered his speech, along with representatives of the LGBTQAI+, Indigenous peoples, and black communities. It was the first time these minorities supported and showed up for an official event of this magnitude.[4]

Another significant occurrence during Petro's presidential inauguration was represented by Simon Bolivar's sword. As mentioned also in Chapter 2, the M-19 guerrilla became public when it stole Bolivar's weapon from the museum which housed it. It was their way of launching the movement. After 17 years of being snatched, in 1991, the M-19 returned it to the government as a peace offering and to demonstrate their willingness to work toward peace. Carlos Pizarro was part of the initiative. Since then, the sword has been kept in a security vault of the Republic Bank in Bogotá, and in 2020, it went to the Palacio de Nariño (Palace of Nariño) or presidential residency. As a strong reference and commitment to achieve peace, Petro asked for the sword to be present during his inauguration. He requested the item from president Iván Duque, who at the moment was still in power and denied lending the sword, arguing that it was too dangerous to take it out of the Palace due to the contested past of the artifact. This response shocked the audience, but Petro went on with the ceremony. After all the speeches, when Colombians finally proclaimed him as the next president, he ordered some guards to bring the sword, and so it happened. This was a definitive moment for Petro's government; the image of the sword coming to him was a landmark, which journalists and politicians interpreted as leaving behind a violent past to build a peaceful future. When the item arrived to Petro's sight, he stated,

> this sword represents a lot for us and do not want to bury it again. I want to put it into a sheathe, as the liberator, its owner, said, when justice in the country is achieved. It belongs to the people and that is why we wanted here in this moment and place.[5]

Petro referred to the sword as a reconciliation icon.

The other speech that deserves attention was given by Vice President Francia Márquez. For many, this was the highlight of the inauguration because for the first time, a black woman swore to serve the country. Her words were also special. Using inclusive language, Márquez referred to her masculine and feminine ancestors and then used gender-neutral terms to include other minorities. She made sure to address Colombia's cultural diversity and all the groups historically excluded, coining the saying, "Until dignity becomes a habit" (hasta que la dignidad se vuelva costumbre).[6] Complementing Márquez's discourse was her family, her husband, parents, and son. Their presence demonstrated that all Colombians should and must be part of policy making and decision taking.

Before the presidential inauguration and as an event that helped to reinforce the new government's purposes, on June 28th, the Truth Commissioners appointed by President Juan Manuel Santos during his second mandate, 2014–2018, submitted their final report to the country. After four years of fieldwork and research throughout all Colombian regions, the team delivered 23 volumes that addressed topics such as emigration, exile, massacres, genocide, disappearances, forced labor, sexual violence, and many other issues related to the recent armed conflict. The report provides detailed information, data, and statistics about the atrocities committed against civilians during the recent armed conflict in Colombia. Descriptions are so vivid and brutal that readers generally need some time to get through them; however, they are the proof that Colombians are willing to face their difficult pasts, talk about them, understand what happened to them and their lost loved ones, and work through those painful memories. The following is one of the thousands of testimonies collected by the Truth Commissioners:

> The Pit
> 
> For them, the river was a cemetery. For us it was where we washed, where we bathed, where collected water for our household activities. On Sundays people prepared rice and potatoes. Do you know what rice and potatoes mean for us, blacks who live near the river? Think that in Popayán [Cauca's Department capital] this is the typical food most appreciated by the *payanese*. That is what it meant for us. If it was not made with yellow potato, it did not work. But the river was also the space where we gathered with our children. While the mother washed, the father played with the kids, they played football. They made rice and shared it with others, they cooked together. It was a community space. That ended. People could not go to the river because at any time [armed groups] they would come and kill us. Also, at any moment dead bodies started to float near those who were bathing or washing. Lifeless bodies. Of course, fishing decreased radically. Instead of catching a fish they would get a hand, a foot. My husband was a fisherman, he did several things, but he enjoyed fishing. My older brother was also a fisherman. Fish started to taste like oil. People stopped eating fish, why catch them if nobody is going to eat them? There was a time when nobody consumed river fish. The river stopped being a recreational space, of family gatherings, or work. They converted the river, symbol of life, into a cemetery.[7]

Unfortunately, testimonies such as the above are not uncommon in Colombia. The internal war has touched the lives of every citizen in different ways. One of the main impacts the Truth Commission Report is having on Colombians relates to the fear victims and survivors had of speaking out. However, since June 28th, many citizens have come forward, are letting some of their guards down, and are willing to confront their violent pasts as difficult as this might be. The disposition to look at the atrocities endured and face them is creating new possibilities of remembrances, thus, for historical memories. This is also because the Truth Report delved on topics which had only been touched upon or of which only the surface was known, such as the war's effect on nature, the silences and sounds produced by the armed actors, how communities such as the LGBTQAI+, indigenous peoples, afro descendants, children and teenagers, the treatment of the bodies during the conflict, and resistance. According to, one of the Truth Commissioners and anthropologists, Alejandro Castillejo,

# Final Thoughts 177

who does what he has called "ritual readings" of the volume he coordinated, *Cuando los pájaros no cantaban. Historias del conflicto armado en Colombia* (*When Birds did not Sing. Histories of the Armed Conflict in Colombia*), these exercises help in the healing Colombians need.

> Once the reading is over, we use other sounds to close and then we open the meeting for conversation. Here the participants resume the histories they heard, which are war stories. They become pedagogical devices, vehicles to create historical memories, and people end up talking about all this.[8]

I believe that the sense of hope Colombians are starting to feel since June 2022 is directly related to the fact that, after a long time, they feel heard and acknowledged. Their voices matter and having that attention encourages victims and survivors to step up and confront their difficult pasts. This also relates to Andreas Huyssen's statement about thinking about memories for the present and future, as mentioned in previous chapters of the book. The fact that people and their communities have a safe space to gather, read, listen, and talk about their memories, atrocities, and resistances will sure enrich the production of historical memories in the country. They will be more even, less one sided, and most definitely, not state drive.

These hopes and expectations, which come after more than ten years of right-wing and center heads of state, which have eroded the confidence of Colombians, are also focusing on the construction and launching of the National Memory Museum of Colombia. Currently, under construction, the venue has undergone several changes not only related to its directors but also its policies. As mentioned in Chapters 3 and 4 of this text, in 2011, Law 1448, also known as Law for Victims and Land Restitution, paves the way for the creation of the National Center for Historical Memory, CNMH, with the aim to design and create a memory museum to make visible the casualties and promote memories, histories, and lives of the country's violence. To make this possible, it is necessary to join the state, private sector, civil society, and international forces. Therefore, the museum's objectives are focused on shedding light on what happened to get to the truth, respecting the diversity of memories, bringing dignity to the victims, reconstructing the social fabric the war destroyed, and fortifying the civil society to avoid atrocities' repetition.[9]

However, the museum has been in the spotlight in recent years due to the lack of continuity in its policies which are reflected in the frequent changes regarding its director. Despite being a museum created for the victims and survivors of the Colombian internal war, Darío Acevedo, ex-director of the National Center for Historical Memory, was a conflict denier. He was appointed during the right-wing presidency of Iván Duque and strived to create a national narrative in which the survivors of violence lost ground. Acevedo's postures not only unsettled victims' associations but also politicians, academics, and journalists. He was well known for distorting the Colombian conflict and for sugarcoating the terms used to refer to brutalities. For example, he would not use words such as "war," "resistance," and "resilience," because he did not consider the atrocities committed by the National Army, for instance, were that serious or pervasive.[10] In addition, he asserted that the Colombian guerrillas enacted terrorist attacks rather than acts of political violence. On February 3, 2020, Acevedo's beliefs about the armed conflict caused the International Coalition of Sites of Conscience (ICSC) to remove the CNMH from their list, causing Colombia's isolation from the international memory community.[11] In addition, one of Acevedo's most polemic moves was to privilege the members of the Federación Colombiana de Ganaderos (Colombian Federation of Land and Cattle Owners-Fedegán) whose close relations with paramilitary groups are notorious. On February 24, 2020, Fedegán and the CNMH signed an agreement to "tell the hidden history of Colombia," implying that the victims' voices highlighted in several reports published before Acevedo assumed the CNMH leadership are questionable and that the versions of Fedegán's members must have priority.[12] Fortunately, when Petro and Márquez took office, Acevedo was forced to resign. Immediately thereafter, the JEP, Special Jurisdiction for Peace, of Colombia made a petition to the General Attorney's Office and called Acevedo for a deposition. Currently, he is under investigation for showing disrespect toward the victims and their memories.[13] Under Acevedo's leadership of the CNMH, the museum had more than three directors, who left the position after deeply disagreeing with Acevedo. For instance, on November 5, 2021, director Laura Montoya handed in her resignation to Acevedo. They had deep disagreements about the way in which the museum should handle the victim's participation in the institution. While Acevedo's leadership privileged conflict denial approaches and narratives, Montoya was concerned about what would be the best way to ease the victims' associations who had retired their archives from the CNMH. She also advocated for giving the lead role in the institution to the victims and conflict survivors.[14] Another director that only lasted for two months was Laura María Ortiz, apparently due to the lack of continuity in the CNMH policies related to the museum.[15] In April 2022, before his resignation, Acevedo appointed Rosario Rizo as the museum's director.[16] Since Acevedo's resignation, the CNMH has had no leadership, which has slowed down the museum's timeline.

Concurring with Colombian historian Sebastián Vargas, the National Museum of Memory in Colombia is necessary because to achieve national reconciliation and healing, it is not possible to privilege one kind of victim and its memory over others. This statement reminds us of what Jelin and Rothberg asserted about competing and hierarchical memories. Thus, it is necessary to provide a historical perspective on the war. The victims and survivors of atrocities participation is crucial for their reparation, as mentioned by Gloria Ramírez and Gloria Quintero in Chapter 3, and by Soraya Bayuelo in Chapter 4. They not only deserve dignity but also a place and space within Colombian society;

thus, the National Museum of Memory should not be exclusively devoted to the victims but to all citizens. As stated by Vargas, an all-inclusive venue can promote empathy, which is key for no repetition, and allows us to approach the violence issue as a long-duration historical phenomenon.[17] This means that the National Museum of Memory has not only the purpose of recovering and dignifying the victims and their voices but also the commitment to explain to all citizens the historical contexts and processes that made violence such a prominent actor in Colombia. Along these lines, the mission of the museum is to help in the elaboration of non-official accounts of the armed conflict.

> We showcase the violent acts and how people resisted them, making sure a plurality of voices. [...] this is not a place only for the direct victims of the country's internal war. It is for all citizens. It is a space in which we want to promote discussions, reflections, and activities related to everyone's historical memories.[18]

The museum is still under construction. Its director planned the inauguration for 2022 but due to the recent events, like Acevedo's resignation, the JEP investigating him, and the new government, today is unsure when the institution will open its doors. Nevertheless, the museum already has an assigned space in Bogota, and its construction is taking place.

According to journalist Daniel Schwartz, a memory museum in Colombia is not the same as one in Argentina, Germany, Chile, or Japan because as many historical memory initiatives in the country, it is being made amid the war. El Mochuelo, community museum addressed in Chapter 4, is an example of how some social groups come together and resist even when violence is ongoing. In addition, Schwartz emphasizes the Latin American trend mentioned throughout the whole book which states that memories are not only explanations of the past but also one of the ways people use to express their present and foresee their future.[19]

What is certain is that Colombian museums are diversifying. Supported by the field developed by Peter Vergo's *The New Museology* (1989), museum professionals started to question the conventional role of the institution as a place devoted to elitist knowledge and authority. This trend coincided with the Colombian violence of the 1980s and encouraged reflections about the role of museums in representing and displaying the country's recent history. That is how the directors and curators of the National Museum of Colombia, created as a shrine for science, adopted some of the principles of the new museology since the early 1990s.

The new museology suggested new conceptual frameworks, but Colombians were also devising alternative ways of thinking about museums based on their lived experiences with political violence and their efforts to remember the past. On one hand, state agents realized the need to include marginalized voices of victims of brutalities in official venues. In this context, the directors of the National Museum of Colombia struggled with ways to display the recent armed conflict and to consider different perspectives and actors tied to the violence. On the other hand, historically underrepresented rural communities found that the new museology echoed many of their concerns: To focus on stories rather than objects, to create inclusive narratives, to privilege underrepresented voices, to question authority and a unitary perspective of the world, and to represent and display what is culturally relevant for them.

The shift of Colombian museums, however, goes beyond state versus periphery. Curators, academics, and communities understand that the idea of a hegemonic metanarrative is something in crisis. Instead, they realize, following A.W. Eaton and Ivan Gaskell, that museums are becoming acentric.[20] This means that curators and museum professionals have the fundamental awareness of the importance of acknowledging even-handedness and equity. They face challenges in their decision-making process because the polarization bred by internal warfare complicates the former, while full representation of all Colombian rural and urban communities bedevils the latter. Therefore, memory museums and exhibitions surged as the response of many communities for inclusion in nation building and the production of historical memories. In this context, invisible, peripheral, and historically underrepresented social groups decided to create grieving spaces where they could gather to heal, reflect on what happened to them, and design strategies to prevent violence from recurring.

*Museums, Exhibitions, and Memories of Violence in Colombia, 2000–2014: Trying to Remember* has aimed to address the fundamental question of what a museum and its social roles and functions are. In Chapter 1, I show how elitist sectors of Colombian society felt that including "controversial" artifacts in the National Museum collections threatened the political narrative as well as the conventional nature of the institution. The adverse reactions forced the director and museum professionals to withdraw their initiative to acquire and display a guerrilla's towel. Chapter 2, also devoted to the politics of memory at the National Museum of Colombia, analyzed why certain national figures, such as ex-guerrilla Carlos Pizarro Leongómez and politician Luis Carlos Galán Sarmiento, do deserve a place in the shrine. In comparing these two cases, I suggest that the latter exhibition succeeded not only because Pizarro was more palatable to cultured urbanites as but also because he was a martyred politician who had renounced armed struggle for electoral politics. Rather, Pizarro's life story conformed to the class and aesthetic sensibilities of a museum devoted to official knowledge and narratives.

Chapters 3 and 4 of *Trying to Remember* aim to complexify understandings of museums in Colombia by addressing two peripheral memory sites and exhibitions. Chapter 3, focused on the inhabitants of Granada, Antioquia, analyzed their memory site at the Hall of Never Again, which community organizers insist is not a museum. For these villagers, museums are places for the embalmed, spaces created by and devoted to the elite class. In this viewpoint, conventional static display spaces would ill serve the needs of the community. In Chapter 4, I explored an example of a different exhibition format used by local communities traumatized by violence: The Traveling Museum of the Memory and Identity of Montes de María. Being the only peripatetic museum in Colombia, this space advances our understanding of local communities' considerations of the format and role of these institutions and what they should do and represent. For the 15 townships that compose the Montes de María region, an itinerant museum was the best alternative they found to reach as many people as possible affected by violence. A conventional, stationary structure would not have served them well. Moreover, as a memory museum, the residents of Montes de Maria insisted on crafting a venue that celebrates cultural resilience as well as mourning loss.

One of the major differences between state and grassroots representations of violence in museums and exhibitions is the treatment they give to the artifacts found in their displays. Conventionally, the first type of venue remains constrained by the character of their collections, still being object centered. In the second kind, it is possible to find displays more story-centered and exhibitions in which the exhibited pieces illustrate the desired narrative. However, with the advent of the new museology, curators of state and grassroots sites are attempting to accommodate the ideas and terms of the communities they seek to represent. This is an ongoing challenge. Another difference between official and alternative memory sites encountered in the four case studies concerns the cultural value judgments exercised by museums in sanctioning particular tastes, behaviors, and markets. However, these ideas, challenged by the new museology, give voice not only to professionals but also to community leaders to define the cultural narratives they wish to show to the public. In this sense, memory sites and exhibitions in Colombia are challenging how people supposedly must behave in and derive from museums, upending their traditional roles as enforcers of social discipline.[21]

When I was finishing this manuscript, the Colombian government appointed museologist and Professor William López as the director of the National Museum of Colombia.[22] Also, the architect María Valencia Gaitán, granddaughter of Jorge Eliécer Gaitán, took over as director of the National Center for Historical Memory.[23]

## Notes

1 Semana, "Francia Márquez Denuncia Atentado En Su Contra y Otros Líderes En Cauca," Semana.com Últimas Noticias de Colombia y el Mundo, August 29, 2020, https://www.semana.com/nacion/articulo/francia-marquez-denuncia-atentado-en-su-contra-y-otros-lideres-sociales-con-armas-y-granadas/612547/
2 "'Venimos a recuperar lo perdido': Discurso De Roy Barreras En La Posesión Presidencial De Petro," Cambio Colombia, accessed September 14, 2022, https://cambiocolombia.com/articulo/politica/venimos-recuperar-lo-perdido-discurso-de-roy-barreras-en-la-posesion-presidencial.

**182** Final Thoughts

3 Semana, "¿Quién Es María José Pizarro, La Senadora Que Le Puso La Banda Presidencial a Petro?" Semana.com Últimas Noticias de Colombia y el Mundo, August 8, 2022, https://www.semana.com/nacion/articulo/quien-es-maria-jose-pizarro-la-senadora-que-le-puso-la-banda-presidencial-a-petro/202231/.
4 "El Poder De Los Símbolos, El Concepto Del Pueblo Durante La Posesión De Gustavo Petro," Cambio Colombia, accessed September 12, 2022, https://cambiocolombia.com/articulo/radar/el-poder-de-los-simbolos-el-concepto-del-pueblo-durante-la-posesion-de-gustavo-petro.
5 Mar Romero, "¿Por Qué La Espada De Bolívar SE Robó El 'Show' En La Toma De Posesión De Gustavo Petro?" France 24 (France 24, August 8, 2022), https://www.france24.com/es/am%C3%A9rica-latina/20220808-por-qu%C3%A9-la-espada-de-bol%C3%ADvar-se-rob%C3%B3-el-show-en-la-toma-de-posesi%C3%B3n-de-gustavo-petro.
6 Maria Camila Renteria Benavides et al., "El Juramento De Francia Márquez Ante Sus Ancestros En Su Posesión Como Vicepresidenta," elpais.com.co, August 7, 2022, https://www.elpais.com.co/politica/el-juramento-de-francia-marquez-ante-sus-ancestros-en-su-posesion-como-vicepresidenta.html.
7 Alejandro Castillejo and Nathalia Salamanca, *Cuando los pájaros no cantaban. Historias del conflicto armado en Colombia*. Volumen testimonial de la Comisión para el esclarecimiento de la verdad, la convivencia y la no repetición (Bogotá: Comisión de la verdad, versión digital), 137.
8 Andrés Ortiz, "Entrevista: La Comisión De La Verdad Pone En Escena Historias De Vida Tras La Guerra," Colombia Visible, May 5, 2022, https://colombiavisible.com/entrevista-la-comision-de-la-verdad-pone-en-escena-150-historias-de-vida-tras-la-guerra/.
9 ¿Qué es el museo?: Museo de Memoria de Colombia, accessed September 24, 2022, https://museodememoria.gov.co/sobre-el-proyecto/que-es-el-museo-de-memoria-de-colombia/.
10 "'Darío Acevedo niega el conflicto armado': Iván Cepeda," *Semana*, May 11, 2019, https://www.semana.com/nacion/articulo/dario-acevedo-niega-el-conflicto-armado-cepeda/639073
11 "Sacan a Colombia de la más importante red internacional de la memoria," *El Tiempo*, February 3, 2020, https://www.eltiempo.com/unidad-investigativa/sacan-a-colombia-de-la-mas- importante-red-internacional-de-memoria-historica-458448
12 "Vamos a firmar un convenio con el Centro Nacional de Memoria Histórica: Fedegán," El Espectador, February 20. 2020, https://www.elespectador.com/colombia2020/pais/vamos-firmar-un-convenio-con-el-centro- nacional-de-memoria-historica-fedegan-articulo-906215
13 El Espectador, "Jep Pide a La Fiscalía Investigar a Darío Acevedo, Exdirector De Centro De Memoria," ELESPECTADOR.COM, August 13, 2022, https://www.elespectador.com/judicial/jep-pide-a-la-fiscalia-investigar-a-dario-acevedo-exdirector-de-centro-de-memoria/.
14 El Espectador, "Renuncia Laura Montoya, Directora Del Museo De Memoria Histórica," ELESPECTADOR.COM, November 5, 2021, https://www.elespectador.com/colombia-20/renuncia-laura-montoya-directora-del-museo-de-memoria-historica/.
15 "Renunció La Directora Del Museo De La Memoria, Tras Solo Dos Meses En El Cargo," infobae (infobae, March 30, 2022), https://www.infobae.com/america/colombia/2022/03/30/renuncio-la-directora-del-museo-de-la-memoria-tras-solo-dos-meses-en-el-cargo/.

16 "Rosario Rizo Navarro Se Posesionó Como Directora Del Museo De Memoria De Colombia," Centro Nacional de Memoria Histórica, April 23, 2022, https://centrodememoriahistorica.gov.co/rosario-rizo-navarro-se-posesiono-como-directora-del-museo-de-memoria-de-colombia/#:~:text=Rosario%20Rizo%20Navarro%20se%20posesion%C3%B3%20como%20directora%20del%20Museo%20de%20Memoria%20de%20Colombia,-Ante%20Dar%C3%ADo%20Acevedo.

17 Sebastian Vargas Alvarez, "El Museo Nacional De La Memoria En Colombia: ¿Qué Exhibir? ¿Cómo Hacerlo?" Universidad del Rosario (Universidad Nacional de Colombia, January 1, 1970), https://pure.urosario.edu.co/en/publications/el-museo-nacional-de-la-memoria-en-colombia-qu%C3%A9-exhibir-c%C3%B3mo-hace.

18 ¿Qué es el museo? Museo de Memoria de Colombia, accessed September 26, 2022, https://museodememoria.gov.co/sobre-el-proyecto/que-es-el-museo-de-memoria-de-colombia/.

19 Daniel Schwartz Cambio, "Un Museo Para La Memoria," Cambio Colombia (Cambio Colombia), accessed September 26, 2022, https://cambiocolombia.com/opinion/puntos-de-vista/un-museo-para-la-memoria.

20 A.W. Eaton and Ivan Gaskell, "Do Subaltern Artifacts Belong in Art Museums?" in *The Ethics of Culture Appropriation*, eds. James O. Young and Conrad G. Brunk (Malden, MA and London: Blackwell Publishing Ltd, 2009), 235–268.

21 Hilde Hein, *The Museum in Transition*.

22 Radio Nacional de Colombia, "William Alfonso López Es El Nuevo Director Del Museo Nacional," Museo Nacional de Colombia | William Alfonso López, nuevo director, accessed November 7, 2022, https://www.radionacional.co/cultura/museo-nacional-de-colombia-william-alfonso-lopez-nuevo-director.

23 El Colombiano, "María Valencia Gaitán Se Posesionó Como Nueva Directora Del Centro Nacional De Memoria Histórica," www.elcolombiano.com (ElColombiano.com, November 3, 2022), https://www.elcolombiano.com/colombia/posesion-maria-valencia-gaitan-nieta-de-jorge-eliecer-gaitan-como-la-nueva-directora-del-centro-nacional-de-memoria-historica-OL19038987.

# BIBLIOGRAPHY

**Archives**

Centro Nacional de Memoria Histórica (CNMH)
Museo Itinerante de la Memoria e Identidad de Los Montes de María, El Mochuelo
Museo Nacional de Colombia
Salón del Nunca Más
Red Colombiana de Lugares de Memoria
Jurisdicción Especial para la Paz, JEP

**Exhibition Catalogues**

Pizarro, María José and Catalina Ruíz, curators. *Hacer la paz en Colombia, "Ya vuelvo", Carlos Pizarro. Documentación Exposición.* Bogotá-Catalunya: Museo Nacional de Colombia, Casa América Catalunya, Fundación Carlos Pizarro, Ministerio de Cultura de Colombia, 200 Culturaes Independencia Bicentenario de las Independencias 1810–2010, 2011: 1.

**Interviews and Oral Histories**

Aristizábal, Carlos Abel. Interview by Author. Granada, Antioquia, Colombia. May 9, 2017.
Bayuelo, Soraya. Interview by Author. Austin – TX, Carmen de Bolívar – Colombia. May 18, 2017.
_____. Interview by Author. New York, Bogotá. July 12, 2022.
Botero, Clara Isabel. Interview by Author. Austin – TX, Bogotá – Colombia.
Castro, Daniel. Interview by Author. Bogotá, Colombia. August 8, 2018.
Castro, Giovanni. Interview by Author. Austin – TX, Pasto, Nariño – Colombia.
Cuervo de Jaramillo, Elvira. Interview by Author. Bogotá, Colombia, February 9, 2017.
de Angulo de Robayo, María Victoria. Interview by Author, February 12, 2017.

Giraldo, Claudia Milena. Interview by Author. Granada, Antioquia, Colombia. May 10, 2017.
Hernández, Bexielena. Interview by Author. Austin – TX, Santa Marta, Magdalena, Colombia, August 15, 2017.
Lara, Patricia. Interview by Author. Austin – TX, Bogotá – Colombia. July 15, 2019.
Montoya, Jaime. Interview by Author. Granada, Antioquia, Colombia. May 12, 2017.
Pizarro, María José. Interview by *La Silla Vacía,* September 16, 2010.
Quintero, Gloria. Interview by Author. Granada, Antioquia, Colombia. May 9, 2017.
_____. Interview by Author. Granada, Antioquia, Colombia. August 14, 2017.
Ramírez, Gloria. Interview by Author. Granada, Antioquia, Colombia. August 14, 2017.
_____. Interview by Author. Granada, Antioquia, Colombia. May 12, 2017.
_____. Interview by Author. New York – Bogotá, Colombia. April 25, 2022.
Rees, Laurence. Interview by PBS. https://www.pbs.org/auschwitz/about/.
Romano, Francisco. Interview by author. Bogotá – Colombia, June 4, 2020.
Ruíz, Catalina. Interview by Author. Bogotá, Colombia. February 14, 2017.
*Siete Digital.* Periodismo regional. Interview: "Cuando la guerra pasa por la vida de uno arrasa con todo." August 27, 2015, https://sietedigital.wordpress.com/2015/08/27/entrevista-cuando-la-guerra-pasa-por-la-vida-de-uno-arrasa-con-todo/

### Newspapers

*El Colombiano El Espectador El Heraldo*
*El Mercurio El Mundo*
*El Nuevo Herald El Nuevo Liberal El País*
*El Tiempo El Universal La Nación La Patria*
*The Guardian*
*The Washington Post*

### Journals

Revista *Semana*
Revista *Cromos*
Revista *Cambio*

### Websites

AMA y no olvida. Museo de la memoria contra la impunidad. http://www.museodelamemorianicaragua.org/
Asociación de Usuarios Campesinos de Colombia, ANUC. http://anuc.co/dynamicdata/historia.php
BBC News Latin America & Caribbean. "Profiles: Colombia's armed groups." http://www.bbc.com/news/world-latin-america-11400950
Bravinder, Tristan. "New Scholarship on the Origins of Latin American Museums." *The Iris. Behind the Scenes at the Getty.* July 26, 2018. http://blogs.getty.edu/iris/new-scholarship-on-the-origins-of-latin-american-museums/
Caracola Consultores. "Museo Itinerante de la Memoria." http://www.caracolaconsultores.com/MIM/

Casa América Catalunya. "Juan Manuel Santos, presidente electo de Colombia, se 'lleva' nuestra exposición "Ya vuelvo" al Museo Nacional de su país." http://americat.barcelona/es/juan-manuel-santos-presidente-electo-de-colombia-se-lleva-nuestra-exposicion-ya-vuelvo-al-museo-nacional-de-su-pais

Casa América Catalunya. "María José Pizarro abre en el Museo Nacional de Colombia la exposición sobre su padre muerto." http://americat.barcelona/es/septiembre-21-maria-jose-pizarro-abre-en-el-museo-nacional-de-colombia-la-exposicion-sobre-su-padremuerto

Casa América Catalunya. "Más de 50.000 personas visitan en el Museo Nacional de Bogotá la muestra 'Hacer la paz en Colombia. Ya vuelvo. Carlos Pizarro.'" http://americat.barcelona/es/mas-de-50-000-personas-visitan-en-el-museo-nacional-de-bogota-la-muestra-hacer-la-paz-en-colombia-ya-vuelvo-carlos-pizarro

Castro, Giovanny. "Inicia en Cartagena el primer vuelo del 'Mochuelo.'" http://mimemoria.org.

Colprensa. "Ataques Del Clan Del Golfo: Campesinos De Los Montes De María Piden Seguridad," Paro armado: campesinos de los Montes de María piden seguridad por ataques del Clan del Golfo, accessed July 21, 2022, https://www.radionacional.co/noticias-colombia/paro-armado-campesinos-de-los-montes-de-maria-piden-seguridad-por-ataques-del

Colprensa. "¿Regresa El Terror a Los Montes De María? Consejos Territoriales Lanzan SOS," www.eluniversal.com.co, May 5, 2022, https://www.eluniversal.com.co/regional/regresa-el-terror-a-los-montes-de-maria-consejos-territoriales-lanzan-sos-CE6512400

Colprensa. "Rubén Darío Acevedo Se Defendió Ante La Jep Por Caso Del Museo Nacional De Memoria," www.elcolombiano.com (ElColombiano.com, July 11, 2022), https://www.elcolombiano.com/colombia/ruben-dario-acevedo-se-defendio-ante-la-jep-por-caso-del-museo-nacional-de-memoria-AI18011706.

Costa-Kostritsky, Valeria. "The Fall of the Conquistadores," Apollo Magazine, August 26, 2021, https://www.apollo-magazine.com/colombia-statues-conquistadores-toppling/#:~:text=On%2016%20September%202020%2C%20members, the%20south%2Dwest%20of%20Colombia

Cristancho, José Gabriel. "Gonzalo Sánchez: trayectoria de una experiencia de memoria de la violencia," in Colombia. *Revista Colombiana de Educación*, no. 61, (2011): 73–88. Retrieved October 16, 2021, from http://www.scielo.org.co/scielo.php?script=sci_arttext&pid=S0120-39162011000200004&lng=en&tlng=es.

"Críticas a Justicia y Paz," February 2014, https://www.elheraldo.co/editorial/criticas-justicia-y-paz-142647

Cultura, Recreación y Deporte. "Ley 397 de 1997 (Ley General de Cultura)." https://www.culturarecreacionydeporte.gov.co/es/ley-397-de-1997-ley-general-de-cultura

"'Darío Acevedo niega el conflicto armado': Iván Cepeda," Semana, May 11, 2019, https://www.semana.com/nacion/articulo/dario-acevedo-niega-el-conflicto-armado-cepeda/639073

Dejusticia. "El Museo Nacional De La Memoria, Un Deber Moral." https://www.dejusticia.org/column/el-museo-nacional-de-la-memoria-un-deber-moral/

Esquema Ley 975. Unidad Nacional de Fiscalías para la Justicia y la Paz, 2012. http://www.fiscalia.gov.co:8080/Esquema975.htm

El Heraldo. "Más De 40 Casos emblemáticos, elevados a crimen de lesa humanidad," *El Heraldo*, accessed July 26, 2022, https://www.elheraldo.co/colombia/mas-de-40-casos-emblematicos-elevados-crimen-de-lesa-humanidad-617164.

"El Poder De Los Símbolos, El Concepto Del Pueblo Durante La Posesión De Gustavo Petro," Cambio Colombia, accessed September 12, 2022, https://cambiocolombia.com/articulo/radar/el-poder-de-los-simbolos-el-concepto-del-pueblo-durante-la-posesion-de-gustavo-petro.

"En 2019 más de 25.000 personas fueron víctimas de desplazamiento forzado," January 3, 2020, https://www.rcnradio.com/colombia/en-2019-mas-de-25000-personas-fueron-victimas-de-desplazamiento-forzado.

Fernández Suárez, Isabel. "La Toalla de Tirofijo, Pieza de Museo," ABC, http://www.abc.es/hemeroteca/historico-16-02-2001/abc/Gente/la-toalla-de- tirofijo-pieza-de-museo_12880.html.

Fiscalía General de la Nación. "Ley 975 de 2005 (Por la cual se dictan disposiciones para la reincorporación de miembros de grupos armados organizados al margen de la ley que contribuyan de manera efectiva a la consecución de la paz nacional y se dictan otras disposiciones para acuerdos humanitarios)," https://www.fiscalia.gov.co/colombia/wp-content/uploads/2013/04/Ley-975-del-25-de-julio-de-2005-concordada-con-decretos-y-sentencias-de-constitucionalidad.pdf.

French Embassy in Bogotá, "Apoyo de Francia al Centro de Memoria Histórica." http://www.ambafrance-co.org/Apoyo-de-Francia-al-Centro-de.

Fundación Carlos Pizarro Leongómez. "Inauguración "'YA VUELVO. Carlos Pizarro, una vida por la paz.'" http://www.carlospizarro.org/index.php/proyectos/exposiciones/item/33- exposicion-ya-vuelvo-barcelona-espana

Gallo Tapias, Laura. "Recuerdos de un sobreviviente del Palacio," Crónica Política y Sociedad, https://cerosetenta.uniandes.edu.co/recuerdos-de-un-sobreviviente-del-palacio/.

Hauenschild, Andrea. "Claims and Reality of New Museology: Case Studies in Canada, the United States, and Mexico," http://museumstudies.si.edu/claims2000.htm#2.

"Hay Futuro Si Hay Verdad: Informe Final Comisión De La Verdad," Hay futuro si hay verdad | Informe Final Comisión de la Verdad, accessed August 31, 2022, https://www.comisiondelaverdad.co/hay-futuro-si-hay-verdad, 576.

Human Rights Watch. "World Report 2011: Colombia. Events of 2010," https://www.hrw.org/world-report/2011/country-chapters/colombia.

Ibermuseos. *Roundtable of Santiago de Chile, 1972. Vol. 1*, May 23, 2022, http://www.ibermuseos.org/en/resources/publications/mesa-redonda-de-santiago-de-chile-1972-vol-1/.

International Center for Transitional Justice. "What Is Transitional Justice?" https://www.ictj.org/about/transitional-justice.

International Committee of Memorial Museums in Remembrance of the Victims of Public Crimes. "What Is ICMEMO," http://icmemo.mini.icom.museum/about/what-is-ic-memo/

International Council of Museums. "ICOM Approves a New Museum Definition," accessed September 14, 2022. https://icom.museum/en/news/icom-approves-a-new-museum-definition/#:~:text=NetworkICOM%20approves%20a%20new%20museum%20definition&text=The%20new%20text%20reads%3A, exhibits%20tangible%20and%20intangible%20heritage.

International Council of Museums. "Museum Definition," https://icom.museum/en/standards-guidelines/museum-definition/

"Jep Pide a La Fiscalía Investigar a Darío Acevedo, Exdirector De Centro De Memoria," *El Espectador*, August 13, 2022, https://www.elespectador.com/judicial/jep-pide-a-la-fiscalia-investigar-a-dario-acevedo-exdirector-de-centro-de-memoria/.

# Bibliography

La cola de rata. "Restaurando a Granada," http://www.traslacoladelarata.com/2013/04/22/restaurando-a-granada/

"La pandemia cambió la forma cómo nos relacionamos con el arte: Directora del Museo Nacional," Interview. *Semana*, July 18, 2021, https://www.semana.com/mejor-colombia/articulo/cuando-veo-entrar-a-un-nino-al-museo-nacional-pienso-que-no-va-a-ser-el-mismo-al-salir-juliana-restrepo/202100/

La Silla Vacía. "¿Ya vuelvo?" http://lasillavacia.com/elblogueo/lospina/22837/ya-vuelvo.

Lugar de la memoria, la tolerancia y la inclusión social. "Quiénes somos," https://lum.cultura.pe/el-lum/quienes-somos

Ministerio de Salud y Protección Social de Colombia, "Grupos-Etnicos," Inicio, accessed July 19, 2022, https://www.minsalud.gov.co/proteccionsocial/promocion-social/Paginas/grupos-etnicos.aspx.

Montemariaaudiovisual. "Quiénes somos," https://montemariaaudiovisual.wordpress.com/quienes-somos/

Museo Nacional de Colombia. "Hacer la paz en Colombia: Ya vuelvo, Carlos Pizarro," http://www.museonacional.gov.co/exposiciones/pasadas/Paginas/Hacerlapazen Colombia12.aspx.

"Museum Definition." ICOM, http://icom.museum/the-vision/museum-definition/

Ocampo López, José Antonio. "Gobierno de Mariano Ospina Pérez." *Historia 2*. http://www.banrepcultural.org/blaavirtual/biografias/ospimari.htm.

Ortiz, Andrés. "Entrevista: La Comisión De La Verdad Pone En Escena Historias De Vida Tras La Guerra," Colombia Visible, May 5, 2022, https://colombiavisible.com/entrevista-la-comision-de-la-verdad-pone-en-escena-150-historias-de-vida-tras-la-guerra/

PBI Colombia. "Trujillo Massacre," https://pbicolombia.org/2016/07/08/trujillo-massacre/

Perry, Jimena and Elizabeth O´brien. "Opinion: Colombia Is in Crisis, and Vaccine Nationalism Is Making It Worse," Latino Rebels (Latino Rebels, May 20, 2021), https://www.latinorebels.com/2021/05/19/colombiacrisisvaccinenationalism/.

Programa de las Naciones Unidas para el Desarrollo. "Los Montes de María: análisis de la conflictividad," http://www.undp.org/content/dam/undp/projects/COL/00058220/Analisis% 20conflcitividad%20Montes%20de%20Maria%20PDF.pdf.

Puentes, Adriana Lucía. "¿Cuántos líderes sociales han sido asesinados durante 2019?" *El Colombiano*, September 18, 2019, https://www.elcolombiano.com/colombia/paz-y-derechos-humanos/lideres-sociales-asesinados-en-colombia-durante-2019-hasta-septiembre-segun-indepaz-PH11611439. "¡Van 18 líderes sociales asesinados en los 14 días de 2020!", January 14, 2020, https://noticias.caracoltv.com/lidera-la-vida/van-18-lideres-sociales-asesinados-en-los-14-dias-de-2020-ie35596.

"¿Qué es ca Comisión de la Verdad?" Comisión de la Verdad Colombia, accessed July 13, 2022, https://web.comisiondelaverdad.co/la-comision/que-es-la-comision-de-la-verdad.

"¿Qué es el Museo de Memoria de Colombia?" Museo de Memoria de Colombia, http://museodememoria.gov.co/sobre-el-proyecto/que-es-el-museo-de-memoria-de-colombia/

Radio Nacional de Colombia, "Comunidades En Los Montes De María Denuncian Intimidaciones De Grupos Armados," Denuncian intimidaciones de grupos armados en los Montes de María, accessed July 21, 2022, https://www.radionacional.co/noticias-colombia/denuncian-intimidaciones-de-grupos-armados-en-los-montes-de-maria.

RCN Radio. "Dejaré de lado mis opiniones para dirigir el Centro de Memoria Histórica: Darío Acevedo," https://www.rcnradio.com/colombia/dejare-de-lado-mis- opiniones-para-dirigir-el-centro-de-memoria-historica-dario-acevedo

"Renovación, historia y virtualidad en la agenda del Museo Nacional," *El Nuevo Siglo*, April 4, 2022, https://www.elnuevosiglo.com.co/articulos/02-26-2021-renovacion-historia-y-virtualidad-en-la-agenda-del-museo-nacional

Renteria Benavides, Maria Camila et al. "El Juramento De Francia Márquez Ante Sus Ancestros En Su Posesión Como Vicepresidenta," elpais.com.co, August 7, 2022, https://www.elpais.com.co/politica/el-juramento-de-francia-marquez-ante-sus-ancestros-en-su-posesion-como-vicepresidenta.html.

"Renuncia Laura Montoya, Directora Del Museo De Memoria Histórica," *El Espectador*, November 5, 2021, https://www.elespectador.com/colombia-20/renuncia-laura-montoya-directora-del-museo-de-memoria-historica/

"Renunció La Directora Del Museo De La Memoria, Tras Solo Dos Meses En El Cargo," infobae (infobae, March 30, 2022), https://www.infobae.com/america/colombia/2022/03/30/renuncio-la-directora-del-museo-de-la-memoria-tras-solo-dos-meses-en-el-cargo/

"'Retiramos los archivos porque el CNMH está trabajando con victimarios': Asociación Minga," *El Espectador*, March 11, 2020, https://www.elespectador.com/colombia2020/pais/retiramos-los-archivos-porque-el-cnmh-esta-trabajando-con-victimarios-asociacion-minga-articulo-907534

Romero, Mar. "¿Por Qué La Espada De Bolívar SE Robó El 'Show' En La Toma De Posesión De Gustavo Petro?" France 24 (France 24, August 8, 2022), https://www.france24.com/es/am%C3%A9rica-latina/20220808-por-qu%C3%A9-la-espada-de-bol%C3%ADvar-se-rob%C3%B3-el-show-en-la-toma-de-posesi%C3%B3n-de-gustavo-petro.

"Rosario Rizo Navarro Se Posesionó Como Directora Del Museo De Memoria De Colombia," Centro Nacional de Memoria Histórica, April 23, 2022, https://centrodememoriahistorica.gov.co/rosario-rizo-navarro-se-posesiono-como-directora-del-museo-de-memoria-de-colombia/#:~:text=Rosario%20Rizo%20Navarro%20se%20posesion%C3%B3%20como%20directora%20del%20Museo%20de%20Memoria%20de%20Colombia,-Ante%20Dar%C3%ADo%20Acevedo

Rutas del conflicto. "La masacre de Granada 2001," http://rutasdelconflicto.com/interna.php?masacre=537.

"Sacan a Colombia de la más importante red internacional de la memoria," *El Tiempo*, February 3, 2020, https://www.eltiempo.com/unidad-investigativa/sacan-a-colombia-de-la-mas-importante-red-internacional-de-memoria-historica-458448

Salamanca, Fernando. "Lo que el Museo Nacional no ha podido exhibir," Kienyke, https://www.kienyke.com/historias/lo-que-el-museo-nacional-no-ha-podido-exhibir Sarmiento, Diana. "Semana de la memoria," http://7urdianasarmiento.blogspot.com/2010/11/semana-de-la-memoria.html.

SB, teleSUR. "Fernando Londoño Llama a 'Hacer Trizas' Acuerdo Con FARC-EP," Sitio, teleSUR, May 7, 2017, https://www.telesurtv.net/news/Fernando-Londono-llama-a-acabar-maldito-acuerdo-con-FARC-EP-20170507-0016.html.

Semana, "¿Quién Es María José Pizarro, La Senadora Que Le Puso La Banda Presidencial a Petro?" Semana.com Últimas Noticias de Colombia y el Mundo, August 8, 2022, https://www.semana.com/nacion/articulo/quien-es-maria-jose-pizarro-la-senadora-que-le-puso-la-banda-presidencial-a-petro/202231/.

Schwartz, Daniel. "Un Museo Para La Memoria," Cambio Colombia (Cambio Colombia), accessed September 26, 2022, https://cambiocolombia.com/opinion/puntos-de-vista/un-museo-para-la-memoria.
Sierra, Álvaro. "La escala de la violencia y sus responsables," Semana, Julio 2013, https://especiales.semana.com/especiales/escala-violencia-colombia/quienes-asesinaron-220000-colombianos.html.
The Center for Justice and Accountability. "Colombia: The Justice and Peace Law," https://cja.org/where-we-work/colombia/related-resources/colombia-the-justice-and-peace-law/
Turkewitz, Julie. "Why Are Colombians Protesting?" The New York Times (The New York Times, May 18, 2021), https://www.nytimes.com/2021/05/18/world/americas/colombia-protests-what-to-know.html.
UN Educational, Scientific and Cultural Organization, UNESCO. "Convention for the Safeguarding of the Intangible Cultural Heritage," https://ich.unesco.org/en/convention.
Unidad de Víctimas. "Ley 1448 de 2011 (Por la cual se dictan medidas de atención, asistencia y reparación integral a las víctimas del conflicto armado interno y se dictan otras disposiciones)," https://www.unidadvictimas.gov.co/sites/default/files/documentosbiblioteca/ley-1448-de-2011.pdf.
_____. "Víctimas conflicto armado," Unidad para la atención y reparación integral a las víctimas, https://www.unidadvictimas.gov.co/es.
Valdés Correa, Beatriz. "¿Por Qué Se Recrudece La Violencia En Los Montes De María?," El Espectador, August 15, 2020, https://www.elespectador.com/colombia-20/conflicto/por-que-se-recrudece-la-violencia-en-los-montes-de-maria-article/
Vargas Alvarez, Sebastian. "El Museo Nacional De La Memoria En Colombia: ¿Qué Exhibir? ¿Cómo Hacerlo?" Universidad del Rosario (Universidad Nacional de Colombia, January 1, 1970), https://pure.urosario.edu.co/en/publications/el-museo-nacional-de-la-memoria-en-colombia-qu%C3%A9-exhibir-c%C3%B3mo-hace.
"'Venimos a recuperar lo perdido': Discurso De Roy Barreras En La Posesión Presidencial De Petro," Cambio Colombia, accessed September 14, 2022, https://cambiocolombia.com/articulo/politica/venimos-recuperar-lo-perdido-discurso-de-roy-barreras-en-la-posesion-presidencial.
Violencia en los Montes de María. "Violencia en los Montes de María," http://violenciamontesdemaria.blogspot.com/

**Published Works**

Abello, Martha Nubia. ¡Basta Ya! Colombia. Memories of War and Dignity. Bogotá: General Report of the Historical Memory Group, 2013.
Adam, Thomas R. The Museum and Popular Culture. New York: American Association for Adult Education, 1939.
Aguilera Díaz, María. Montes de María: Una subregión de economía campesina y empresarial. Cartagena: Banco de la República, 2013.
Alape, Arturo. Manuel Marulanda, Tirofijo. Colombia: 40 años de lucha guerrillera. Argentina-México: Editorial Txalaparta, 2000.
Alcino, Valeria Fabiana. "Voces de la ausencia/poética de la memoria en la obra Evidencias (2010) de Norberto Puzzolo, Museo de la Memoria, Rosario, Argentina. Sonido, silencio e imagen durante la dictadura argentina (1976–1983)." IV Congreso Internacional de investigación en artes visuales: ANIAV, 2019.

Arnold de Simine, Silke. "Memory Museum and Museum Text: Intermediality in Daniel Libeskind's *Austerlitz*." *Theory, Culture & Society*. SAGE: Los Angeles, London, New Delhi, and Singapore, Vol. 29, No. 1 (2012): 14–35.

———. *Mediating Memory in the Museum. Trauma, Empathy, Nostalgia*. London: Palgrave MacMillan, 2013.

Arthur, Paige. "How 'Transitions' Reshaped Human Rights: A Conceptual History of Transitional Justice." *Human Rights Quarterly*, Vol. 31, No. 2 (May 2009): 321–367.

Barahona de Brito, Alexandra. "Transitional Justice and Memory: Exploring Perspectives." *South European Society and Politics*, Vol. 15, no. 3 (September 2010): 359–376.

Bartlett, Frederic. *Remembering. A Study in Experimental and Social Psychology*. Cambridge: Cambridge University Press, 1932.

Becker, Carol, James Clifford, and Louis Gates. *Different Voices: A Social, Cultural, and Historical Framework for Change in the American Art Museum*. Washington, DC: Americans for the Arts, 1993.

Bennett, Tony. *The Birth of the Museum. History, Theory, Politics*. London and New York: Routledge, 1995.

Bilbija, Ksenija, and Leigh A. Payne, eds. *Accounting for Violence. Marketing Memory in Latin America*. Durham, NC: Duke University Press, 2010.

Blair, Elsa. *Desaparición forzada*. Balance de la contribución del Centro Nacional de Memoria Histórica al esclarecimiento histórico. Bogotá: Centro Nacional de Memoria Histórica, 2018.

Botero, Clara Isabel. "La construcción del museo comunitario de San Jacinto, Montes de María, Bolívar." *Boletín de historia y antigüedades*, Vol.101, No. 859 (2014): 493–515.

———. *El redescubrimiento del pasado prehispánico de Colombia: viajeros, arqueólogos y coleccionistas, 1820–1945*. Bogotá: Instituto Colombiano de Antropología e Historia, Universidad de Los Andes, 2012.

Bourdieu, Pierre. *Distinction. A Social Critique of the Judgement of Taste*. Translated by Richard Nice. Cambridge, MA: Harvard University Press, 1984.

Brennan, Michael. "Why Materiality on Mourning Matters." In *The Materiality of Mourning. Cross-Disciplinary Perspectives*. Edited by Zahra Newsby and Ruth E. Touson. Abingdon and New York: Routledge, 2019.

Brulon, Bruno. "Decolonising the Museum? Community Experiences in the Periphery of the ICOM Museum Definition." *Curator: The Museum Journal*, Vol. 64, No. 3 (2021): 439–455.

Burnett Tylor, Edward. *Primitive Culture* Vol I. London: Dover Publications, [1873] 2016.

Carrigan, Anna. *El Palacio de Justicia. Una tragedia colombiana*. Bogotá: Editorial Ícono, 2009.

Castillejo, Alejandra and Nathalia Salamanca, *Cuando los pájaros no cantaban. Historias del conflicto armado en Colombia*. Volumen testimonial de la Comisión para el esclarecimiento de la verdad, la convivencia y la no repetición. Bogotá: Comisión de la verdad, 2022.

Castro, Giovanni, Soraya Bayuelo Castellar, and Italia Isadora Samudio Reyes. "Museo itinerante de la memoria y la identidad de los Montes de María: tejiendo memorias y relatos para la reparación simbólica, la vida y la convivencia." In *Estudios para la paz: representaciones, imaginarios y estrategias en el conflicto armado*. ed. Ciudad Paz-ando. Bogotá: Universidad Distrital, 2013, 159–174.

Cauvin, Thomas. *Public History: A Textbook of Practice*. 2nd Edition. New York and London: Routledge, 2022.

Chapin, David, and Stephen Klein. "Forum: The Epistemic Museum." *Museum News*, Vol. 71, No. 4, (July/August 1992): 60–61, 76.
Clifford, James. *Routes: Travel and Translation in the Late Twentieth Century*. Cambridge: Harvard University Press, 1997.
Cohen, David. *The Combing of History*. Chicago, IL: The University of Chicago Press, 1994.
Cook, Susan E. "The Politics of Preservation in Rwanda." In *Genocide in Cambodia and Rwanda*. Edited by Susan E. Cook. Piscataway, NJ: Transaction Publishers, 2006, V–XI.
de los Ríos, Edwin, Carmen Andrea Becerra Becerra, and Fabián Enrique Oyaga Martínez. *Montes de María: entre la consolidación del territorio y el acaparamiento de tierras. Aproximación a la situación de Derechos Humanos y el Derecho Internacional Humanitario en la región (2006–2012)*. Bogotá: Publicaciones ILSA, 2012.
Dixon, Micaela. "The Unreliable Perpetrator: Negotiating Narrative Perspective at Museums of The Third Reich and the Gdr. P." *German Life and Letters*, Vol. 70, No. 2 (April 2017): 241–261.
Douglas, Mary. *Purity and Danger. An Analysis of Concepts of Pollution and Taboo*. New York: Routledge, 1966.
———. *Risk and Blame. Essays in Cultural Theory*. New York and Canada: Routledge, 1992.
Duncan, Carol, and Alan Wallach. "The Universal Survey Museum." In *Museum Studies: An Anthology of Contexts*. Edited by Bettina Messias Carbonell. Malden: Blackwell Publishing, 2004, 46–62.
Eaton, A. W., and Ivan Gaskell. "Do Subaltern Artifacts Belong in Art Museums?" In *The Ethics of Culture Appropriation*. Edited by James O. Young and Conrad G. Brunk: 235–268. Malden, MA and Oxford: Blackwell Publishing Ltd., 2009.
Ehrenreich, Robert and Jane Klinger. "War in Context: Let the Artefacts Speak." In *Does War Belong in Museums? The Representation of Violence in Exhibitions*. Edited by W. Muchitsch. Bielefeld: Museumsakademie Joanneum, 2013, 145–154.
Johannes Fabian. "On Recognizing Things. The "Ethnic Artefact" and the "Ethnographic Object," *L'Homme*, No. 170, ESPÈCES D'OBJETS (avril/juin 2004); 47–60, Published by EHESS, accessed November 28, 2016, 20:09 UTC, Stable URL: http://www.jstor.org/stable/40590211.
Fonseca Barrera, Alejandra, and Sebastián Vargas. "Museo Memoria y Tolerancia de la ciudad de México. Aproximación crítica con dos contrapesos." *Intervención*. enero-junio, No. 11 (2015): 73–82.
Forero, Andrés. "Sí, el Caribe también tiene sabor: producción de identidades regionales en el Museo del Caribe." In *Baukara, bitácoras de antropología e historia de la antropología en América Latina*. Bogotá: Universidad Nacional de Colombia, 2013. No. 4 https://www.humanas.unal.edu.co/baukara/files/1914/5506/3779/Baukara_4.pdf
Forero Parra, Michael Andrés. "Colombia's National Memory Museum: Architecture from a Gender Perspective." ICAMT Annual 44th Conference, September 6–8, 2018. Espoo & Helsinki, Finland.
"Francia Márquez Denuncia Atentado En Su Contra y Otros Líderes En Cauca," Semana.com Últimas Noticias de Colombia y el Mundo, August 29, 2020, https://www.semana.com/nacion/articulo/francia-marquez-denuncia-atentado-en-su-contra-y-otros-lideres-sociales-con-armas-y-granadas/612547/

Frisch, Michael H. *A Shared Authority: Essays on the Craft and Meaning of Oral and Public History*. Albany: State University of New York Press, 2011.
García Márquez, Gabriel. *Living to Tell the Tale*. Translated by Edith Grossman. New York: Vintage International, A Division of Random House Inc., 2003.
Garduño, Ana. "Mexico's Museo de Artes Plásticas. The Divergent Discourses of 1934 and 1947." In *Art Museums of Latin America. Structuring Representation*: 31–44. Edited by Michele Greet and Gina McDaniel Tarver. New York: Routledge, 2018.
Garrard-Burnett, Virginia. *Terror in the Land of the Holy Spirit: Guatemala under General Efraín Ríos Montt 1982–1983*. New York: Oxford University Press, 2010.
Geertz, Clifford. *Conocimiento local. Ensayos sobre la interpretación de las culturas*. Translated by Alberto López Bargados. Barcelona, Buenos Aires, Mexico: Ediciones Paidós, 1994.
_____. *Los usos de la diversidad*. Translated by María José Nicolau La Roda, Nicolás Sánchez Dura, and Alfredo Taberna. Barcelona: Ediciones Paidós, 1996.
_____. *La interpretación de las culturas*. Translated by Alberto L. Bixio. Barcelona: Editorial Gedisa, 2003.
Gómez, Adolfo León. *Los Secretos del Panóptico*. Bogotá: Imprenta de M. Rivas & Cía, 1905.
Gómez Gallego, Jorge Aníbal, José Roberto Herrera Vergara, and Nilson Pinilla Pinilla. *Informe final: Comisión de la verdad sobre los hechos del Palacio de Justicia*. Bogotá: Universidad del Rosario, Fundación Hanns Seidel, Comisión de la verdad Palacio de Justicia, 2010.
Halbwachs, Maurice. *On Collective Memory*. Translated by Lewis A. Coser. Chicago, IL and London: The University of Chicago Press, 1992.
Hall, Stuart. *Representation: Cultural Representations and Signifying Practices*. London: Sage Publications, 1997.
Hall, Stuart, and Paddy Whannel. *The Popular Arts*. Durham, NC and London: Duke University Press, [2018] 1964.
Hartog, François. "Time and Heritage." *Museum International*, Vol. 57, No. 3 (2005): 7–18.
Hein, Hilde S. *The Museum in Transition. A Philosophical Perspective*. Washington, DC: The Smithsonian Institution, 2010.
Hernández Sabogal, Myriam. *Una nación desplazada: Informe nacional del desplazamiento forzado en Colombia*. Bogotá: Centro Nacional de Memoria Histórica, 2015.
Herz, John H. *From Dictatorship to Democracy: Coping with the Legacies of Authoritarianism and Totalitarianism*. Westport, CT: Greenwood Press, 1982.
Huyssen, Andreas. *Present Pasts: Urban Palimpsests and the Politics of Memory*. Stanford, CA: Stanford University Press, 2009.
Jackins, Ira. "Franz Boas and Exhibits: On the Limitations of the Museum Method in Anthropology." In *Objects and Others. Essays on Museums and Material Culture*. Edited by W. G. Stocking. Madison: University of Wisconsin Press, 1995, 75–111.
Jaramillo, Jefferson, and Carlos del Cairo. "Los dilemas de la museificación. Reflexiones en torno a dos iniciativas estatales de construcción." *Memoria y Sociedad*, Vol. 17, No. 35 (2013): 76–92.
Jelin, Elizabeth. *State Repression and the Labors of Memory*. Translated by Marcial Godoy-Anativia and Judy Rein. Minneapolis: The University of Minnesota Press, 2003.
Jelin, Elizabeth Jelin and Wendy Gosselin. *The Struggle for the Past How We Construct Social Memories*. New York: Berghahn, 2021.
Karp, Ivan, Christine Mullen Kreamer, and Steven D. Lavine, eds. *Museums and Communities: The Politics of Public Culture*. Washington, DC: Smithsonian, 1992.

Karp, Ivan and Steven D. Lavine, eds. *Exhibiting Cultures. The Poetics and Politics of Museum Display*. Washington, DC: Smithsonian Institution, 1991.

Klein, Kerwin Lee. "On the Emergence of Memory in Historical Discourse." *Representations*, No. 69, Special Issue *Grounds for Remembering* (Winter, 2000): 127–150. https://doi.org/10.2307/2902903.

LaCapra, Dominick. *Representing the Holocaust*. Ithaca, NY and London: Cornell University Press, 1994.

Lazzara, Michael J. "The Memory Turn." In *New Approaches to Latin American Studies. Culture and Power*. Edited by Juan Poblete. New York: Routledge, 2018, 14–32.

Lazzara, Michael J. and Fernando A. Blanco, eds. *Los Futuros de La Memoria En América Latina: Sujetos, Políticas y Epistemologías En Disputa*. Chapel Hill: University of North Carolina Press, 2022.

Lessa, Francesca. *Memory and Transitional Justice in Argentina and Uruguay. Against Impunity*. New York: Palgrave-McMillan, 2013.

Lévi-Strauss, Claude. *Race and History*. Paris: UNESCO, 1952.

Lykes, M. Brinton, and Hugo van der Merwe. "Exploring/Expanding the Reach of Transitional Justice." *International Journal of Transitional Justice*, Vol. 11, No. 3 (November 1, 2017): 371–377.

MacCall, Vikki, and Clive Gray. "Museums and the 'New Museology': Theory, Practice, and Organisational Change." *Management and Curatorship*, Vol. 29, No. 1 (2013): 1–17.

Martínez Velasco, Camila. "La cultura popular entra al museo: curaduría participativa en el Museo Nacional de Colombia (2005–2011)." In *Cuadernos de Curaduría. Aproximaciones a la historia del Museo Nacional*, No. 18. Bogotá: Museo Nacional de Colombia, 2021, 91–108. https://museonacional.gov.co/Publicaciones/cuadernos-de-curaduria/Paginas/cuadernos-de-curaduria-18.aspx

Mcdonald, Sharon. "Is 'Difficult Heritage' Still Difficult? Why Public Knowledge of Past Perpetration May No Longer Be So Unsettling to Collective Identities." *Museum International (English edition)*, Vol. 67, No. 1–4 (2015): 6–22.

_____. *Difficult Heritage. Negotiating the Nazi Past in Nuremberg and Beyond*. New York: Routledge, 2009.

Méndez, Juan E. "Victims as Protagonists in Transitional Justice." *International Journal of Transitional Justice*, Vol. 10, No. 1 (March 2016): 1–5.

Molano, Alfredo. *Desterrados. Crónicas del desarraigo*. Bogotá: El Áncora Editores, 2001.

Morales de Gómez, Teresa. "La Casa de las aulas. Sede del Museo de Arte Colonial en Bogotá." *Credencial Historia*, Vol. 138 (June 2001). https://www.banrepcultural.org/biblioteca-virtual/credencial-historia/numero-138/la-casa-de-las-aulas-museo-de-arte-colonial-en-bogota

Murillo Sandoval, Juan David. "De Lo Natural y Lo Nacional. Representaciones de la Naturaleza Explotable en la Exposición Internacional de Chile de 1875." *Historia*, Vol. 48, No. 1 (2015): 245–276.

Nora, Pierre. *Realms of Memory. The Construction of the French Past*. Vol I. Translated by Lawrence D. Kritzman. New York: Columbia University Press, 1996.

O'Donnell, Guillermo, Philippe C. Schmitter, and Laurence Whitehead. *Transitions from Authoritarian Rule: Comparative Perspectives*. Baltimore, MD: John Hopkins University Press, 1986.

Ortega, Naila Katherine Flor. "Eduardo Santos y el mecenazgo cultural: la donación al Museo Nacional de Colombia." In *Cuadernos de Curaduría. Aproximaciones a la historia del Museo Nacional*, No. 14. Bogotá: Museo Nacional de Colombia, 2008, 115–143. https://

museonacional.gov.co/Publicaciones/cuadernos-de-curaduria/Documents/2019/Cuadernos_de_curaduria_14.pdf

Ospina, Roberto Romero. *Unión Patriótica. Expedientes contra el olvido*. Bogotá: Centro de Memoria, Paz y Reconciliación, Agència Catalana de Cooperació al Desenvolupament, Alcaldía Mayor de Bogotá, Bogotá Humana, 2012.

Pabón, Rosemberg. *Así nos tomamos la embajada*. Bogotá: Editorial Planeta, 1984.

Palacios, Marco. *Between Legitimacy and Violence: A History of Colombia, 1875–2002*. Translated by Richard Stoller. Durham, NC: Duke University Press, 2006.

———. *Violencia pública en Colombia, 1958–2010*. Bogotá: Fondo de Cultura Económica, 2012.

Parejo González, Enrique. *La Tragedia del Palacio de Justicia. Cúmulo de errores y abusos*. Bogotá: Editorial Oveja Negra, 2010.

Paz Otero, Víctor. "Éste es otro paseo." *El Espectador*, March 3, 2001. National Museum of Colombia Archive.

Pécaut, Daniel, and Liliana González. "Presente, pasado y futuro de la violencia en Colombia." *Desarrollo Económico*, Vol. 36, No. 144 (January–March, 1997): 891–930.

Pérez Benavides, Amada Carolina and Sebastián Vargas Álvarez. "Perspectives on Public History in Colombia." *International Public History*, Vol. 4, No. 2 (2021): 143–152. https://doi.org/10.1515/iph-2021-2027.

Perry, Jimena. *Caminos de la antropología en Colombia: Gregorio Hernández de Alba*. Bogotá: Universidad de Los Andes, 2006.

Pizarro, Juan Antonio. *Carlos Pizarro*. Bogotá: Círculo de Lectores, 1992.

Pizarro Leongómez, Eduardo. *Las Farc (1949–2011). De guerrilla campesina a máquina de guerra*. Bogotá: Grupo Editorial, Norma, 2001.

Plazas Vega, Luis Alfonso. *La batalla del Palacio de Justicia*. Bogotá: Intermedio Editores, 2000.

Podgorny, Irina and Maria Margaret Lopes. "Trayectorias y desafíos de la historiografía de los museos de historia natural en América Del Sur." *Anais do Museu Paulista: História e Cultura Material*, Vol. 21, No. 1 (2013): 15–25.

Prakash, Gyan. "Museum Matters." In *Museum Studies. An Anthology of Contexts*. Edited by Bettina Messias Carbonell. Malden: Blackwell Publishing, 2004, 317–324.

Proyecto. "*Renovación del guion y el montaje museográfico del Museo Nacional de Colombia.*" *Guión Sala 7. Memoria y Nación*. Museo Nacional de Colombia, Bogotá.

Rajca, Andrew C. *Dissensual Subjects: Memory, Human Rights, and Postdictatorship in Argentina, Brazil, and Uruguay*. Evanston, IL: Northwestern University Press, 2018.

Ramírez, Gloria, and Lorena Luengas. "Salón del Nunca Más, Granada. Un proceso comunitario. Oriente Antioqueño." In *Museos, comunidades y reconciliación. Experiencias y memorias en diálogo. XIV Cátedra de Historia Ernesto Restrepo Tirado*. Bogotá: Museo Nacional de Colombia, Universidad Externado de Colombia, 2009, 24–60. https://www.museonacional.gov.co/Publicaciones/catedra/Documents/XIV_catedra_historia_MNC.pdf

Rancière, Jacques. (Steven Corcoran, Translator). *Dissensus: On Politics and Aesthetics*. London and New York: Continuum International Publishing Group Ltd, 2010.

Rekdal, Per B. "About the Beauty of War and the Attractivity of Violence." In *Does War Belong in Museums? The Representation of Violence in Exhibitions*. Edited by. W. Muchitsch. Bielefeld: Museumsakademie Joanneum, 2013, 123–130.

Riaño Alcalá, Pilar, and María Victoria Uribe, "Constructing Memory amidst War: The Historical Memory Group of Colombia." *International Journal of Transitional Justice*, Vol. 10, No. 1 (March 2016): 6–24.

Ricoeur, Paul. *History, Memory, Forgetting*. Translated by Kathleen Blamey and David Pellauer. Chicago, IL and London: The University of Chicago Press, 2004.

Robledo, Santiago. "Las colecciones industriales del Museo Nacional de Colombia." In *Cuadernos de Curaduría. Aproximaciones a la historia del Museo Nacional*, No. 17. Bogotá: Museo Nacional de Colombia, 2020, 10–48. https://museonacional.gov.co/Publicaciones/cuadernos-de-curaduria/Documents/2020/17.pdf

Rodrigues-Carvalho, Claudia Marcelo Carvalho, and Wagner Martins. "From Museu Real to Museu Nacional/UFRJ, Rio de Janeiro, Brazil: Past and Present Fragments." *Revista del Museo Argentino de Ciencias Naturales*, Vol. 14, No. 2 (2012): 223–228.

Rodríguez Prada, María Paola. "Origen de la institución museal en Colombia: entidad científica para el desarrollo y progreso." In *Cuadernos de Curaduría. Aproximaciones a la historia del Museo Nacional*. Bogotá: Museo Nacional de Colombia, 2008, 1–21. https://museonacional.gov.co/el-museo/historia/nacimiento-museo/Documents/Aproximacionesalahistoria06.pdf

Roldán, Mary. *Blood and Fire. La Violencia in Antioquia, Colombia, 1946–1953*. Durham, NC and London: Duke University Press, 2002.

Roth, Michael. *Memory, Trauma, and History: Essays on Living with the Past*. New York: Columbia University Press, 2012.

Rothberg, Michael. *Multidirectional Memory: Remembering the Holocaust in the Age of Decolonization*. Stanford, CA: Stanford University Press, 2009.

Rúa Delgado, Carlos Felipe. "Los momentos de la justicia transicional en Colombia." *Revista de Derecho*, Vol. 43 (2015): 71–109.

Salge, Manuel. *El principio arcóntico del patrimonio. Origen, transformaciones y desafíos de los procesos de patrimonialización en Colombia*. Bogotá: Ediciones UniAndes, 2019.

Sánchez, Gonzalo. *La Masacre de El Salado: esa guerra no era nuestra*. Bogotá: Centro Nacional de Memoria Histórica, 2009.

_____. "Testimonio, Justicia y Memoria. Reflexiones preliminares sobre una trilogía actual." *Estudios Políticos*, Vol. 53 (2018): 19–47.

_____. *Guerras, Memoria e Historia*. Medellín: La Carreta Editores, 2006.

_____. *Memorias, Subjetividades y Política: Ensayos Sobre Un País Que Se Niega a Dejar La Guerra*. Bogotá: Editorial Planeta Colombiana, Crítica, 2020.

Sarlo, Beatriz. *Tiempo pasado: cultura de la memoria y giro subjetivo*. Buenos Aires: Siglo Veintiuno Editores, 2005.

Schubert, Karsten. *The Curator's Egg: The Evolution of the Museum Concept from the French Revolution to the Present Day*. London: Ridling House, 2009.

Segura, Martha. *Itinerario del Museo Nacional*. Tomo I. Bogotá: Instituto Colombiano de Cultura, Museo Nacional de Colombia, 1995.

Segura, Martha. *Itinerario del Museo Nacional*. Tomo II. Bogotá: Instituto Colombiano de Cultura, Museo Nacional de Colombia, 1995.

Sierra Becerra, Diana Carolina. "Historical Memory at El Salvador's Museo de la Palabra y la Imagen." *Latin American Perspectives*, Vol. 43, No. 6 (2016): 8–26.

Stam, Deirdre C. "The Informed Muse: The Implications of 'The New Museology' for Museum Practice." *Museum Management and Curatorship*, Vol. 12 (1993): 267–283.

Stern, Steve. *Reckoning with Pinochet. The Memory Question in Democratic Chile, 1989–2006*. Durham, NC: Duke University Press, 2010.

Taborsky, Edwina. "The Discursive Object." In *Objects of Knowledge, New Research in Museum Studies* 1. Edited by Susan Pearce. London and Atlantic Highlands, NJ: The Athlone Press, 1990, 50–78.

Tamm, Marek. "Beyond History and Memory: New Perspectives in Memory Studies." *History Compass*, Vol. 11, No. 6 (2013): 458–473.

Tavera, Gonzalo. "Informe del bibliotecario nacional." en Anales de la Universidad Nacional de los Estados Unidos de Colombia, n°. 89, Bogotá, febrero de, 1879.

Teitel, Ruti G., "Transitional Justice Genealogy." *Harvard Human Rights Journal*, Vol. 16, (Spring 2003): 69–94.

Téllez Castañeda, Germán. "La arquitectura y el urbanismo en la época republicana, 1830–40/1930–35." In *Nueva Historia de Colombia*. Edited by Álvaro Tirado Mejía. Bogotá: Editorial Planeta, 1989, Vol 2, 223–251.

Uribe, María Victoria. *Antropología de la inhumanidad. Un ensayo interpretativo sobre el terror en Colombia*. Bogotá: Editorial Norma, 2004.

Uribe, María Victoria, and Pilar Riaño Alcalá. "Memory Amidst War: The Historical Memory Group of Colombia." *International Journal of Transitional Justice*, Vol. 10 (2016): 6–24.

Uribe, María Victoria, and Teófilo Vásquez. *Enterrar y Callar: Las masacres en Colombia, 1980–1993* Vol. II. Bogotá: Comité Permanente por la Defensa de los Derechos Humanos 1995.

Vergo, Peter. *The New Museology*. London: Reaktion Books, 1989.

Veysel, Apaydin. *Critical Perspectives on Cultural Memory and Heritage: Construction, Transformation and Destruction*. London: UCL Press. Kindle Edition. 2020.

Viejo-Rose, Darcia. "Cultural Heritage and Memory: Untangling the Ties That Bind." *Culture & History Digital Journal*, Vol. 4, No. 2 (2015): e018. https://doi.org/10.3989/chdj.2015.018.

Villa Martínez, Martha Inés. *Granada: Memorias de guerra, resistencia y reconstrucción*. Bogotá: Centro Nacional de Memoria Histórica, 2016.

Villalón, Roberta, ed. *Memory, Truth, and Justice in Contemporary Latin America*. London: Rowman and Littlefield, 2017.

Villamizar Herrera, Darío. *Las guerrillas en Colombia: Una historia desde los orígenes hasta los confines*. Bogotá: Penguin Random House Grupo Editorial Colombia, Kindle Edition, 2017.

Winter, Jay. *Sites of Memory, Sites of Mourning: The Great War in European Cultural History*. Cambridge, MA: Cambridge University Pres, 1988.

———. "The Generation of Memory: Reflections on the 'Memory Boom' in Contemporary Historical Studies." *Canadian Military History*, Vol. 10, No. 3, ( Article 5, 2001): 57–66.

Wolff Rojas, Tatiana. "Pensamientos sobre la representación de la memoria traumática en el Museo de la Memoria y los Derechos Humanos (mmdh), Santiago de Chile." *Intervención*, Vol. 7, No. 13, (enero-junio 2016): 61–73.

# INDEX

Note: **Bold** page numbers refer to tables and *italic* page numbers refer to figures.

Abello, Martha Nubia 20, 21
Acevedo, Darío 26, 121
Adams, T.R. 111
Alape, Arturo 62
Alianza Democrática M-19 81
Allen, Woody 143–144
Arbeláez, Jotamario 44
Arenas, Jacobo 60
Ariès, Philippe 112
Aristizábal, Carlos Abel 115
Arnold di Simine, Silke 11–12
art museums 24
Arthur, Paige 118
Asociacion de Victimas de Granada, Asovida (Association of Victims of Granada) 105
Association of Trujillo's Relatives Victims (AFAVI) 21
autobiographical memory 13, 108, 109, 137, 149
Autodefensas Unidas de Colombia (AUC) 130
Avelar, Idelber 116

Bachelet, Michelle 25
Barahona de Brito, Alexandra 118
Barreras, Roy 174
Bartlett, Frederic 148
Bayuelo, Soraya 143, 148–150, 157–158, 160–161, 163, *164*, 178–179

Belalcázar, Sebastián de 4
Bennett, Tony 11–12, 34
bipartisan violence 18
Blanco, Fernando 8
Boas, Franz 51
*Bogotazo* 58
Bolivar, Simon 35, 59, 174–175
Bonilla, Rodrigo Lara 84–86
Borrero, Misael Pastrana 53
Botero, Clara Isabel 39, 165–166
Botero, Fernando 47, 56
Bourdieu, Pierre 10–11, 46–47, 113, 145
Braudel, Fernand 112
Brennan, Michael 92, 138–139
Brulon, Bruno 111

Cairo, Carlos del 44
Caribbean Museum 166–167
Carrigan, Ana 78
Carlos Pizarro Leongomez Foundation 93
Castillejo, Alejandro 20–21, 176–177
Castro, Daniel 83
Castro, Giovanni 156–157
Catalan Agency for International Development Cooperation (AECID) 162
Center of Information for the Collective Memory and Human Rights 124
Chapin, David 107
civil armed conflict (1899–1902) 39
civil rights 5

## Index

Cohen, David 34–35
collective 10, 106–109, 129, 134, 143, 145, 149, 156–158, *162*, 163, 167–170; memory 13, 50–51, 116, 132, 137–138; self-preservation 27
Colombia 2–14, 116, 154–156, 173–181; cultural diversity 27–28; immaterial/intangible heritage 145–149; Massacres **127–128**; memory museums and exhibitions 21, **22–23**, 23–26; National Museum 32–64, 69–100, 113, 165; public policies 106; transitional justice 117–121; violence 15–21;
Colombian Communist Youth (JUCO) 75
Colombian Communist Party 75
Colombian Institute of Anthropology and History (ICANH) 166
Colombian Memory Sites Network 21, **22–23**
Columbus, Christopher 5
Comision de Implementacion y Monitoreo de la Ley Victimas (CIMLV) 119
communities 146, 169; black 27, 40, 156, 174; collective memories 137–138; El Mochuelo 160; grassroots 3, 5, 14; healing process 106; LGBTQ 150; LGBTQIA 160; memory 11, 178; Montes de María 166; rehabilitation 105; romanticization 110; rural 3, 21, 100, 132, 180
Conservative Misael Pastrana Borrero (1970–1974) 60
Convention for the Safeguarding of the Intangible Cultural Heritage 146
Cook, Susan E. 35
Cuervo de Jaramillo, Elvira 32–36, 40, 42–49, 52–56, 63, 64, 69, 71–74, 83–84, 93
culture/cultural: capital 10, 38–39; definition of 27; diversity 27–28, 40, 41; empowerment 112; inventory exercise 13
Current of Socialist Renewal (CRS) 55

Departamento Administrativo Nacional de Estadistica (DANE) 27
difficult heritage 8, 36, 72
Dixon, Micaela 63
Douglas, Mary 27–28, 50
Duque, Iván 2, 4, 17, 120, 121, 154, 169, 173, 175, 177

Echandía, Alfonso Reyes 78–79
Ehrenreich, Robert 51
Ejercito de Liberacion Nacional (ELN) guerrilla 17, 19, 58, 127, 130
El Mochuelo 144–149, 156
exhibitions, in Colombia and Latin America 21, **22–23**, 23–26
The Extraditables (Los Extraditables) 86

"false positives" process 123
FARC-EP 1, 2, 17, 19, 20, 32–36, 45, 55–63, 75, 120, 130–131, 153
Feldman, Joseph 6
Felipe, Andrés 36
Foucault, Michel 34
Frisch, Michael H. 169

Gaitán, Jorge Eliécer 58
Gaitán, María Valencia 181
Galán, Luis Carlos 46, 47, 53, 56, 70, 82–88, 174
*Galán vive* (Galan Lives) exhibition 70
Gamba, Nicolás Pereira 38
Garrard, Virginia 98
Garzón, Jaime 47
Gaviria, José Obdulio 116
Gay, Peter 112
Geertz, Clifford 27–28, 158
Getty Research Institute Symposium 6
*Glass Houses: Paul Rivet and Human Diversity* 36
González, Beatriz 40, 54, 72–73
Granada *114 see* Hall of Never Again
grassroots 4, 11, 12, 181; communities 3, 5, 14; memory 121, 139, 167; proliferation of 116
guerrillas 1, 11, 16
Gulf Clan 155

Halbwachs, Maurice 13, 34–35, 108, 109, 134–135, 148, 149
Hall of Never Again 12, 105–107, 144–145, 149; autobiographical and collective 108–109; *bitácoras* 134–138; characteristics 115; Community Center 121–122; display of 125, *126*; entrance to 124, *124*; false positives 123; Granada's church 122, *122*; ICOM 109–112; inhabitants 131; massacres 126, **127–128**; memory 114–117; National Museum of Colombia 113; transitional justice, Colombia 109, 117–121; violence 131

Hall, Stuart 47
Hartog, Francois 145–146
Hein, Hilde S. 107
Hernández de Alba, Gregorio 40
Hernández, Bexielena 150–151, 163
Hernández, Ester E. 6
Herz, John H. 117
historical memory 2, 3, 6–11, 13–16, 26–28, 90–92, 145; Colombia 71; El Mochuelo 147–149; policies 173; *Ya vuelvo's* sensible reception 95–99
*History, Memory, Forgetting* (Paul) 147, 149
Histórico, Pacto 2
human rights violations 5
Hurtado, Álvaro Gómez 52, 53
Huyssen, Andreas 146, 177

internal war 1–2, 13, 21, 26, 35, 58, 152, 173, 176, 180
International Committee of Memorial Museums in Remembrance of the Victims of Public Crimes (ICMEMO) 24
International Coalition of Sites of Conscience (ICSC) 178
International Council of Museums (ICOM) 109
International Federation for Public History (IFPH) 4, 6

Jaimes, Luis Alberto Morantes 60
Jaramillo, Jefferson 44
Jelin, Elizabeth 5, 7–10, 25, 34–35, 46, 47, 109
Jiménez de Quesada, Gonzalo 4
Johannes Fabian 49–50

Karp, Ivan 11–12
Klein, Hilde 11–12
Klein, Stephen 107
Klinger, Jane 51

La Catedral (The Cathedral) 55
Latin American Roaming Art (LARA) 51
La Violencia 17–18, 59
Lazzara, Michael 7, 8
Le Roy Ladurie, Emmanuel 112
Leal, Jaime Pardo 82–83
Lejeune, Max 98
Levina, Steven 11–12
*lieux de mémoire* (sites of memory) 14, 116
Liberal Alberto Lleras Camargo (1958–1962) 60

Lopes, Maria Margaret 11–12, 24
López, William 181
Law for Victims 177

MacDonald, Sharon 36, 51–52, 71–72
Marcuse, Herbert 75
Marín, Pedro Antonio 32
Márquez, Francia 2, 175
Márquez, Miguel Maza 85
Marx, Karl 75
massacres 16–18, 58; El Salado 153, 155, 156; Granada 125–126, **127–128**; 129–132; Las Brisas 165; Montes de María 150–151, **151**, 152, *159*
McDonald, Sharon 8
Mejía, Adriana 48
Mejía, José Jaramillo 44
Memoria y nacion (Memory and Nation) 73
memory/memories 8–16; Colombia 21, **22–23**, 23–26; collective 3, 11, 50–51, 116, 132, 137–138, 178; definition of 10; grassroots 121, 139, 167; museums 21, **22–23**, 23–26, 177, 179; *see also* historical memory
memory sheet 160
Méndez, Juan E. 118
military outrage, National Museum of Colombia 88–89
Ministerio de Salud (Ministry of Health) 27
Molano, Alfredo 20
Montes de María 143–157, **151,** 153, 158, *159,* 160
Montoya, Jaime 132
Moody, Jessica 146
Moore, Henry 54
Moreiras, Alberto 116
Movimiento 19 de Abril, M-19 (April 19th Movement) 70
multidirectional memory concept 10
Museo de la Memoria (Memory Museum) 25
Museo del Holocausto (Holocaust Museum) 25
museums 3, 4, 6–7, 9–14, 27, 106–118; CNMH policies 178; definition of 110; memory 21, **22–23**, 23–26, 177, 179; Montes de María, El Mochuelo 143–170, 181; National Museum of Colombia 32–64, 69–100, 180

Namuy Misak community 4
National Association of Peasant Users of Colombia (ANUC) 150

## Index

National Center for Historical Memory (CNMH) 19, 58, 151
National Front (1958–1974) 60
National Library of Colombia 42
National Museum of Colombia 69–71; Conservative Party 32; Cuervo de Jaramillo's initiative 44–49; cultural conceptions 34; FARC-EP 33, 35, 36, 56–63, **57**; headquarters of 42–43; historic artifacts 49–56; history of 36–42; innovative pathways 71–74; memory venues 35; *Ya Vuelvo*, exhibition reactions 81–89; *Ya Vuelvo*'s sensible reception 95–99
*The New Museology* (Vergo) 107, 179
Nora, Pierre 14
Nuevo Liberalismo (New Liberalism) party 85
Nunca Mas (Never Again) slogan 117

O'Donnell, Guillermo 117
Operacion Ballena Azul (Operation Blue Whale) 75
Ospina, Lucas 81
Ossa, Bernardo Jaramillo 70, 87, 174

Palacios, Marco 15, 18–19, 20
paramilitaries 15–21, 58, 126, **127–128**; 129–133, 150–155
Pastrana, Andrés 32, 55
Paths of Memory and Peace 133
Paz Otero, Víctor 48
Peace Accord in 2016 4
Peace Agreement of 2016 1
Pecaut, Daniel 18
Pérez Benavides, Amada Carolina 3
Petro, Gustavo 2, 19, 173–175
Pinochet, Augusto 25
Pizarro Leongómez, Carlos 64, 69, 70, 74, 153; Carlos Pizarro Leongómez: Elite to Commander of M-19 74–81; *Ya vuelvo* 89–95, *92*
Pizarro Leongómez, Eduardo 62
Pizarro, María José 69–70, 81, 90–93, 96–98, 138, 174
"Pizarro's deaths" 91
Plazas Vega, Luis Alfonso 89
Podogrny, Irina 11–12, 24
political rights 5
political violence *see also* National Museum of Colombia
Pombo, Fidel 39
Pombo, Roberto 59

Popular Liberation Army (EPL) 55, 58, 93
"pornography of violence" 98
Posso, Rafael 165
Prakash, Gyan 11–12, 35
Pumarejo, Alfonso López 39

Quinta de Bolivar (Villa of Bolivar) 75
Quintin Lame Armed Movement (MAQL) 55
Quintero, Gloria 105, 114, 125–126, 129, 133, 134, 139, 178–179

Rajca, Andrew C. 7, 108, 125
Ramírez, Gloria 105, 109, 123, 133, 148, 178–179
Rancière, Jacques 108
Registro Uegis de V de Vtro (Unique Victim Registry) 57
Rekdal, Per B. 36
remembrance 7–10, 12, 14, 21, 23, 45–47, 125, 147–149, 170; Pizarro Leongómez, Carlos 89–95
*Remembering: A Study in Experimental and Social Psychology* (Bartlett) 148
Remhi Project 123
Retrato de Carlos (Portrait of Carlos) 93
Restrepo, José Francisco 153
Revolutionary Independent Labor Movement 53
Riaño Alcalá, Pilar 15, 119
Richard, Nelly 116
Ricoeur, Paul 9, 10, 147, 149
Rincón, Héctor 44–45
*Río abajo* (Downriver) 124
ritual readings 177
Rivero, Mariano de 37
Rivet, Paul 37, 39–40
Roca, José 51–52
Rodríguez Gacha, Gonzalo 86, 87
Rodríguez, María Paola 38
Roldán, Mary 20, 21
Roth, Michael 34–35
Rothberg, Michael 10, 34–35, 71, 170
Rúa Delgado, Carlos Felipe 119
Ruíz, Catalina 79, *79,* 89–91, *92*

Salon del Nunca Mas (Hall of Never Again) 105
Samper, Ernesto 81
Sánchez, Diana 26
Sánchez, Gonzalo 5, 9, 14, 17, 20, 26, 131–132, 152, 156

Santos, Eduardo 39
Santos, Juan Manuel 1, 71, 120, 175
Sarlo, Beatriz 34–35, 116
Schlereth, Thomas J. 111–112
Schmitter, Philippe C. 117
Schwartz, Daniel 179
Second Peace Process (1989–1990) 94
Siege Operation Democracy and Liberty 76
Sikkink, Kathryn 5
Simon Bolivar Guerrilla Coordinating Board 55
social fabrics 3
Society of Jesus Maximum School 42
Spanish International Cooperation Agency for Development 115
Special Peace Jurisdiction 12, 119
Stern, Steve 11–12, 14, 46
Suez Canal crisis (1956) 98

Taborski, Edwina 112
Tavera, Gonzalo A. 38
Taylor, Edward 27
Teitel, Ruti G. 118
Tejipaz 132–133
Thomas, Keith V. 112
Tirado, Ernesto Restrepo 39
Tirofijo's towel *see* National Museum of Colombia
Torres, Jerónimo 37
transitional justice, Colombia 109, 117–121, 138
traveling museum: Black communities 156; Caribbean Museum 166–167; Collective 167–170; decision-making process 180; El Mochuelo 144–149, 156–163, *162, 164,* 165–170; Gulf Clan 155; immaterial/intangible heritage, Colombia 145–150; LGBTQIA community 160–161; Millennium Development Goals 162; Montes de María 143–157, **151**, 153, 158, *159,* 160; paramilitary demobilization 154; Tree of Life 163, *164,* 165; UNESCO 147–148

"Tree of Life" 163, 165
Truth Commission 1

Unamuno, Aurelia 6
Union Patriotica (UP) 80, 87
Unit for the Victims Assistance and Reparation 56
Uribe, María Victoria 15, 20, 21, 119
Utrera, Eduardo 50

Vargas, Sebastián 3
Vargas, Virgilio Barco 86
Vásquez, Fabio Ochoa 87
Vásquez, Teófilo 18, 20
Vélez, Álvaro Uribe 15, 17, 71, 89–90, 105, 116–117, 119, 157
Vélez, Manuel Marulanda 32, 59
Vergo, Paul 11–12
Vergo, Peter 24, 107, 179
Veysel, Apaydin 145
victims, definition of 16, 119
Villamizar, Darío 20
Villamizar, Herrera 21
violence 3, 7, 9–14, 109, 138–139, 166–167; at El Mochuelo 157–165; in Colombia 15–21, 179; in Montes de María 150–157; political 27, 32–64, 69–100, 178, 179; representations 121–126, 129–134; social fabrics 144
Vizcaíno, Milciades 120

War of Marquetalia 60
War of Villarrica 60
Whitehead, Laurence 117
Wolff, Navarro 78
Workers Revolutionary Party (PRT) 55
Wrigley, E. A. 112

*Ya vuelvo:* exhibition 70; historical memories 95–99; National Museum of Colombia 88–89
Yerushalmi, Yosef 116

*Zakhor: Jewish History and Jewish Memory* (Yerushalmi) 116